The Gateshead

Book

of

Days

JO BATH
& RICHARD F. STEVENSON

First published 2013

The History Press
The Mill, Brimscombe Port
Stroud, Gloucestershire, GL5 2QG
www.thehistorypress.co.uk

British Library Cataloguing in Publication Data.
A catalogue record for this book is available from the British Library.

ISBN 978 0 7524 6867 9

Typesetting and origination by The History Press
Printed in India

JANUARY 1ST

1907: On this day, one of Gateshead's most famous quayside personalities was seen for the last time. Thomas Ferens, more commonly known as 'Tommy on the Bridge', was a beggar who became famous locally because of his 'strong' personality and his near-constant presence on the quayside. As his nickname suggests, Tommy was usually found on a bridge, begging from tourists and locals alike. Born in the early 1840s, he was an orphan by the age of 5 and was partially paralysed in both hands, and completely blind. Unable to work for a living, Tommy began begging from an early age. Indeed, although he later became synonymous with the Swing Bridge, his career in fact started on the older, stone Tyne Bridge that was on the same site until 1876. Apparently it was his belief that neither the Gateshead nor the Newcastle police could arrest him for begging so long as he straddled the border between the two authorities! He was known to shout insults when his earnings were insufficient, even angrily throwing money into the Tyne on occasion. Before long he had become something of a tourist attraction himself and picture postcards of him were sold to visitors to Gateshead. Unfortunately on this cold, snowy January day, Tommy was found lying unconscious near to Bridge Street. The police took him to the Workhouse Hospital in Bensham, where he died twenty minutes later. He had been a fixture 'on the bridge' for forty years. (Walton, C., *Old Gateshead*, No. 41)

January 2nd

1940: On this day, Gateshead lost one of its most respected citizens. Local historian John Oxberry was born in Windy Nook in 1857. Although he dedicated his later life to the town of his birth, he emigrated to New Zealand as a young man, eager to seek wealth and fortune in the gold mines of Otago. Disappointed with his luck there, he returned home and worked for Gateshead's authorities in various capacities until eventually becoming Superintendent Registrar in 1917 – a job he held until retiring in 1930. Throughout his working life and retirement, Oxberry tirelessly strived to research, make public, and preserve Gateshead's history. Clarence Walton, himself a great collector of Gateshead's historical scraps, sums it up beautifully: 'Mr Oxberry's diligent and painstaking investigation covering a period of many years, his toilsome task of collecting and indexing practically every word and import printed about his beloved home town, but which to him was a labour of love, gives him without dispute the honour of being Gateshead's greatest historian.' In 1937 Oxberry was elected Honorary Freeman of the Borough in recognition of his services, and received a silver casket in the Shipley Art Gallery. His death was the long-term result of an accident at home in 1939, from which he never truly recovered. (Walton, C., *Scrapbook*, Gateshead Library)

JANUARY 3RD

1540: On this day, Stella's nuns were made homeless and unemployed! As long ago as 1149, William de St Barbara, Bishop of Durham, granted an area of Stella 'with all its appurtenances in woodland, champian [fields], roads, ways, metes, boundaries, mills, and meadows, Waters, fish-dams, and fisheries, free of forest-right and pasturage of the Bishop's hogs, to St Bartholomew and the Nuns of Newcastle.' Although ownership changed hands, a nunnery remained on the same site for nearly 400 years, with the nuns enjoying the use of the land and the support of wealthy local families. Then came Henry VIII. From 1536 to 1541, Henry's Dissolution of the Monasteries was responsible for the closure of most of the monasteries and nunneries in the kingdom, and Stella's was one of the last to be suppressed during this scheme. Indeed, its future prospects seemed good when it escaped the first round of suppressions in 1537, and it was re-founded and preserved. But by 1540 the vast lands and great building supported only one prioress and nine nuns. So, for economic as much as religious reasons, it was closed. Stella Hall was built on the site of the – now ruined – nunnery. Visitors to the Hall have included Italian general and politician Garibaldi, a statue of whom was found in a garden on the Stella estate. (Bourne, W., *History of the Parish of Ryton*, 1896 / isee.gateshead.gov.uk)

JANUARY 4TH

1886: On this day, the 'Felling Ghost' was captured. According to the press, 'For the past six weeks considerable excitement has been caused in the vicinity of Holly Street, Felling, by the appearance of what was supposed to be a ghost ...' This apparition would be seen lurking behind walls, rattling closed windows and doors. When seen, it 'would give an unearthly moan and disappear again in the darkness.' This night, however, the ghoul was surprised by a man brandishing a poker. Giving chase (wearing nothing but his shirt), the man screamed 'For God's sake, stop the ghost!' A crowd gave chase, forcing the 'ghost' to seek shelter – in the police station! Unsurprisingly, the phantom proved to be a simple burglar, very much alive, and thankful for the police's protection from an angry mob threatening to give him a 'good coating of tar and feathers'. He was tried on January 12th. The *North-Eastern Daily Gazette* reports that the two lawyers involved seemed oddly obsessed with Shakespeare. When one spoke of the accused going to sleep, his opposite number interrupted 'perchance to dream'. The first then went on to quote Hamlet's words to his dead father, asking why his 'dread corpse' had returned. Eventually the judge was forced to ask them to simply relate the facts, without resorting to poetry. (*Liverpool Mercury* / *North-Eastern Daily Gazette*)

JANUARY 5TH

1832: On this day, W. Maclean of the Central Health Board wrote to the Newcastle Board of Health concerning an alarming rumour. It seemed that, only three weeks after a cholera outbreak began, Gateshead had set up a temporary hospital for sufferers. But – perhaps because of the sheer number of patients – the whole set-up was thought to be 'highly inadequate and improper'. Maclean had been told that 'five children were actually placed in one bed, and three in another bed in that hospital' – perhaps no worse than they would have had at home, in some cases, but certainly far from ideal for the seriously ill! Maclean demanded an explanation for how these circumstances could arise, 'which, if founded in truth, must prove highly disgraceful to the members of the Board.' The cholera epidemic certainly hit Gateshead hard. When the local Board of Health met eight days later, they reported that cholera deaths had now reached 124 in Gateshead (compared to 204 in the much larger Newcastle). It didn't help that Newcastle had closed its doors to vagrants, as part of its public health measures, so any strays visiting Tyneside wound up on the south bank. By the time that year's epidemic had run its course in Gateshead, over 400 had been infected and around 150 had died in the town. (www.nationalarchives.gov.uk / Morris, R., *Cholera 1832*, Taylor & Francis: 1976)

JANUARY 6TH

1989: On this day, footballer Andy Carroll was born in Gateshead. Carroll started playing for Newcastle United in 2006, after initially showing talent while attending Brighton Avenue Primary School and Joseph Swan Secondary School. His meteoric rise creates an amazing list of achievements. He made his début for Newcastle United on November 2nd 2006 in a UEFA cup win against Palermo. Although he did not score that day, at only 17 years and 300 days old, he became the youngest player to represent United in Europe. In 2007 he was the recipient of the Wor Jackie Milburn Trophy for young players with outstanding potential. On July 29th that year he scored his first senior goal during a friendly against Italian giants Juventus, putting his left-footed shot past World Cup winning goalie, Gianluigi Buffon. He secured his position as United's main striker during the 2009/10 season, where his seventeen goals helped Newcastle gain promotion. His reward was the coveted Newcastle Number 9 shirt – as worn by legends such as Hughie Gallacher, Jackie Milburn, Malcolm MacDonald, Andy Cole and Alan Shearer. Carroll had achieved much, and was still only 22 years old. Then came a day of heartbreak for Newcastle fans: on January 31st – the last day of the transfer window – just before the 11 p.m. deadline, Carroll was unexpectedly signed by Liverpool for £35 million. At the time of writing, this is still the record for the most expensive British player of all time. (www.sport.co.uk)

JANUARY 7TH

1839: This day has gone down in history as 'Windy Monday'. A little past midnight, a hurricane – described by an eyewitness as 'resistless fury and appalling magnitude ... [which] bore a closer resemblance to a west Indian tornado than the storms which, however fierce, visit the temperate regions of our globe' – swept across the country. It howled across Tyneside in the small hours, and hit hardest in Gateshead. In Chopwell, around 20,000 trees were uprooted. By morning, the streets of Gateshead were strewn with debris, bricks and tiles, 'as if the town had stood a siege'. Almost every building on Gateshead Fell had been damaged (many lost their roofs), as had the new Cholera Memorial. The *Fox* steamboat had been blown from its moorings and flung against the bridge, where it sank. There were several major injuries – one man broke a leg in the collapse of the 115ft tower of the Brandling Junction Railway Company, while another broke both arms trying to cross Scotswood Bridge. John Errick was even more unlucky – he was crushed to death by the fall of a 75ft tower at Abbot & Co.'s ironworks, while his friend only just escaped the falling debris. (Fordyce, J., *Local Records*, 1867)

January 8th

1611: On this day, a charter was signed 'rebranding' a long-standing Gateshead institution. The Hospital of St Edmund the King and Martyr (not to be confused with Gateshead's other medieval hospital, the Hospital of St Edmund the Bishop and Confessor), had been providing for the poor of Gateshead for over 300 years, financed by rents and coal revenue from its estates. It even survived the Reformation, although by the 1590s its finances and administration were deeply muddled, and it was only able to support three elderly people. There were even suspicions that some of the administrators were trying to pervert the hospital estates by getting private use out of them. The Common Council applied to King James I for letters patent for the institution to be re-founded – apparently not realising that technically it wasn't anything to do with them! But it worked, and on this day St Edmund's was replaced by the Hospital of King James. Even with royal backing, however, the hospital's decline continued. By the eighteenth century, its cottages were in such disrepair they were pulled down, and hens reportedly roamed freely in its chapel! (Carlton, I., *A Short History of Gateshead*, Gateshead Corporation, 1974 / Manders, F., *A History of King James's Hospital, Gateshead*, King James's Hospital Trustees: 1974)

January 9th

1701: On this day, Revd Theophilus Pickering bequeathed £300 per year to maintain a free school in Gateshead, in a room adjoining St Mary's Church, Oakwellgate. Named the Anchorage School, this – the oldest school in Gateshead – was in a suitable location, as it is believed that an anchoress (a female hermit who volunteered to be 'anchored' to one room or cell for a lifetime of devotion) provided religious instruction on the site from 1340. We know that there was, at least briefly, a school there a little before 1701 because in 1693, minutes from a vestry meeting discharged John Tennant from teaching in the anchorage any further because he had come there 'without the consent of, and in opposition to, Mr George Tullie, rector of the parish'. But perhaps Tennant gave the rector the idea that a school would be an asset to the Church. Pickering's bequest stipulated that the school's master had to teach children in the basics of Latin and Greek, grammar, geography and mathematics, as well as how to keep accounts, and 'the art of navigation, or plain sailing' – important skills for getting a good job on the Tyne. Thanks to Pickering's zeal and generosity, the Anchorage flourished and by 1827 there were about ninety children. Theophilus Pickering – if the records are correct – lived to be 108 or 109 years old! (www. gateshead-grammar.com / Lang, A., *The St Mary's Story*, Gateshead Council, 2009)

January 10th

1886: Around this date, there was a severe and prolonged period of bitter weather at Tyneside. The Swan Pond in Sheriff Hill froze solid, and Mr Elliot, Chief Constable of Gateshead, had the idea of raising funds for the Royal Victoria Infirmary by charging for the use of the pond as an ice rink. The problem was that this was January, with few hours of daylight, so a source of illumination was needed. The pond was a long way from Newcastle's electricity supply stations. Fortunately, Tyneside was a crucible of electrical innovation. Elliot approached Clarke, Chapman & Co. engineering works, whose new staff member, Charles Parsons, had recently invented a new kind of portable generator, called the 'turbo-dynamo'. This steam turbine was shortly to make all earlier forms of power station generator redundant. Elliot persuaded the company of the publicity value of working together and the compact engine, mounted on two wheels, was pulled by a horse to Swan Pond. Joseph Swan provided electric lights made to his own patent, also very new at the time. So many people paid just to say they had skated by electric light, that £100 was raised for the RVI over the course of three days – although it was much too crowded for anyone to really get much skating done! (Weightman, G., *Children of Light*, Atlantic Books, 2011)

JANUARY 11TH

1849: On this day, Marley Hill Colliery's owners felt the wrath of their workers. Miners' conditions and pay were poor at this time. Marley Hill's miners had signed their employment bonds with Bowes & Co., on the understanding that they would receive at least 4s per day. But they were only getting 2s 6d to 3s 6d, and they had to buy their own candles, powder and equipment. When they spoke up about their concerns and talked of unionisation, the mine owners' immediate response was to throw them, their families, and their possessions out of their (company-owned) homes. Furthermore, ejected miners were told that they would be arrested for trespass should they ever return to Bowes & Co. land. In response, the remaining Marley Hill miners went on strike, forcing the owners to buy coal for their coke ovens from the nearby Hobson Pit instead. On the night of January 11th, a group of fifteen armed and disguised men approached the Hobson Pit and menacingly ordered its workers away. They then placed a cask of gunpowder onto the boilers and the resulting explosion caused irreparable damage. With their supply of coal now removed, Bowes & Co. issued a £50 reward for information leading to the arrest of the culprits. In a show of solidarity in the face of injustice, nobody ever came forward. Surely this must be one of the few *deliberate* boiler explosions in the history of coal mining. (ourgateshead.org)

January 12th

1740: By this day the year's continuing bitter winter had finally reached the point where the people might as well use the Tyne as a road. It had frozen over in December, ships could not move, and indeed many were damaged by the press of ice. On this day, the inhabitants of Tyneside took to the ice until the river resembled a market, with stalls selling meat and drink and entertainment including foot races, and even a football match (this being the sort of football with teams of hundreds, a huge 'pitch', and very few rules). The next day, Sir John Fenwick of Bywell held a birthday party on the river for his son – he erected a tent on the ice, where they actually roasted a sheep, and also travelled across the ice in a carriage. The river was still frozen a month later, at which point the coal owners hired 200 men to start cutting a channel through the ice, a mile and a half long, from the staithes to the open water. It took them a week, but by that time a great mass of ice had travelled downstream, which needed clearing out. That done, Sir Henry Liddell tried to extend the channel to other staithes, but stopped when two men drowned. The thaw did not arrive until February 24th. (Sykes, J., *Local Records*, i, 1833)

JANUARY 13TH

1923: On this day the funeral was held at Gateshead East Cemetery of unemployed furnace-man, and respected Communist party member, Alexander Fullarton. It was a colourful affair: the coffin was draped in the red flag of his party, and his twenty-four pall-bearers wore red ribbons. The 1,000 attendees wore red rosettes and ties, and sang 'The Red Flag' and 'We'll keep the Red Flag Flying Here'. There was, however, a farcical element to the proceedings. Fullarton's coffin had to be taken out through the window of his tiny house. At the funeral itself, crowds and marshals turned up to the wrong grave. When the mistake was noticed, a thousand pairs of feet rushed to the correct spot, trampling the ground and damaging other graves. (*Oxberry's Scraps*)

———— •◆• ————

1934: On this day, a rugby team completed a nine-week, 5,200-mile tour around Britain, in Gateshead. Indeed, since the team in question was the Australian Rugby League XIII, they had travelled 10,500 miles beforehand! They were entertained before the game in Newcastle, where players from Newcastle, New South Wales, enjoyed meeting the Lord Mayor of Newcastle, England. The Australian coach, confusingly called Mr H. Sunderland, commented over the post-match dinner at Gateshead Town Hall 'we have in Australia … a minority of people who sometimes make rude noises at sporting functions, but you have in England sporting people whom it has been a delight to meet.' (*Newcastle Journal*)

JANUARY 14TH

1786: On this day, members of the Gateshead Fell Gang were apprehended. The *Newcastle Courant* on January 21st reported that, 'four persons belonging to the notorious gang of thieves and shop-lifters, called the Bishop Auckland Gang, otherwise the Barlow Gang, otherwise the Gateshead-Fell-Gang, so called from several of them residing at these places, and from numbers of them frequently rendezvousing there, were observed reconnoitring the Linen Drapers shops in this town, and traced to an Alehouse in Pipewellgate, where they were apprehended and brought back ...' The four caught on this occasion were Elizabeth Thompson, Walter and Jane Clark, and Eleanor Murray (known as Gardiner). Whilst Walter Clark apparently escaped, a House of Correction document suggests that two further members of the gang were captured later in the year. The description of one, Abraham Smith, paints quite a portrait of the eighteenth-century criminal: 'he was lately a soldier in the Fencibles in America; he appears to be about 21 years of age, 5ft 5ins high, has a dark or swarthy complexion, long dark brown hair, curled at his ears, black eyes, and now wears an old slouched hat, a black neckcloth, an old blue halfwide coat, with white metal flat buttons, an old red double breasted waistcoat, and trowsers.' One of their number was not quite as lucky as Clark: Francis Russell was 'whipped around the Sandhill' for his crimes. (*Newcastle Courant*)

January 15th

1814: On this day, a courageous Dutchman enabled the people of Gateshead and Newcastle to have some fun! The frost was so bitterly cold that the entire breadth of the Tyne, along the stretch from Redheugh to the Glasshouse Bridge at Ouseburn, was frozen over. Tempting though it was to attempt to walk and skate upon it, the people of both towns knew the dangers of the river that divided them. Nervously, one Dutch sailor agreed to test the ice by attaching two cow bones to the soles of his shoes as blades and lowering himself onto the surface. He took with him a long stick, just in case he needed to hold himself in position until help arrived, should the ice have broken. Luckily, he found the ice was solid, and the crowd joyfully joined him. The townsfolk of the North East have always known how to throw an impromptu party, and party they did! For three weeks young, old, rich, poor, men, women and children all enjoyed the ice. Wealthy MPs skated amongst (temporarily) unemployed keelmen and sailors. Booths selling liquor were soon erected on the ice and fires lit for warmth. There were races, with and without skates. Prizes included items of clothing, alcohol and even a leg of mutton. Games of quoits and football, fruit and cake stalls, fiddlers, pipers, and horse and cart rides all added to the village fête atmosphere. (Sykes, J., *Local Records*, ii, 1833)

JANUARY 16TH

1829: On this day, the bells of St Mary's church, Gateshead, rang in celebration of the birthday of the honourable Charles William Lambton, son of Lord Durham. This was not in itself remarkable – church bells rang for many such occasions. Indeed, many churches throughout County Durham rang their bells for Lambton too. But St Mary's had the Union Society of Change Ringers performing at their best! They rang 4,536 changes of grandsire triples – a method of ringing seven bells in every possible mathematical permutation. St Mary's bell tower held eight bells. In grandsire triples, the ringers start with rounds. This is when the bells are rung in sequential order, starting with the lightest bell, number one, and going in through two, three, four, five, six, seven and finally the heaviest bell, the tenor, eighth. The sequence of the first seven bells was then changed in pattern, with the tenor bell always being rung eighth to keep the rhythm going. According to Sykes, it 'was a feat which had never been performed on these bells on any similar occasion before.' It took a very long and gruelling two hours and fifty-eight minutes to ring the changes! (Sykes, J., *Local Records*, ii, 1833)

January 17th

2011: On this day, Gateshead's skyline began to change forever as its residents said goodbye to one of its most distinctive buildings. Derwent Tower was more commonly known as the Dunston Rocket because of its distinctive shape. Architect Owen Luder's brutalist design featured a single, multi-faced tower surrounded by flying buttresses, and its similarities to a rocket were not lost to the Gateshead people when building began in 1969 – the year of the moon landing. Completed in the 1970s, at twenty-nine storeys and over 280ft in height, it dominated the skyline of Gateshead. To stabilise the poor building ground, a special form of foundation had to be created, more commonly associated with sea harbours – a reinforced concrete caisson was built before being sunk into the ground and the tower was then built on top. This caisson was intended to become a car park for residents, but it flooded badly almost immediately. Other problems faced by residents as the tower began to deteriorate included dead and diseased pigeons in the external water tanks, faulty lifts, broken water pumps, electrical faults, disintegrating masonry and cladding, damp and condensation, poor lighting and rising crime. By 2007, when the building was evacuated, only forty of the 196 flats were occupied. Councillor Mick Henry, who began the demolition process, proved a master of understatement when he said that 'the housing in this block was poor and people didn't want to live here anymore.' (*Evening Chronicle*)

JANUARY 18TH

On this day (in an unknown year, and a fictional world) ten-year-old Jane Eyre packed her bags to leave Gateshead Hall, getting ready to set off for Lowood School. In Charlotte Brontë's *Jane Eyre*, the eponymous heroine goes to Gateshead Hall to live with her aunt and cousins, after her parents' death. Alternately ignored and abused by her relatives, Jane suffered many indignities, including a claustrophobic panic when she was locked in the 'red room' where her uncle died (he is said to be buried under a vault of 'Gateshead Church'). She finally left the hall on January 19th and only returned once as an adult, visiting her aunt on her death bed. Gateshead Hall, of course, is as fictional as its inhabitants, and in fact there is nothing to specifically tie the hall and its surroundings, as described by Brontë, to the real Gateshead. The inhabitants of Gateshead may empathise with the brief external descriptions of the 'leafless shrubbery ... cold winter winds ... wet lawn and storm-beat shrub ... and ceaseless rain'. But in fact the hall is thought by some to be based on Stone Gappe Hall, where Brontë worked as a governess – which is in Yorkshire. (Brontë, C., *Jane Eyre*, Wordsworth Editions: 1992)

January 19th

1953: On this day, an inquest decided that a Gateshead man had died after a mining accident. The unusual part of this story is that John Graham Robinson of Windy Nook had sustained his injuries a whole decade earlier. In July 1942, a large stone had fallen from the roof of Heworth Pit and landed on Robinson. The unfortunate man never worked again. The coroner pronounced that he had died of a compound fracture of the spine 'attributable to the injury received in 1942'. (*Gateshead Post*)

———•◆•———

1969: Also on this day a referee felt over-exposed! The referee – whose name is not mentioned in the newspaper article – was due to officiate in a match for the Gateshead and District Sunday Football League. On two previous occasions he had begrudgingly agreed to change in the open in full view of the dozens of spectators and players. On this occasion – a chilly January day – he had had enough, and refused to referee the game. He sent a letter to the Council demanding changing facilities at Moss Heaps and Peggy's Bank playing fields. Council spokesmen replied that previous attempts at providing facilities had failed. These had included a 'cupboard' that was destroyed, a school that banned all football teams after its facilities were abused, and a railway sleeper van that was burnt-out. Eventually, teams moved to the well-equipped Whitehouse Lane instead. (*Gateshead Post*)

JANUARY 20TH

1836: On this day, John Usher was sworn in as Gateshead's first police constable. One week later (in the Gateshead Force's fastest ever promotion) he became superintendent. Newcastle didn't have a police force until a week or two later, and didn't have anyone patrolling the streets until May. Gateshead, meanwhile, recruited six constables in March – although they only worked at weekends between 5 p.m. and midnight, for 1s 6d per night! They joined eight night watchmen who were already working weekends 9 p.m. to 5 a.m., and weekdays 10 p.m. to 5 a.m. In 1836 Usher was hard at work chasing thieves and handling cases relating to obstruction of the turnpike road. Within a couple of years, Gateshead Police Force had two lock-ups: one in the Town Hall and the other at the end of the bridge (though this did not have iron bars until 1843). In the 1840s the force had the use of rattles, sticks, and after 1846, leg irons. By then, wages were 17s a week for an eleven-hour day (plus a free suit and two pairs of shoes per year). But in 1853 the Gateshead police were forbidden to carry sticks and were ordered to 'control their tempers'! Usher himself later went on to be the borough's workhouse master, Superintendent of Births and Marriages, and later Superintendent of Cemeteries. (Pyke, E., 'Gateshead Borough Force', *Northumbria Bobby*, Winter 2009, http://www.thisisgateshead.com)

January 21st

1970: On this day, a child was in the bad books! Nine-year-old Linda Smith of Beacon Lough had, the previous day, decided to go to Brownies. She did not tell her parents where she was going, simply pausing to pick up her knitting before walking out of the door of her house and apparently disappearing. Several hours passed, and as the night drew in, her worried parents called the police. A full-scale search was mounted, with dozens of police officers and dogs systematically searching the streets of Gateshead overnight. In the morning – just as the second shift of police officers was starting – Linda was found in a house a few streets away, still clutching her knitting. In her words: 'I went to Brownies with my friend and I was scared to come home because it finished too late, so I went to her house instead … when she opened the door I sneaked up the stairs without her parents seeing me. When she came to bed she gave me a blanket and a pillow from her doll's cot and I went to sleep under the bed.' After a night of blissful ignorance over the trouble and worry she had caused, Linda was reunited with her parents who said, 'it was a terrible ordeal, we were up all night imagining all sorts of awful things.' Linda promised never to do it again! (*Evening Chronicle*)

January 22nd

1886: On this day, nothing happened. At least, nothing happened in the Gateshead Borough Police Court. The *Tyneside Echo* reports that 'The Magistrate's Clerk (Mr Robson) announced to the magistrates that he was very happy to inform them that they had that morning a maiden session. They had not a single case on the list, a state of things that had not occurred for 20 years.' Rather than twiddle their thumbs, the magistrates asked Robson what was done in this event. Robson then advised that last time, in 1865, he 'had the pleasure of presenting ... the presiding magistrate with a pair of white kid gloves. He had great pleasure in performing a similar ceremony this morning.' The mayor congratulated the Chief Constable on the remarkably low crime-rate and terminated court proceedings for the day. (*Tyneside Echo*)

———◆———

2007: Also on this day, a special ceremony of remembrance was held to remember a Canadian pilot called James D'arcy Lees Graham, who was killed in an accident at High Marley Hill on February 10th 1942. His Hawker Hurricane left RAF Usworth safely, but as weather conditions worsened, D'arcy, as he was known, failed to pull out of a dive from low cloud and crashed into a snow-covered orchard on the hill. He was only 24. (www.sunnisidelocalhistorysociety.co.uk)

January 23rd

1900: On this day, Gateshead was heartily proud of its men! Over forty volunteers from the town signed up to join the 5th Battalion of the Durham Light Infantry to fight in the Boer War, and were sworn in during a hugely patriotic ceremony. Together they enjoyed a hearty dinner and a 'smoking concert' (a concert during which one may smoke!) in the Drill Hall, Bensham. They then marched in full kit, including side arms, to the Town Hall. On the way they were cheered on by Gateshead residents who sang and chanted, despite the atrocious weather. A platform had been erected for the swearing-in ceremony, with the men stepping up six at a time. Colonel Proctor officiated and welcomed the men. Interestingly, he also made an apology that not all of the 280 men that applied could be accepted – he selected 'as good a body of men as they would see in the whole corps, who would be a credit to their country.' In Saltwell Park and Durham Road, two memorials commemorate the Gateshead men who died during the Boer War, 1899–1902. Doubtlessly, many of the names written on those memorials would have been amongst those that were read out so proudly today.

JANUARY 24TH

1889: On this day, the so-called 'Flying Butcher' committed murder in Wrekenton. Edward Wilkinson brutally stabbed Police Constable John Graham of Gateshead's borough force with a large butcher's knife before beating him to death with his own truncheon. It seems that Graham had testified against Wilkinson earlier that day on a charge of disorder, resulting in a fine. Clearly Wilkinson, a butcher by trade, had exacted revenge. Horrifically, the crime took place in broad daylight, in full view of 'a number of bystanders, who appear to have been paralysed with fear, as they did nothing until Wilkinson had left the spot,' according to *Reynold's Newspaper*. If the journalist sounds disapproving of the witnesses for not intervening, he does at least concede that Graham died 'almost immediately'. Graham, only 29 years old, left a widow and four children. For once Victorian justice proved swift. Wilkinson was found in Sunderland on the same night with the knife secured against his leg with a garter. When asked about the crime, he answered, 'I know all about that.' On January 30th a verdict of wilful murder was returned by the coroner's jury. Wilkinson was committed for trial on February 1st, and hanged on the 23rd, less than a month after the murder. (*Reynold's Newspaper / The Monthly Chronicle of North-Country Lore and Legend*)

JANUARY 25TH

1824: On this day, David Shafto Hawks was the first person to play Gateshead's new church organ. This was no mean feat, considering that David had been blind since early infancy. The son of wealthy industrialist Sir Robert Shafto Hawks, he had composed and published marches for military bands at 9 years old, and later specialised in composing Tyrolean, Scottish and Welsh airs, often dedicated to his mentor, Thomas Thompson of St Nicholas', Newcastle. David had already shown 'a most amazing proof of musical genius and early proficiency' when playing the previous organ at St Mary's church, aged just 17. Indeed, there had been an organ in St Mary's since at least 1672, when one is mentioned in the accounts. If that same organ was still in place by the 1820s – and no other is mentioned in the meanwhile – then one can only imagine its state of repair. The new organ was built and erected by Wood, Small & Co. of Edinburgh, but today's event was a purely local affair. David played 'in a most masterful style' and sermons were preached by Revd Charles Thorp of Ryton and Revd John Collinson of Lamesley. The church was crowded from morning to afternoon, filled with Gateshead's ordinary folk as well as the great and the good. Collections raised over £46 in total towards the £525 cost of the organ, supplemented by private donations, pew rents and public subscriptions. (Sykes, J., *Local Records*, ii, 1833 / Lang, A., *The St Mary's Story*, Gateshead Council, 2009)

JANUARY 26TH

1922: On this day, local newspapers reported the shocking news that women had partaken in Burns Night celebrations! The *Evening Chronicle* wrote that 'For the first time in the 36 years of its being, the anniversary dinner of the Gateshead Burns Club was graced by the presence of the lasses. Of the company of 250 enthusiastic Scots ... there were nearly as many ladies as men – which is how the Bard himself would have it.' A new toast of 'The Lasses' was made in acknowledgement, but it was believed by many that a lot of the traditional male 'fun' might be prohibited because of delicate female sensibilities. A Mrs Morrison responded, 'Though our presence here tonight may be a restraint on the surroundings, I think you men will be all the better for it tomorrow,' which raised laughter from men and women alike. (*Evening Chronicle*)

------ • ◆ • ------

2011: Also on this day, film-buffs were given the chance to own a piece of history. The demolition of Trinity Street Car Park had started in July 2010, but today saw the first chance for fans to buy pieces of it in a souvenir tin for £5. Each tin came with a certificate from Owen Luder (*see* January 17th), the architect of the iconic car park. The building was famously known as the *Get Carter* car park; hit-man Jack Carter, played by Michael Caine, threw businessman Cliff Brumby from the top in the 1971 classic film (*see* September 3rd). (www.bbc.co.uk/news)

JANUARY 27TH

1746: On this day, the Duke of Cumberland and his men received a warm welcome in Gateshead. Warm, that is, because of the heat from a burning mansion. The Protestant Duke was on his way north to try and stop the progress of Bonnie Prince Charlie's Catholic army. Tonight he was to stop in Newcastle. To get there he passed through Gateshead, and close to Gateshead House, a mansion owned by a Catholic man, Sir Thomas Riddell. Behind its high walls there was even a Catholic chapel. The Riddells were not there that night – perhaps understandably, given the nature of the duke's visit – and they left their gardener, Woodness, to look after their property. Reports suggest that the crowds of Protestant supporters in Gateshead did not actually intend to burn the building. It seems that many of them scaled its walls to get a clearer view of the royal visitor. Nonetheless, Woodness, keen to defend his employer's property, promptly set the dogs on the trespassers. Many were bitten and the angry mob gave chase. Although Woodness appears to have escaped, the crowd's desire for revenge led to them setting fire to the building. By the time the duke arrived (actually about 1 o'clock in the morning of the 28th), the fire was burning frightfully against the night sky. What became of Woodness, the unfortunate gardener whose zeal for Gateshead House's protection inadvertently led to its destruction, we do not know. (Sykes, J., *Local Records*, i, 1833)

JANUARY 28TH

1417: On this day, Gateshead regained legal control of one third of the Tyne Bridge. The bridge – and the river below it – had been a key point of contention between Newcastle and Gateshead for many years. Newcastle was determined to restrict any development on the Gateshead side, and ideally take the bridge over entirely. In 1383, Newcastle burgesses ordered the building of a tower at the south side of the bridge, and took away the boundary stones from the middle of the overpass, claiming the entire thing. Two years later they challenged the Bishop of Durham to show where, in the charters, it said they should not have jurisdiction over the entire river. In 1412 an agreement seemed to have been reached, with Newcastle burgesses agreeing that the bishop had jurisdiction of the bridge as far as 'the place that is called Jargonhole'. But the Court of Chancery wasn't convinced that this was a genuine agreement, and demanded further proof. It was not until this day, five years on, that the victory was won, with Newcastle Corporation handing over the 1383 bridge tower. But, as Manders puts it, 'the bishop had won a battle but was steadily losing the war', as decisions relating to the river itself increasingly were settled in Newcastle, especially after 1454 when the king granted conservatorship of the Tyne to the town. (Welford, R., *History of Newcastle*, W. Scott, 1884 / Manders, F., *A History of Gateshead*, Gateshead Corporation, 1973)

JANUARY 29TH

1929: On this day, the Prince of Wales stopped here for a cuppa. Making a trip around the coal mining areas of the North, the prince reached High Spen just in time to meet the miners coming in from the night shift. It seems that one man, Robert Farrage, jokingly invited the future King Edward VIII in for tea. Imagine his surprise when his grimy hand was shaken and the offer accepted! Bob took him into his three-roomed house at 6 Front Street, where ten Farrages lived. Here Isabella Farrage was making a meal. Apparently, she wiped her hands on her apron before taking the proffered hand of the prince. An awkward silence was broken when the couple's daughter entered the room. 'Martha, here's the Prince of Wales to see you,' said Isabella. The startled Martha was met with a cheery, 'How do you do?' from their visitor, which put everyone at ease. The prince probably needed refreshment after his depressing visit to Winlaton. A miner, Frank McKay, had arranged to show the state of poverty and poor health some miners were living in. Unfortunately, when the Prince turned up at the McKays' cottage, the blinds were drawn. Frank's wife had just died and he was away making funeral arrangements. The prince simply patted Frank MacKay's daughter on the head, advised her to 'cheer up', and continued his tour. (*The Western Daily Press* / Pears, T.W., *High Spen and District*, ebook, 2010)

JANUARY 30TH

1848: On this day, 15-year-old Hannah Greener was buried in Winlaton. As far as we know, she was the first person to ever die from anaesthesia. Although she died in Newcastle's Infirmary, Hannah was born in Path Head, Winlaton. Her unmarried mother, Hannah Shippen, died during her birth. Her father, John Greener, moved around the North East looking for employment so Hannah lived with various family members. According to one witness at her inquest she was 'much trashed around' by some of her foster parents. Eventually she moved in with her father, who had settled in Winlaton. Hannah suffered from severely ingrown toenails, and by 1848 had already endured one successful operation to remove a nail from her big toe. On that occasion she had been given ether, but it had given her a bad head. Fatefully, the decision was made to switch to chloroform – still a new discovery – for the next operation. Dr Meggison, who administered the chloroform with a handkerchief, was surprised to see Hannah's face turn white. Her mouth spluttered 'as if in epilepsy' so Meggison quickly gave her water and brandy. Despite his efforts, she died within minutes. The inquest found that Hannah had died from congestion of the lungs but that 'no blame could be attached to Dr Meggison'. (Knight, P., 'An Unexplained Death: Hannah Greener and Chloroform', *Anaesthesiology*, 2002 / Pears, B., *The Short, Sad Life and Tragic Death of Hannah Greener*, unpublished)

January 31st

1949: On this day a magistrate heard evidence in a confusing and unusual breaking, entering and theft case. James Cassidy, a bricklayer of Park Road in Gateshead, was sentenced to six months' imprisonment for three crimes. Firstly, he was found guilty of breaking into and entering the Grey Horse Inn with the intention of stealing. He was also found guilty of two further counts of theft – both from Laws stores in Gateshead. This seemed like a straightforward case because Cassidy had already confessed to all three crimes. However, during the trial Cassidy suddenly changed his plea from 'guilty' to 'not guilty' for the latter two counts. Regarding the two thefts from Laws, Cassidy announced in court that he had falsely confessed to those crimes because he was 'afraid of being bashed around by the police'. When asked why, he replied that he 'had been told by several people and I was afraid of getting the same myself'. Cassidy admitted that no actual threats had been made by the police and that he had been treated well and given medical assistance for cuts sustained whilst smashing the pub window. Strangely, he maintained his plea of 'guilty' for the first crime, admitting breaking a window whilst drunk to obtain entry to the pub to get more alcohol. He even noted that 'they had put bars in the windows since' the last time he had broken into the same pub! (*Gateshead Post*)

FEBRUARY 1ST

1840: On this day there was a terrible shipping accident on the Tyne, close to Friar's Goose. According to Fordyce's *Local Records*, 'the London *Merchant Steamer* was going down the river on her voyage to London, and the brig *Good Intent*, from Lynn, laden with flour, was sailing up, towed by the steam-tug *Margaret*, when they came violently in contact with each other. The *Good Intent* was struck on the larboard (port) bow, and in a few minutes went down. The crew had just time to save their lives.' This entry reminds us just how busy – and dangerous – the River Tyne was in its industrial heyday. On the Gateshead side of the river, coal mines (like that at Friar's Goose), glassworks, ironworks, engineering works, cement factories and a whole range of chemical works stood cheek by jowl. Most goods were transported by sea, either to London or abroad, using the Tyne as the link from the warehouse. Millions of tonnes of imports and exports travelled this way in the nineteenth century. With increased trade and traffic came increased problems. Danger was not limited to the river itself, but spread to its quays and buildings. Days like this – featuring accidents, explosions, fires or violence – were all too commonplace. (Fordyce, T., *Local Records*, 1867)

February 2nd

1871: On this day, a Gateshead theatre manager gave his disappointed customers their money back. The Alexandra Theatre stood at the corner of Oakwellgate and the High Street. Managed by Mr Edwins, it was Gateshead's first theatre, having opened on November 14th 1870. Today's performance was to feature Laura de Braham's *troupe* of four Parisian dancers, performing what was billed as 'the Can Can'. This sounds like a very loose interpretation! 'Three women were on the stage, two representing characters of their own sex, while the third represented a man … a young girl sprung forward and joined them. Their manoeuvres were obscene, and the one habited in male attire was almost in a state of nakedness. Towards the conclusion she performed the trick designated by clowns "splits".' Unfortunately for cast and audience alike, Gateshead's mayor and chief constable had both seen earlier performances. Chief Constable Elliott judged it 'immoral' – whilst he had seen the Can Can danced before, he had seen 'nothing like what he saw at the Alexandra'! The mayor had never seen 'anything more beastly' in his life and officially banned the 'Parisian ballet'. So it was that Mr Edwins had to step onto his stage, apologise for this evening's cancellation and offer a refund. Unsurprisingly, 'many availed themselves of [his] kindness.' The Alexandra itself closed, permanently, only four months after opening and later became a place of worship for Gateshead's Salvation Army and Baptists. (*The Era*)

FEBRUARY 3RD

1953: On this day, author Garry Hogg gave a stark warning to the Gateshead Tea Club. Hogg, a travel writer, was promoting his latest work, *The Turf Beneath My Feet*, as part of a lecture tour of Britain. Two hundred members of the Tea Club gathered in the Bewick Hall, probably expecting a relaxing talk involving photographs and anecdotes. Certainly they would have welcomed Hogg's readings of the works of Thomas Hardy, Hugh Walpole and Sheila K. Smith, and his reminiscences of countryside walks. Next, however, the author used the occasion to vociferously warn the assembled book lovers of the anti-social dangers of … television. To quote Hogg's eloquent battle-cry: 'Television is modern civilisation's greatest menace … it will make us a nation of non-readers, of anti-socialites, of glassy-eyed people, content to watch the petty pieces of actors on screen.' It is easy to imagine the tone and actions of the orator during his rant, and also the stunned reaction of the tea-sipping audience! Retrospectively, Hogg's comments seem to foreshadow many opinions held today. But it should be remembered that in 1953, the BBC was airing such socially threatening shows as *Muffin the Mule*, *Panorama* and the coronation of Elizabeth II; hardly the tell-tale signs of an oncoming population of glassy-eyed couch potatoes! It may also be of interest that one of Hogg's better-known books, written in 1958 and still in print, is the exceptionally graphic *Cannibalism and Human Sacrifice*! (*Gateshead Post*)

FEBRUARY 4TH

1941: On this day, John Steel – future drummer with The Animals – was born in Gateshead. He remembers his childhood as full of music: 'My sisters were fond of musicals, my brother tended to be touching on jazz … and my dad liked Bing Crosby.' He learned the piano as a child, apparently due to a parental belief that someone who could play well would always be able to make a living. He then switched to jazz trumpet. Steel studied at Newcastle College of Art and Industrial Design, and was a founder member of The Pagan Jazzmen – which was soon transformed by the discovery of rock and roll. At this point Steel began to play drums – because the band's drummer wanted to move to guitar! After a few shifts in line-up (including time as The Kansas City Several, and the Alan Price Rhythm and Blues Combo), the band emerged as The Animals, named for their wild stage act. The group's bluesy rock was at the centre of a booming musical scene in early 1960s Tyneside, encouraging talk of a distinctive Tyne sound to rival that coming from the Mersey. But that never fully materialised, and The Animals' career was dramatic but brief. Currently, John Steel still tours as Animals and Friends. (www.earlyblues.com)

FEBRUARY 5TH

1916: On this day, a terrible tragedy occurred on Bensham Bank. Young tram driver Leonard Jane had left Saltwell Park with the No. 7 tram. Around 7.30 p.m. he stopped outside the Ravensworth Arms as another tram, parked outside St Cuthbert's church, was blocking his route. Leonard engaged his handbrake and walked up the bank to consult the driver. Unfortunately, he had not informed the conductress. Thinking he was still aboard, she continued letting on passengers, expecting that soon the bell would ring and the tram would move. Leonard hadn't known about a secondary 'slipper' brake and had, understandably, not engaged it. The increasing weight of the vehicle made it slip its handbrake, and it rolled down the steep slope with gathering speed. The trolley soon came off the electric overhead cable, plunging the whole tram into darkness. Suddenly the tram came to the sharp bend leading onto Saltwell Road, where it toppled. Amazingly, nobody on board was killed, although many were injured. Not so lucky were the four people crushed beneath it. A family of three – Vaisey and Jane Morrell and their 7-year-old son Foster – had been crossing the tracks on the way to the nearby picture house. Tragically, the fourth victim was Private Hutchinson, a Durham soldier who was on leave; he had survived action at the Somme, only to be killed on home soil. In 2011, children from Kelvin Grove Primary School wrote and recorded a moving song to commemorate the tragedy. (*Evening Chronicle*)

FEBRUARY 6TH

1985: On this day, local press reported how one Gateshead business was bucking the unemployment trend! In a period of history where North-Eastern miners, shipyard workers and metal workers were famously hit by a huge rise in unemployment and strike action, one industry was actively searching for men – the stripping industry! Having employed female strippers for years, local businesswoman Ann Robertson had had the brainwave of targeting hen and 'ladies-only' nights by employing men to dance and strip. Like a real-life, local version of the Sheffield-based film *The Full Monty*, her business grew up in one of the most economically hard-hit areas of Gateshead. In an interview with the *Gateshead Post*, Robertson said, 'all we look for in a male stripper is good looks, masculinity and an original act. Every person I employ is one person less for the Government to worry about. The income is steady, well above average earnings and no one can say we're not fulfilling a demand.' The report then mentions her 'famous five' of 'fire-eating Geno, Dominic and his snakes, leather-clad Zorro, the terrifying Victor and gentlemanly Bowie.' Interestingly the subsequent week's *Post* saw another article about the Robertson Agency – asking for public help in sourcing a large snake for one of her star line-up. Apparently Dominic's 10ft Indian python, Barnaby, had died shortly after the first article, and he needed a replacement for his act! (*Gateshead Post*)

FEBRUARY 7TH

1855: On this day, the 'dirty little back lane out of Newcastle' got a little bit cleaner! Dr Johnson's famously damning description of eighteenth-century Gateshead seems in many ways accurate. Certainly clean water, decent sanitation and basic public hygiene facilities were sorely lacking. But on this day, two years after the 1853 cholera epidemic, Oakwellgate Baths were opened. These were Gateshead's first public baths and washhouses and cost £4,300 to build. William Hall, the Borough Engineer, designed an impressive building, capped off with the Gateshead civic arms and motto. They were used by around 400 people a week, but the costs put others off: 'warm baths – first class sixpence; second class two-pence; cold baths – two-pence and one penny respectively while washing was charged for at one penny per hour.' Carlton reports, 'the washing facilities included "ingenious" wringing machines'. By 1914, the building was being used as a factory, and it eventually fell out of use altogether. The building was Grade II listed, but falling foul of fire and vandalism, it was mostly demolished in the 1990s. Part of its wall has been incorporated into the Sage Gateshead's car park. (Carlton, I., *A Short History of Gateshead*, Gateshead Corporation, 1974)

FEBRUARY 8TH

1813: On this day was formed, in Gateshead, the Melon Lodge of the Order of Free Gardeners. The Free Gardeners was one of many friendly societies which flourished at the time (Gateshead also had Freemasons, Oddfellows, and the Lodge of Free and Easy Johns). The Free Gardeners traced their origins to late seventeenth-century Scotland, where 'free' (ie non-professional) gardeners met for mutual support, developing 'secrets' and multiple branches. The organisation reached the North East with a regiment of the Forfar militia stationed in North Shields. St George's Lodge, North Shields, beget the St Michael Pineapple Lodge, who met in Newcastle's Flesh Market. They in turn warranted the Melon Lodge. Neither seems to have had much interest in gardening, unlike Adam's Lodge, Sunderland, which held actual flower shows. (Mackenzie, E., *Historical Account of Newcastle*, 1827)

———— • ◆ • ————

2003: On this day, volunteers gathered at the Baltic Art Gallery to learn about participating in Antony Gormley's 'Domain Field' artwork. Gormley explained the project – and over two days, 240 local people, aged 5-95, were selected from over 900 applicants. A gallery was given over to a team of sculptors who worked to make full body plaster casts of each person. Each cast was then used as the basis for a unique 'body' made of stainless steel bars, and the 900 figures positioned across a whole floor of the gallery. (Baltic media release)

FEBRUARY 9TH

1930: On this day, one of Gateshead's unsung benefactors was born. Derek Oyston was a science teacher at Hookergate Grammar School. Known to be eccentric – he kept a cushion stuffed full of pink ribbon in his classroom – he was well liked by both pupils and staff. He was also homosexual. One of his pupils remembers: 'Far from thinking Derek was gay, we really thought that Derek and the school secretary … were an item. They certainly got on very well together and we often saw them talking and laughing together. Again in retrospect, they both had some involvement in out-of-school amateur dramatics, so that probably accounted for their friendship.' However, at some point in his school career, Oyston was apparently dogged by homophobic abuse from some of the pupils, which sadly contributed to the health problems that eventually led to his retirement in 1971. But for all of his contributions and achievements as a teacher, it was in death that he had most impact. When Oyston died in 2005, he left the bulk of his considerable estate to the Campaign for Homosexual Equality, an organisation that used the money to create an award for the prestigious London Lesbian and Gay Film Festival, the Derek Oyston Award. The annual award recognises the achievements of those that make films that document and reflect the experience of campaigning for lesbian and gay rights – an extraordinary legacy. (www.ageofdiversity.org.uk)

FEBRUARY 10TH

1800: On this day, Sir Joseph Cowen was born in Greenside. From humble, working-class beginnings (starting out as an apprentice chain-maker), Cowen managed to climb the social and political ladder, eventually becoming Chairman of the Tyne Improvement Committee (for which he was given a knighthood in 1871), a Durham Justice of the Peace, an Alderman, and Liberal MP for Newcastle (from 1865 until his death in 1873). His father, one of a long line of workers at Crowley's Ironworks, founded a factory in Blaydon Burn when the ironworks closed in 1816. Sir Joseph inherited this factory and greatly enlarged it, founding Joseph Cowen & Co., a brick-makers specialising in fine-quality fire-bricks. A fighter for the rights of the working man, Cowen always ensured that his workers and their families were well looked after – even arranging for Blaydon to be connected to his factory's gas lighting system! He was also a shrewd businessman, successful enough to display his factory's wares in the 1851 Great Exhibition. He bought Stella Hall, where his family would remain for generations. His son, also called Joseph, had a career that eclipsed even his father's – he too was a great businessman, MP and political activist, but also became an influential newspaper editor. ('Millionaires and how they became so', *Tit-Bits*, 1884 / *Oxford Dictionary of National Biography*)

February 11th

1916: On this day, a policeman had a lucky escape. Constable William Smith, of the Gateshead Police Force, was passing an indoor shooting range just off the High Street when a bullet whizzed by within 12in of his head, smashing through a window. Smith found the culprit immediately – it was Jane Chapman of Plough Yard, who managed the shooting range for a Mr Wilson. Finding out whether she did it deliberately or accidentally, however, was rather trickier. Constable Smith entered the range to interview Mr Wilson. Wilson immediately pointed the finger of suspicion at Chapman, alleging that she had been using the Winchester repeating rifle to shoot at Wilson himself! Constable Smith took her into custody and marched her off towards the station. *En route* Chapman said to Smith, 'I was only cleaning the rifle. Here's a pound note. Don't say anything about it.' Amazingly, Chapman's lawyer followed this line of defence, saying that, 'Sometimes the rifles get jammed, and the only way to get rid of the cartridge then is to fire off the rifle … It was her duty to clean and oil the rifles, and she was doing this on the day in question.' Even more amazingly, the court accepted this and Chapman was merely handed a £2 fine for not observing appropriate precautions. (*Evening Chronicle*)

February 12th

2001: On this day, fugitive 'Wild Bill' was knocked down and killed while making a daring escape attempt. 'Wild Bill' was the name given to a 12-stone wild boar, which saw an opportunity to avoid the slaughterhouse as he was being loaded onto a van in Chopwell. He managed to make it 10 miles over the borough border into Durham. On the A692, however, he was hit by a car and died of head injuries. The driver – a 40-year-old man – was unharmed, but very surprised. Perhaps Wild Bill was searching for his kin – a press report warns its readers: 'Wild Bill's cousins, some of which grow to more than 6ft long, weigh more than 20st and run at 30mph, are roaming the North-East … A report suggests that numbers could reach almost 3,500 by 2012 and, after more than 300 years of extinction in Britain, boars like Wild Bill will become a common sight once again.' Journalistic hyperbole aside, another wild boar *had* terrorised part of Gateshead just three years before. In July 1998 residents of a housing estate in Felling witnessed a boar attacking foals in a nearby field. When they tried to intervene, the huge, tusked creature gave chase. Eventually a police marksman shot him before any further harm could be done. Several others, also thought to be escapees, were spotted in Chopwell Woods in late 2001, and at least one was shot. (*The Northern Echo / Evening Chronicle*)

FEBRUARY 13TH

2012: On this day, a Gateshead couple were banned from keeping animals for three years. The reason – they had kept a pet marmoset in their front room! According to the RSPCA, 18-month-old Marley was treated as a member of the family by his owners. A spokesperson said that 'it isn't necessary to have a special licence to keep a marmoset but they are extremely difficult to look after correctly and shouldn't be owned by anyone who isn't expert in their needs.' Judging from the report, Duncan Johnston and Patricia Wilson were not experts. They gave him a parrot's cage to live in and he shared the room with two dogs. Speaking after her case was heard at Gateshead's Magistrates Court, Wilson, of Rawling Road, Low Fell revealed that she had bought Marley for £900 from a friend – on Facebook! She clearly meant no harm to the creature, however, saying, 'Marley and I bonded straight away and I loved him.' Her father, a neighbour, added that, 'it was just like having a new baby in the family. He used to come over to ours and he would ride around on my dog's back.' The RSPCA commented that 'this marmoset was lucky in many ways, although his needs weren't being met he didn't come to any physical harm in the care of Johnston and Wilson ... Marley is now in the kind of environment he requires, surrounded by his own kind.' (*Northern Echo*)

February 14th

1934: On this day, Sir Vincent Raven, KBE, died. Although born in 1859 in Norfolk and buried in Suffolk, it is the former Greenesfield Locomotive works on Fletcher Road in Gateshead that bears a memorial plaque with his name on it. In 1876 the young engineer began an apprenticeship in the town with North Eastern Railways. Through hard work and grand ambitions, he gained seniority and responsibilities in the firm, becoming its Chief Assistant Locomotive Superintendent in 1893 and eventually its last Chief Mechanical Engineer in 1910. A frustrated visionary, his plans for rail transport in the North were extremely progressive. It has been said that he was well ahead of the times in which he lived, particularly in his promotion of electric railways. Unveiling the aforementioned plaque in 2012, Gateshead's mayor, Joe Mitchison, commented, 'even now we think of electric trains as something modern, high tech almost. Raven was well ahead of his time; if circumstances hadn't changed, the North East would have been a world leader in high speed electric trains. There is a very good chance that world railway history would have been totally different. His passion for electric trains was proved to be well founded and today most of the passenger trains that link the North East to London and Edinburgh are the direct descendants of Raven's pioneering work.' (www.guardian.co.uk)

FEBRUARY 15TH

1937: On this day, a brand new cinema was opened by actress Gracie Fields. Originally known as Black's Regal, the cinema was built at 306 High Street. It was the most opulent cinema in Gateshead and boasted a magnificent Compton organ which was played during performances and intervals. Today, Mayor Alderman White officiated at the opening ceremony before Fields performed from the Regal's rooftop. Fields was at the time the nation's highest paid film and music star, but she still interrupted a holiday in glamorous St Moritz to come to Gateshead for the occasion! Crowds of several thousand stopped traffic in the streets as she sang. In 1944 the cinema was taken over by the Odeon chain, and in 1945 it was renamed the Gateshead Odeon. The 'Rochdale Lass' continued to entertain and lift British spirits throughout the war years and the austerity of the 1950s, and the same can be said of the building she opened for Gateshead's residents. By the 1960s and 1970s, however, both were in decline – Fields, due to ill health, and the Odeon in the face of stiff competition from television. In 1975, the doors on the cinema's final performance closed. Gracie Fields died in 1979. By that time, the once glamorous Odeon had become a bingo hall. (Manders, F., *Cinemas of Gateshead*, Gateshead Council, 1995)

FEBRUARY 16TH

1998: On this day, The Angel of the North was officially unveiled – although its arrival and construction took much longer than one day. On February 14th, it took three low-loaders five hours to bring the pieces of the 20m tall sculpture from Hartlepool Steel Fabrications Ltd on Teesside to its current position. It travelled at no more than 15mph and enjoyed a police escort all the way! On the 15th, a large crowd gathered to watch the Angel's ascension as cranes slowly lifted it to its feet. Today, designer Antony Gormley was at the site to welcome his now iconic creation. The former Turner prize-winner said that today was 'an extraordinary day, really, really extraordinary. Hundreds of people have turned up and the feeling that I get from the atmosphere here today is like the best birthday party any sculpture could have.' According to most, its 54m wingspan and 200 tonnes weight marked it out, not only as an inspiring monolithic work of art, but also as a great example of North-East engineering and ambition. But it was not without its detractors. Local press coined the phrase the 'Angel of Death', amid fears that its appearance would distract passing motorists on the A1, causing road fatalities. *The Gateshead Post* even produced a silhouetted picture of the 1935 Luftwaffe statue in Berlin, which to some bore a striking resemblance to the Angel! (www.bbc.co.uk/news)

FEBRUARY 17TH

1865: On this day, an aggrieved relative took the law into his own hands. Thomas George Hetherington was the nephew of the recently deceased Thomas Cummins, a magistrate. At this time Gateshead's Temperance Union was well established and was promoting abstention from alcohol as a way of improving the town's working men. Unfortunately, two years earlier Cummins had allegedly been found drunk on Windmill Hills. His recent (non-alcohol related!) demise was used by Mr Lucas, a 'well-known gentleman in temperance circles', as a cautionary tale. Lucas printed flyers for his talk, 'The Last Days of a Gateshead Magistrate; A Lesson of Instruction and Warning', and pasted them all over town. Mr Hetherington, incensed by the smearing of his uncle's good name, stormed to the Temperance Hall to confront Lucas, crying, 'You are a cowardly blackguard. It is an act that no-one with the feelings of a man would be guilty of. And I intend to administer to you a sound horsewhipping' – which he did, much to the delight of the gathering crowds. According to the not-entirely-impartial *Gateshead Observer*, this 'served him right'. Indeed, the whip was 'almost worn away' by its use! Lucas was then turned around and kicked 'on the part that hurts honour more than any part before'. His lecture never did go ahead, and Hetherington escaped punishment for what was perceived by many to be an honourable act. (*Gateshead Observer*)

FEBRUARY 18TH

1850: On this day, Gateshead was mourning the death of a national hero. John William Trotter was christened at St Mary's church in 1770. His parents, George and Dorothy, ran the Goat Inn on nearby Bottle Bank. In 1785, Trotter was apprenticed to Captain Usher, master mariner, under whom his sea career appears to have flourished. His distinguished service for the Royal Navy would be enough to make him an important son of Gateshead, but more was to come. Trotter joined HMS *Leviathan* as master in 1803. Admiral Sir Henry William Bayntun, GCB (1766 – 16 December 1840) was a senior officer in the Royal Navy, whose distinguished career in the French Revolutionary and Napoleonic Wars was a catalogue of the highest and lowest points of the Navy during the conflict. HMS *Leviathan* had a crew of 640 men and 74 guns. On October 21st 1805, *Leviathan* fought at the Battle of Trafalgar. During the battle, Trotter skilfully manoeuvred *Leviathan* into position to attack the Spanish ship *San Augustin. Leviathan* fired a broadside at her at a range of under 50 yards. The determined Trotter then moved it across the *San Augustin's* bow, allowing the gun crews to sweep her decks. Outflanked, the *San Augustin* surrendered in one of the most comprehensive victories of the epic battle. Trotter was 35 years old. For his contribution, he was awarded the Trafalgar Medal – an incredible 43 years later, aged 78! He died on this day, two years later, and was 'interred with all becoming solemnity and respect' in the church where he had been baptised eighty years before. Today, his gravestone stands alone on the west side of St Mary's. (*Newcastle Journal* / Lang, A., *The St Mary's Story*, Gateshead Council: 2009)

FEBRUARY 19TH

1848: On this day, as the *Gateshead Observer* reported, 'at ten minutes to twelve o'clock, an express train, arranged by Messrs. Smith and Sons, newsagents, London, arrived at the Gateshead Station, with the financial statement of Lord John Russell and the debate in parliament of the evening previous. The distance from the metropolis to Gateshead having been performed in six hours and twenty minutes.' The advent of railways evidently helped Gateshead's blossoming newspaper industry as well as its coal industry! Modern high-speed electric trains take three hours to do the same journey, but this was at the time an impressive undertaking. The Gateshead station the article refers to is the one that was built for the Newcastle to Darlington line, which opened in 1844 (and in reality only went as far north as Gateshead – *see* June 19th). Although the Scotswood Railway Bridge had been built in 1839, there was not yet a railway bridge to directly link the north and south lines over the River Tyne. Until the building of the High Level Bridge (*see* June 7th), passengers were instead asked to alight at Gateshead station and then catch a steamer to Newcastle Central station, where they could then continue their journey by rail. When the Team Valley line opened in 1868, a second station was opened in Gateshead. To avoid confusion they were re-named Gateshead East and Gateshead West. Gateshead West eventually closed in 1965 whilst Gateshead East carried on until 1981. (*Gateshead Observer*)

FEBRUARY 20TH

1912: Around this day, London's cultural elite were astir with enthusiasm for the latest theatre première – the social commentary *Rutherford and Son*, written by Githa Sowerby of Gateshead. Githa was born into the Sowerby glass-working dynasty, and while she also wrote other works (including several successful children's books), it was this play that brought her greatest success. Perhaps that was because she was writing about what she knew. While the devastating social and economic satire of *Rutherford and Son* was not a direct reflection of her own life, the play is a no-punches-pulled family saga set against the backdrop of their glassworks! Crucially, 'K.G. Sowerby' did not reveal that she was a woman, and when the audience called 'author!' on the opening night, she stayed in her seat. The next morning, she woke to glowing reviews comparing her to Ibsen. When the press discovered her gender, Githa Sowerby was propelled to brief celebrity as an unwitting feminist icon. It is thought that she hated the attention, and presented an image of an air-headed ingénue to deflect attention – certainly the press presented her as 'just the sort of young woman you may meet by the score on tennis lawns ...' Perhaps this is why her achievement was almost forgotten for many years, and she died in obscurity. One hundred years after its first showing, *Rutherford and Son* has recently been revived, to mixed opinions on its longevity. (Various national press)

FEBRUARY 21ST

1919: On this day, First World War flying ace Thomas Elliott retired. Born in Gateshead in 1898, Elliott was the only child in his family to survive to adulthood. His parents must have been petrified when he joined the war effort in one of the most dangerous occupations – the life expectancy of an airman was just eleven days! Nonetheless, in his Bristol F.2b, Elliott successfully 'bagged' at least eleven enemy planes in his career, achieving the rank of 2nd Lieutenant and the tag of 'ace'. (www. theaerodrome.com)

1969: Also on this day, High Spen began its fight-back! A public meeting was held in response to Spen's Category D listing by Durham County Council. This classification meant that the mining village was to be left to wither on the vine. No new houses or shops were to be built and any vacant properties could be demolished. At the meeting, Blaydon Urban District Council and the local Labour Party publicly vowed to join residents in their fight for survival. MP Bob Woof subsequently raised awareness in Parliament. High Spen survived – in 1974 it came under the jurisdiction of Gateshead Council, who removed the Category D tag and started to regenerate the area. Some Category D villages, such as Chopwell, had similar escapes. Others, like Addison, were not so lucky (*see* September 19th). (www.englandsnortheast.co.uk / Pears, T., *High Spen and District*, ebook: 2010)

FEBRUARY 22ND

1774: On this day the Gateshead Society for the Prosecution of Felons was started, possibly the first of its kind in the country. Formed in response to rising crime, this society resolved to 'use our utmost endeavours to apprehend and prosecute every person who shall commit any Burglary, Felony, Robbery, Theft, Depredation or other Misdemeanour [*sic.*], in or upon the persons or properties of the members.' It included property owners, shopkeepers, and many others who had something worth stealing. (Manders, F. *History of Gateshead*, Gateshead Corporation: 1973)

———◆———

1939: Also on this day, the Team Valley Trading Estate was formally opened by King George VI and Queen Elizabeth (later the Queen Mother). At St George's House the King unveiled a commemorative plaque, an event which attracted 500 people. The royal couple spent three hours on site, touring factories and businesses. The whole event was captured on an early promotional video, including one embarrassing, if small, mishap: an official bow that was due to be untied by royal hands simply refused to slip! Sheepishly, a Team Valley official had to go and find a pair of scissors to (carefully) hand to the King ... (www.nrfta.org.uk)

FEBRUARY 23RD

1745: On this day, the co-founder of Methodism John Wesley crossed Gateshead Fell. He found the paths 'abundantly worse than they had been the day before; not only because the snows were deeper, which made the causeways in many places unpassable ... but likewise because the hard frost, succeeding the thaw, had made all the ground like glass. We were often obliged to walk, it being impossible to ride, and our horses several times fell down while we were leading them ... It was past eight before we got to Gateshead-Fell, which appeared a great pathless waste of white. The snow filling up and covering all the roads, we were at a loss how to proceed; when an honest man of Newcastle overtook and guided us safe into the town. Many a rough journey have I had before, but one like this I never had; between wind, and hail, and rain, and ice, and snow, and driving sleet, and piercing cold.' (*The Journal of John Wesley*)

1898: Also on this day, a beef-dressing competition was held in the Standard Theatre, Gateshead. Beef dressing is slaughtering and dividing the carcass of an animal as quickly as possible. Today, London's Edward Harper took on Gateshead's Matthew Ramsey. The bulls they were dressing each weighed 53st. Ramsey lost, disadvantaged by a bad case of blood poisoning in his left hand. (*Newcastle Weekly Courant*)

FEBRUARY 24TH

1900: On this day, a Swalwell man won the Victoria Cross for bravery in action in South Africa. Originally a Yorkshireman, James Firth lived in Quality Row. He enlisted in the Duke of Wellington's West Riding regiment in 1889, eventually becoming a sergeant. His citation in the *London Gazette* makes gripping reading: 'During the action at Plewman's Farm, near Arundel, Cape Colony, Lance-Corporal Blackman having been wounded and lying exposed to a hot fire at a range of from four to five hundred yards, Sergeant Firth picked him up and carried him to cover. Later in the day, when the enemy had advanced to within a short distance of the firing line, Second Lieutenant Wilson being dangerously wounded and in a most exposed position Sergeant Firth carried him over the crest of the ridge, which was being held by the troops, to shelter, and was himself shot through the nose and eye whilst doing so.' Due to his injuries, the Boer War was over for Sergeant Firth. With typical gallantry it seems that he made a further application to fight in 1914, at the advent of the First World War, but he was denied, again on medical grounds. Sergeant James Firth died of tuberculosis in 1921, aged just 47. In his will he left his son a silver watch, presented to him by the people of Swalwell. (angloboerwar.com)

FEBRUARY 25TH

1885: On this day, the Reading Rooms of Gateshead's first public library opened on Swinburne Street. It had not been an easy job getting to this point. Despite an 1850 Act establishing the principle of free libraries for townspeople, Gateshead seemed reticent to adopt the idea. This was partially due to increased rates. There was also influential opposition from the Mechanics Institute, which had its own members' library (though this was, in truth, more of a middle-class gentlemen's club than something for the common man). When the decision was finally made in 1880, it was only carried by a 681-649 vote in favour! Nonetheless, on this day Lord Northbourne's opening ceremony attracted crowds, eager to see the inspiring Romanesque architecture, including a 'colonnade enriched with festooned pediments'. There were symbolically significant statues of the Greek philosopher Archimedes and renowned Gateshead engraver Thomas Bewick overlooking the entrance. The library proved popular, especially with the 13-20 age group of working men. Indeed, the newspapers of the day reported that the people of Gateshead simply couldn't get enough. One letter to the editor of the *Tyneside Echo* complained that the Reading Room's 9 p.m. closing time was too early for most! The library's first most-borrowed book was *Robinson Crusoe*, possibly because of the widely held (but unsubstantiated) belief that Daniel Defoe wrote it during his brief stay in Gateshead ... (Manders, F., *A History of Gateshead*, Gateshead Corporation: 1973 / *Newcastle Weekly Courant*)

FEBRUARY 26TH

1827: On this day people lined the Gateshead Quays to get a better look at an old man in a boat! Alexander Brodie was described as 'the oldest wherryman on the river Tyne'. A 'wherry' was simply a transportation boat that carried coal, metal, chemicals, bricks or any other locally made produce along the Tyne. The men who piloted and maintained them were tough, skilled and knew the river they worked on better than any. Brodie would have been well used to dealing with the effects of floods. Although we do not know his exact age, it is more than likely that he could remember the awful flood of February 1793, and probably the Great Flood of November 1771 (*see* November 16th). Both of these catastrophes had been caused by rapid thawing after a period of heavy snow and frost. On this day, the cause was the same. The flood waters were not as high as on those two monumental occasions, but were high enough to flood cellars and buildings on both sides of the river, as well as the streets. Sykes reports that 'about 4 o'clock in the afternoon [Brodie] plied a small boat along the Quay … to the amusement of several spectators.' Having navigated the river countless times before, this would be one of the very few times Brodie would have been able to sail along a street! (Sykes, J., *Local Records*, ii, 1833)

February 27th

1849: On this day, Mrs Cail of Gateshead was about to give birth to William Henry Cail, an almost-forgotten key figure in sporting history. Described as 'a dour man of few words' and 'a hard-headed businessman', Cail was an alderman of Newcastle and a politician of some repute. His major love, however, was amateur sports, and it was in this field he would make his mark. In his youth Cail was a keen amateur rower, but was unable to compete with professionals in this sport. He was also a leading figure in the establishment of the first Northumberland County Cricket Club in 1881, which still meets in Jesmond. The previous year he had been instrumental in the formation of the Northumberland Rugby Football Union. He became Treasurer of the national Rugby Football Union and its President from 1892–4. This was a particularly important time in the evolution of the game, being the period of the 'Great Schism' when twenty-two teams from Yorkshire and Lancashire resigned from the amateur-based RFU to form the professionally based Northern League – effectively making Rugby League and Union separate sports. Cail's biggest achievement is probably the creation of a 'home' for English amateur rugby in Twickenham. Cail also managed the England team in a tour of South Africa in 1910 and – interestingly – introduced Stuttgart to rugby in 1865. (Harris, E., *Twickenham Rugby Ground 1906-1910: A Grand Gesture*, Kingston University: 2010)

FEBRUARY 28TH

1931: On this day, Gateshead received news that it was to receive its first automatic traffic signals. At this stage there was no accepted standard phrase to describe traffic lights, so the *Evening Chronicle* ran an article entitled 'Traffic Robots'! It is a shame that the phrase did not catch on ... (*Evening Chronicle*)

❖

1953: Also on this day, Gateshead Football Club had a shot at the big time! The FA Cup Quarter Finals was a stage that the Division Three North team had never reached before. Today at Redheugh Park they faced the mighty Bolton Wanderers, featuring five international players including the legendary Nat Lofthouse. Gateshead's minnows had beaten top-flight and well-known opposition, including Liverpool, Hull and Plymouth, *en route* to this fixture, and it was hotly anticipated by the locals. In the rush for tickets, one woman was badly hurt and needed one leg amputated. A record 17,692 turned up to watch the 'Heed' attempt to carry on their impressive run – which they very nearly did! Gateshead – playing in borrowed black and white stripes – should have been awarded a penalty when Bolton's Eric Bell handled the ball in his own box. Just moments later, Lofthouse's talent and experience combined to score the only goal of the game. Bolton may have won 1-0 today, but they went on to lose 4-3 to Blackpool in the famous 'Matthews' final. But could Gateshead have done any better if that penalty had been given ...? (www.gateshead-fc.com / Esther, G., *Requiem for Redheugh*, Gateshead Council: 1984)

FEBRUARY 29TH

1892: On this day, James Whistler wrote from Paris to Maria Leathart at Bracken Dene, Gateshead, asking to borrow one of his own works of art, 'Purple' and 'Rose: The Lange Leizen of the Six Marks', for exhibition. Maria's husband James was a prominent industrialist, and also a leading patron of the arts, frequently commissioning new pieces, especially from the Pre-Raphaelites. Dante Gabriel Rossetti painted Maria, and Ford Madox Brown painted James himself; the two portraits hung on either side of a fireplace in Bracken Dene. Focussing on landscapes, Leathart also bought or commissioned works by Whistler and other well-known landscape artists. He was not, however, universally liked: archaeologist William Greenwell once wrote to the wife of another landscape painter, Alfred William Hunt, that if Leathart won Hunt's Time and Tide at auction, 'I should regret him getting it more than anyone, for he absolutely is entirely without taste, & is so vainglorious about his "refined" feelings'. James Leathart's interest in art continued, and indeed he normally dealt with correspondence himself, but by 1892 he was in poor health. He was to live another three years, increasingly forced to sell his beloved landscapes in order to stave off financial troubles. Arthur Hughes' Mrs James Leathart and Children (showing only three out of the couple's ten children!), painted at Bracken Dene, can be seen at the Laing Art Gallery. (Newall, C., The Poetry of Truth, Ashmolean Museum, 2004 / www.whistler. arts.gla.ac.uk)

MARCH 1ST

1836: On this day, Gateshead held an election for the Assessors of the Borough. It was the first election to be overseen by George Hawks, who had been elected as Gateshead's first mayor on January 1st 1836. Surviving documents reveal the locations of the first local polling stations: East Ward enjoyed the Justice Room in the Town Hall and the Police Offices in Oakwellgate; South Ward had Kell's Lane School; and finally, West Ward made do with 'The Room, or Shop, No 194 on the West side of High Street.' Quite how much involvement Hawks had with this election is questionable. His reputation as mayor was one of political indolence. Of the ten motions voted on by the Council by October 1836, Hawks abstained from seven and was absent for two! (Original Electoral leaflet, 1836 / Manders, F., *A History of Gateshead*, Gateshead Corporation: 1973)

———•◆•———

1837: Also on this day, the Derwent to Redheugh railway was opened. Its purpose was to link coal mines to the staithes at Hebburn, removing the need for keelboats. Built by the Newcastle to Carlisle Railway Company, this 2¾-mile stretch provided an important link in the route to Carlisle. Indeed, when the famous Carlisle to Newcastle route was formally opened on June 18th 1838, strictly speaking it was actually the Carlisle to Redheugh line! (www.strps.org)

MARCH 2ND

1911: On this day, Robert Spence Watson, a truly great Gateshead man, died. Spence Watson was born into a Quaker family in 1837, and studied in York and London. On his return to Gateshead, there was no facet of north-east life that Spence Watson would not seek to improve. His work and achievements in the worlds of philanthropy, politics, social reform and education gained him a position of huge influence and prestige. He became president of the Literary and Philosophical Society, the National Liberal Association, and Armstrong College (later Newcastle University), and chairman of the first Newcastle Board School. Spence Watson lived at Bensham Grove for much of his life and it was here that he entertained politicians such as William Stewart Gladstone, Russian exiles Stepniak and Kropotkin, and artists and authors including William Morris and Dante Gabriel Rossetti. Being a solicitor and a Liberal, and never afraid of stating his argument or point of view, he even threatened to have Tory Prime Minister Benjamin Disraeli indicted! This was over a circular that the PM had issued, telling British ships to return any escaping slaves to their 'owners'. Spence Watson argued – successfully – that the offending circular effectively promoted kidnap, and the circular was humbly withdrawn. (www.ncl.ac.uk/library/specialcollections / www.watsonburton.com)

MARCH 3RD

1983: On this day, Marley Hill Colliery closed. This was in itself a sad occasion, but it had an extra dimension for the borough. Marley Hill Colliery had been the last remaining working pit in Gateshead. Considering that coal mining had been a massive part of the area's history for at least 600 hundred years, this was a monumental day. It also marked the end of a proud tradition of Gateshead pit ponies. With the closure of this mine, only fifty-four remaining pit ponies were left in the North East – eight in Sacriston Colliery and forty-six in Ellington. One of Marley Hill's pit ponies, however, enjoyed a charmed existence after his involuntary redundancy today. Aged just five when he left Marley Hill, after a brief spell in Sacriston, Pip was moved to Beamish North of England Open Air Museum, just over the border into Durham. There he spent a long and happy retirement meeting visitors, having beautifully illustrated children's books written about him, and even meeting royalty! In 2002, the Princess Royal enjoyed Pip's company so much that she fell behind schedule for the rest of her visit. By his death in 2009, he was one of, if not the last, surviving former pit ponies in England. (*Gateshead Post / Daily Telegraph*)

MARCH 4TH

1875: On this day, a sportsman died in bizarre circumstances. The Prest family had more than its fair share of bad luck (*see* April 20th) in Gateshead. Charles Henry Prest was staying at the Rectory in Bensham, with his brother, Rector Edward Prest. Originally a solicitor, Charles had been a first-class England cricketer and a sprinter of some repute, although he seems to have given up sports in favour of acting about five years before his visit to Gateshead. It appears that he had arrived in poor health, retiring to bed immediately with a fever. The next day, after delivering his breakfast, Mary Henderson – the household nurse – reported hearing Charles singing in his room. Later she passed his door and saw black smoke seeping through, so ran for help. Rector Prest's daughter, Edith Rose Prest, opened the doors and windows to allow the smoke to clear. She saw her uncle's body, on fire, lying between the bed and the washstand. His injuries were truly horrific, with both hands 'burned off' and his 'head and face fearfully scorched'. An enquiry found that he had probably been asleep in a chair next to the fire when he had 'whilst suffering from some fit, fallen forward and become so burned as to occasion his death.' As a footnote, Charles and Edward's brother, William Prest, captained Yorkshire at cricket and co-founded Sheffield Football Club, the world's oldest club still playing association football. (*York Herald*)

MARCH 5TH

1950: In the late evening of this day, Tram 289 made the last-ever tram journey across the Tyne Bridge to Gateshead. The idea of trams crossing the world-famous bridge now seems odd, but in fact improving links between the two electric tram services over the river was one of the main reasons why the New Tyne Bridge was constructed in 1928. Trams became a familiar fixture on the new bridge, but were on their way out by 1950. The rest of the Gateshead tram network ceased to operate only a year later, on August 4th 1951. (Klapper, C., *The Golden Age of Tramways*, David and Charles: 1974)

———◆———

1984: Also on this day, investigations began into the dramatic collapse of one of the six 150ft chimneys of Dunston Power Station. The station was decommissioned in 1981, but the crash, which happened in gale force winds and in the middle of the night, still took officials by surprise. And today officials entered the plant to take a look around. In the event, they found that the chimney's neighbour was liable to go the same way, so in July they gave it a helping hand with a controlled demolition. The other four lasted until full demolition from November later that year. (*The Journal* / www.wikipedia.com)

MARCH 6TH

1903: On this day, the *Jewish Chronicle* reported that several of Gateshead's separate Jewish communities were trying to amalgamate. Although the first Jewish settler we know of was on the 1841 Census in Pipewellgate, the main arrival of Jewish settlers in Gateshead came about after a late-nineteenth-century split from the Newcastle synagogues. This article suggests that the Gateshead settlers did not see themselves as one group. It says: 'For several years the Jewish community of Gateshead has been split into several sections each worshipping in small rooms, not suitable for their purpose. Many of these dissensions, unable to provide for the needs of a congregation, have had to depend on the neighbouring congregation of Newcastle.' The article then reports 'some success now after [a] meeting on Sunday … whereby two parties have agreed to join forces.' This proposed amalgamation happened in August 1903, combining 'the late Chevrah Agdath Achim and Chevrah Kadisha into one body, henceforth called the Beth Hamedrash Chevrah Kadisha.' The article suggests that poverty was a problem for the fledgling community. There were about seventy Jewish families in Gateshead, 'mostly very poor'. With this new spirit of communality, funding for a new synagogue seems to have been forthcoming: 'Mr Max Rubenstein of Dundalk, Ireland, has promised a donation of £75 … Rubenstein is visiting relatives in Gateshead. His offer has been accepted and a donation list has been opened, and upwards of £100 raised in addition to Rubenstein's.' (*Jewish Chronicle*)

MARCH 7TH

1770: On this day, Mary Eleanor Bowes celebrated her coming of age at Gibside Hall. Apparently it was quite a party: 'An ox was roasted whole, which, with other victuals and some hogsheads of strong ale &c., were given to the populace, many hundreds having assembled there to celebrate the day.' But the carefree 21-year-old was not to have a blessed life. Already married to John Lyon, 9th Earl of Strathmore, it is generally accepted that – due to her husband's ill health and inattention – the young countess took several lovers and also endured numerous aborted pregnancies. Incredibly, her second marriage made her first look comparably successful! Andrew Robinson Stoney was a scoundrel with a mysterious past. His first wife had died suspiciously and he was rumoured to have committed all manner of sadistic crimes against his female servants. When he and Mary married, he was 'Stoney broke' and immediately set about attempting to attain her fortune. It seems that Mary was kept a virtual prisoner and physically and mentally abused. In 1785 she finally managed to escape his clutches, and began divorce proceedings – exceedingly rare for a Georgian woman. Stoney responded by kidnapping her! After a cross-country chase, Mary was freed and Stoney was put on trial for his actions, eventually serving three years in prison. Remembered as the Unhappy Countess, Mary never again remarried nor used Gibside for celebrations. (Sykes, J., *Local Records*, i, 1833 / www.sunnisidelocalhistorysociety.co.uk)

MARCH 8TH

1743: On this day, John Wesley paid his first visit to Gateshead Fell. The scene he describes seems about as far away from modern Low Fell as possible: 'In the afternoon I preached on a smooth part of the Fell (or Common) near Chowden[e]. I found we were got into the very Kingswood of the North. Twenty or thirty children ran round us, as soon as we came, staring as in amaze. They could not properly be said to be either clothed or naked. One of the largest (a girl about fifteen) had a piece of a ragged, dirty blanket some way hung about her, and a kind of cap on her head, of the same cloth and colour. My heart was exceedingly enlarged towards them; and they looked as if they would have swallowed me up; especially while I was applying these words, "Be it known to you men and brethren, that through this man is preached unto you forgiveness of sins".' By 'Kingswood', Wesley is referring to the school and congregation he founded near Bristol, where his teachings first took root. In total Wesley made more than thirty visits to Gateshead Fell, sometimes in terrible conditions (*see* February 23rd). Occasionally he resorted to preaching in the open, when the chapels were too small to hold his enthusiastic and sizeable flock. His last visit seems to have been in his 85th year. (www.wesleyhistoricalsociety.org.uk)

MARCH 9TH

1854: On this day, members of the Cholera Inquiry Commission were into the second of three days of data collection. They had been convened to investigate Gateshead's health and sanitation issues, in response to a terrible outbreak of cholera. After previous epidemics in 1831 and 1849, the town should have been well prepared to either combat or prevent later outbreaks. Yet the Commission found that in 1853, '433 persons perished in a few weeks out of a population of 26,000 or thereabouts … being a mortality of about one in sixty during that short period.' Furthermore, in some streets the mortality rates were 'as high as one in 19.5; as many as seven persons out of about 120 being stated to have died in one block of buildings, three out of thirty to have died in one house, and three … in the cellars of another single house.' Even in periods between cholera outbreaks, they found that the 'actual annual death-rate is at least double the natural or necessary death-rate of the place.' Infuriatingly, Gateshead, with its steep slopes towards the Tyne, was found to have had great potential for drainage and sanitation; there was 'no reason whatever why Gateshead should not be a very healthy town.' The Commission's report pointed the finger squarely at the Council, and advised greater expenditure on public sanitation facilities (*see* February 7th). (Cholera Inquiry Commission Report, 1854)

MARCH 10TH

1976: On this day, squash player Vanessa Atkinson was born in Whickham. She ranks as one of the top sportswomen ever to hail from Tyneside, but is not well known in the area because her father, following his work as a civil engineer, took the family to Holland when she was 10 years old. Atkinson's interest in sport began in her Whickham years: she recalls, 'I always loved sport and dabbled at everything at school in Whickham. I loved athletics and won a few races, and I enjoyed gymnastics and netball. I first put my hand on a squash racket at eight and by the time I was 13 or 14 I was taking it much more seriously.' Her father's contract was initially for a year, but was gradually extended, and after five years in which Atkinson increasingly focused on her squash, she was eligible to play as a Dutch national – as she has done ever since. In 2004 she won the highest paid championship in squash, the Qatar Classic, and went on to win the World Open within a fortnight – no surprise then that she was voted World Squash Player of the Year. She also reached world number 1 in the rankings in 2006. (www.sundaysun.co.uk)

MARCH 11TH

1881: On this day, William Wailes died at his home in Saltwell Towers. Originally a tea merchant and grocer in Newcastle, Wailes' company was so successful that he had time and money to concentrate on his hobby and first love – making and designing elegant and boldly colourful glasswork. In 1830 he went to Germany to study art with the famous Franz Mayer & Co. On his return Wailes decided to make the move from talented amateur to professional glass manufacturer. By the 1840s, Wailes had his own studios and glassworks. His talent was showcased in the stained glass of many churches, right across the country. The cathedrals of Chichester and Gloucester both boast his work. Locally, St Mary's and St Cuthbert's of Gateshead both had Wailes' designs, as did many buildings in Newcastle, including St Mary's Catholic Cathedral. Despite the loss of such a great artist, however, Gateshead did benefit enormously from today's sad occasion. Wailes had built the impressive Saltwell Park and Saltwell Towers for his own use. By the 1870s, however, Wailes appears to have had money problems. They were enough for him to sell the park and its Victorian mansion to the Gateshead Corporation for £35,000 (about £1.7m in modern money), on condition that he might continue to live there until his death. (www.gateshead.gov.uk)

MARCH 12TH

1879: On this day, scientist Joseph Swan lectured to around 500 people in Gateshead Town Hall, and demonstrated his latest invention, the first-ever reasonably practical incandescent light bulb. He first demonstrated the improved design at a meeting of the Newcastle-upon-Tyne Chemical Society, and this March lecture was actually its fourth outing. Swan's connection to Gateshead goes far beyond this, however. Born in Bishopwearmouth, he moved to the town around 1845, and began work in his brother's chemist's shop across the river. In 1869, now a partner in the company, Swan and his young family moved to Underhill, an imposing Low Fell property. At the time, he was already working on light bulb designs, but all his inventions – featuring variations on a glass vacuum bulb pierced by two platinum wires connected by a thin piece of carbonised paper – had a very short working life due to an inadequate vacuum. In the large conservatory of Underhill, Swan set up a laboratory and conducted many of his early experiments, relating both to electrical filaments, and also to his other field of research, dry plate photography. In 1878, he had a breakthrough, replacing the paper filament with a carbonised strand of something similar to rayon (essentially in passing inventing the world's first artificial fibre!). As Swan tested his design within the home, Underhill has the distinction of being the first house to be lit by electric light, and some of his early light fittings still survive. (Swan, M.E., *Sir Joseph Wilson Swan*, Oriel Press: 1968)

MARCH 13TH

1576: On this day, Gateshead and Newcastle nearly merged. This was not the first time, either! In March 1553, the Duke of Northumberland actually succeeded in annexing the two towns, pulling Gateshead out of the control of the Bishop of Durham. Unfortunately for him, young Edward VI (whom Northumberland controlled) died only a few months later and Gateshead re-joined County Durham. In 1576, it was the merchants of Newcastle who seized an opportunity to try and annex Gateshead. After Bishop of Durham James Pilkington's death in January 1576, a Parliamentary Bill was hurriedly put together with the aim of doing just that. It was first read to Parliament on this day. The people of Gateshead quickly organised resistance to this threat before the Bill could be read a second time. A petition was dispatched to Lord Burghley, Lord Treasurer of England, stating that the Bill would only serve the 'private profit of a few of the said town of Newcastle'. As Newcastle was viewed by many as having suspiciously Catholic tendencies, this was a good argument during the Protestant reign of Queen Elizabeth I. Contrastingly, the people of Gateshead were portrayed as 'substantial, honest men, faithful and true subjects, as did appear in the late rebellion.' If joined with Newcastle it was feared that Gateshead would be 'replenished with evil-disposed persons and thieves'! The Bill was dropped. (Carlton, I., *A Short History of Gateshead*: Gateshead Corporation: 1973)

MARCH 14TH

1951: On this day, Jackie Milburn helped seven men and two pit ponies survive a mining accident in South Birtley Colliery. The most impressive part of this story is that Newcastle United legend 'Wor Jackie' wasn't even in Birtley at the time. He was instead scoring the first goal in United's 2-1 win in the FA Cup semi-final replay against Wolves! At about 1 a.m. that morning, a sudden fall of clay and water had trapped the miners 30ft below ground level. The first attempt to dig them out very nearly worked, and the rescuers were within 2ft of breaking through to them. Unfortunately a second fall of material undid almost all of their good work – but not before a tube had been pushed through to the tunnel where they were entombed. Through that tube travelled food, drink and – most importantly – updates about the match! The miners confessed that throughout the thirty-four hours before their rescue, they mainly talked about football and in particular Newcastle's chances in the FA Cup Final. All seven men (and both ponies) escaped unharmed or with minor injuries. To celebrate, a newspaper paid for tickets for each man to watch the final against Blackpool, which Newcastle won 2-0, with both goals scored by 'Wor Jackie' himself! (www.chroniclelive.co.uk)

MARCH 15TH

1772: On this day, Revd Andrew Wood was buried in St Mary's church, Gateshead. According to his – long-destroyed – memorial, he was interred 'amidst the tears of his parishioners'. Wood was born on May 29th 1715 and later educated at Baliol College, Oxford. He was made a Chaplain to the King in 1760 and would have still regularly visited the Chapels Royal in St James' Palace after becoming Rector of Gateshead in 1769. He seems to have been a very literary man, constantly either reading books or writing letters to friends and other clergymen. Described by some as 'an uncommonly lively writer' and 'the very soul of festivity amongst the Maids of Honour and Chaplains at St James'', Wood was quite a character. For a bookish man, he preserved his name in history through a most uncharacteristic act. During the Great Flood of 1771 (*see* November 16th), Andrew Wood caught a fever whilst rescuing people from the Tyne, which had burst its banks and washed away the old Tyne Bridge. Unfortunately, his bravery cost him his life, as he never recovered and was dead within four months. Sadly, in June 1772, the *Newcastle Courant* carried a piece advertising the sale of his beloved library. (Nichols, J., *Literary Anecdotes of the Eighteenth Century*, 1812 / Lang, A., *The St Mary's Story*: Gateshead Council: 2009)

MARCH 16TH

1855: On this day, the Right Honourable Thomas Henry Liddell, Baron Ravensworth, was buried in Lamesley, having died nine days previously, aged 80. The funeral was described as 'very private', although this should not be mistaken for meaning 'low-key'. The service was attended only by 'all his children [he had 12!] then in England; by his sons-in-law, the Earl of Hardwicke, Viscount Barrington, and Sir Hedworth Williamson; and by Earl Vane, the Earl of Mulgrave, John Bowes, esq., and N. Wood, esq. (who officiated as pall bearers).' After the service, 'His Lordship's numerous tenantry, as well as a number of persons from Newcastle and Gateshead … followed the remains to the grave.' In his lifetime, the Baron had transformed Ravensworth Castle – only a short walk from his resting place. When he succeeded to the Baronetcy as 6th Baronet (he later became 1st Baron in 1827), the previous Baronet had built a new mansion within the medieval castle walls. In 1808, he knocked this down and employed John Nash to design and build a new Gothic-style house on top. Nash is famous for having built Marble Arch, the Royal Pavilion in Brighton and large parts of Buckingham Palace. The late baron had taken full advantage of his fashionable new home, entertaining famous and prestigious guests on his estate (*see* October 4th) and introducing them to the area. (Fordyce, T., *Local Records*, 1867)

MARCH 17TH

1922: On this day, Ruth Dodds performed in *The Pitman's Pay* in Bill Quay. She was a member of the Progressive Players amateur theatre group, associated with the Independent Labour Party, founded in 1920 and later to be central to the creation of the Little Theatre, Gateshead (*see* October 13th). *The Pitman's Pay* was Dodds' first play and featured the conflict between 1830s union leader Thomas Hepburn (*see* May 4th) and a government agent. It had won the Sheffield Playgoers competition, which should have meant the society would then produce the play – but they refused, leaving the Progressive Players tackling the work themselves, with the men making scenery and the women making costumes. It was performed six times in Newcastle and three in Gateshead before beginning an intermittent tour of the surrounding villages, including this night. Most of the audience would be expected to have links with socialist politics. In her diary, Dodds described the Bill Quay performance as 'the last & worst of our country performances; a horrible dirty inconvenient picture hall, a huge noisy ill-mannered audience, every possible difficulty in entrances & exits, & dressing accommodation, stage space & sitting generally … The local comrades were very nice and kind … But the men made frightfully long speeches! They were just starting a local Labour party, and this was to raise funds.' (Dodds, R., *A Pilgrimage of Grace*, Bewick Press: 1996 / Merkin, R., 'No Space of Our Own' in *Women, Theatre and Performance*, ed. M. Gale: 2001)

MARCH 18TH

1948: On this day, Queen Elizabeth (later the Queen Mother) opened the Queen Elizabeth Hospital in Sheriff Hill – about a decade late! In 1930s Gateshead, hospital accommodation was urgently needed. At the time, the former Workhouse Hospital in Bensham and the Sheriff Hill Isolation Hospital were the only real options, and both lacked modern facilities. In times of pressing need – such as during the First World War and flu epidemics – the stately homes of Whinney House and Saltwell Hall had even been temporarily converted into hospitals. So it was that the Mayor of Gateshead laid the foundation stone for a new, modern hospital on Sheriff Hill in 1938. Unfortunately, building work began just in time for the advent of the Second World War! The hospital was not completed until 1948, although some wards were open from as early as 1943. During a trip to the North East, the Queen arrived to formally open the hospital which bore her name. Pathé newsreel footage survives of her arrival with the mayor watched by thousands of waving well-wishers. After inspecting the new wards, the Queen made her way to the maternity wards, where she spoke to some of Gateshead's newest mothers and youngest residents. (www.britishpathe.com)

MARCH 19TH

1868: On this day, Gateshead had its first ram-raid … According to the press, a horse and gig had been left in the care of an 11- or 12-year-old lad outside the Princess Alice Inn in Wrekenton, by Mr Greaves – a travelling ale-salesman. Mr Greaves was apparently 'totally sober' and quite regularly left the horse with lads outside pubs. Somehow, the horse got away from his young minder and bolted towards central Gateshead. Greaves gave chase, but could not get nearer than three yards away before the horse sped into the distance. The horse, still pulling its gig, raced down Gateshead High Street, 'scattering vehicles and pedestrians in all directions and finally being brought to a standstill by driving … into the large window of Mr Caris, Jeweller … Chains, watches, rings, pens, seals, bracelets and every variety of goods usually found in such shops were swept upon the pavement …' One man, 58-year-old Robert Carr, was knocked over and suffered a fractured leg, telling his friends that he 'would rather have been killed than that his leg should have been broken'. It seems that bystanders immediately dived in – not to help the injured man (or horse), but to steal whatever jewellery they could lay their hands on! Unfortunately there is a tragic end to the story – Carr's leg could not be saved, and after an amputation, he died on April 11th. (*Illustrated Police News / Newcastle Courant*)

MARCH 20TH

1700: On this day the Common Council of Newcastle agreed to the building of three large water cisterns. These, and another at the Side Pant, were fed by 'the new water' – that is, water from Gateshead Fell. At the time, there was much concern about the shortage of 'good and wholesome' water available in Newcastle. So in 1697, it was agreed to hire William Yarnold, a London engineer. He secured all of the available springs on the Newcastle side of the river, but this still was not enough, so he took a large contract for water from across the Tyne, where there was still plenty to spare. From 1700, water from the Heworth wellspring ran through 4in fir and elm pipes, and then across the fell to a pond in Holmes Close in a conduit (and sometimes, an open trench). From there, 3in lead pipes were run through Gateshead and over the Tyne. There were frequent leaks which sometimes damaged cellars in Gateshead. For a price, small branch pipes could be run into individual houses – but in 1712, only twenty-two houses in Gateshead had a direct supply, and well into the eighteenth century such houses had four hours on a Tuesday to draw all the water they wanted for a week! (Brand, J., *The History and Antiquities of Newcastle*, 1789 / Rennison, R., *Water to Tyneside*, Newcastle and Gateshead Water Co.: 1979)

MARCH 21ST

1848: On this day, the Mechanics Institute bazaar was held 'in the new building of the institution in West Street, under the most flattering auspices.' And what a bazaar it was! Although the Institute had been around since 1836, it had previously met in the Town Hall, the Bethesda Chapel and even the Grey Horse Inn. The aim of this bazaar was to raise money to help pay for the new building, which had been completed earlier in the month. Great efforts were made to 'make the exhibition as complete and attractive as possible ... perhaps a more splendid and effective bazaar has never been witnessed in the borough.' Occupying a whole wall was a refreshments table that 'presented almost anything that could tempt the eye or administer to the taste.' Upstairs, amid music and song, the main hall contained 'a splendid and costly profusion of fancy, ornamental and useful objects of art and curiosity ... a fine collection of paintings from the Fine Arts Society ... two large and elegant plate glass mirrors ... a splendid chandelier, studded with glass drops, sent by Joseph Price.' There was even a guest appearance from Eliza Bowes-Lyon, the Countess of Strathmore (who died in Edinburgh later that year), who 'patronized every stall and made several purchases.' (*Newcastle Courant*)

MARCH 22ND

1898: On this day, 33-year-old Charles Smith was executed for murder. The victim, his 30-year-old wife Mary Anne Smith, had been killed in their Pipewellgate home in the early hours of December 27th 1897. On that day, the Scotsman's voice had echoed through the narrow, dingy streets – 'My bonnie wife has been murdered in the water closet!'. Quite why Smith chose these words is not clear, as his wife was not in the water closet at all, but was lying naked on the bed, battered to death. Smith denied murder, despite being discovered standing beside the bed, covered in his 'bonnie wife's' blood, and still drunk. In court Smith, a plasterer by trade, was convicted on the evidence of the couple's 11-year-old son (who later came under the care of Dr Barnardo's). Having arrived home from a drinking session, the couple had seemingly started rowing, and in a fit of drunken rage Charles bludgeoned Mary Anne to death using a broken broom handle. He was found guilty of murder and sentenced to death. This morning he walked 'very firmly' the 100 yards from his cell to the scaffold, and was executed at 8 o'clock by Durham Prison by father-and-son hangmen, James and Thomas Billington. (*North-East Daily Gazette, Middlesbrough*)

MARCH 23RD

1960: On this day, Derwenthaugh Staithes were closed down, after many years of service for the industries of Gateshead. The spot was used as a drop-off point for coal from the mid-eighteenth century, with more and more tracks laid from it to nearby, and not so nearby, pits, like Garesfield, Clockburn, High Spen and Marley Hill. When the Consett Iron Company opened a colliery at Chopwell in the 1890s, they brought the coal by rail to the Derwenthaugh Staithes. These were huge – the second biggest on the Tyne after those at Dunston, with 340m of frontage on the Tyne and another 250 onto the Derwent, and room for fifty keelboats. They also served the Derwenthaugh Coke Works, which worked to turn coal into coke, and then shipped this out. This former industrial heartland has changed almost beyond recognition. The shoreline now hosts hotels, offices, fast-food outlets and a high-technology learning centre. Whereas once the railway along the Tyne transported coal to the staithes, now it is used primarily for passengers visiting the Metrocentre. The grime and soot of the Coke Works has made way for a countryside park – its waggonways becoming public footpaths. Yet lost amongst these symbols of modernisation and change, one small section of the Derwenthaugh Staithes survives as a jetty within Derwenthaugh Marina.

MARCH 24TH

1702: On this day, James Clavering, 1st Baronet of Axwell, was buried in Whickham. He was made Baronet in 1661, and his baronetcy of Axwell lived on, passed down the generations, until 1893. The 1st baronet's will stated that he would provide for the poor of Whickham Parish: 'every Sunday at twelve after divine service to 24 poor people, 24 penny loaves' and every St Andrew's day, '24 coats, petticoats, and Waistcoats of grey russett, to 24 poor men, women, or children'. (Surtees, R., *The History and Antiquities of the County Palatine of Durham: volume 2*, 1820)

———◆———

1933: Also on this day, Dunston welcomed its new power station. Dunston 'B', as it was named, was possibly the first power station to be mainly constructed of glass and steel, rather than concrete, and its super re-heated steam system was at the time the most efficient in the world. There was a need for a new station. The previous one, built in 1910 and from now on named Dunston 'A', was equipped for a 40hz power system, whereas the new National Grid used a 50hz system. The transition was gradual (made even more so by the war), and 'B' was not fully operational until the 1950s. Today's schedule of 'music, song and jest' was a celebration of the completion of its first operational phase. (www.webwanderers.org)

MARCH 25TH

1666: On this day, Lady Day, the hearth tax was introduced in Whickham. The hearth tax was a new idea, based on taxing households according to how many hearths they had, and its records can be extremely valuable to local historians. Three hundred and sixty-seven householders were listed for Whickham, suggesting a population of around 1,600, perhaps more. This was four times the population of a century earlier, even though across County Durham as a whole, the population rose by only 70 per cent. The extra people were incomers, who often stayed only a short time, drawn to the heart of a rapidly expanding coal trade. At the same time, arable land had largely been worked to exhaustion by the burgesses of Newcastle, who had use of it, and the coal beneath, under the 'Grand Lease' scheme. Over 80 per cent lived in houses with only one hearth, and almost all of these were exempt due to poverty – a higher rate than even the poorest parts of Newcastle. This mass of young industrial workers, living in lodgings or temporary shacks, also led to a big gender imbalance in the parish. At the other end of the spectrum, less than 3 per cent of households had more than four hearths. This included Sir Thomas Liddell with eleven, and Sir James Clavering with ten. (Wrightson, K. and Levine, D., 'Death in Whickham' ed. Walter, J. and Schofield, R., *Famine, Disease and the Social Order*, Cambridge University Press: 1989)

MARCH 26TH

1907: On this day at 10.52 a.m., Felling was deafened by a terrifying sound. The Leeds to Newcastle express train was hurtling at full speed between Heworth signal-box and Felling when suddenly, without warning, its engine hit a kink in the line. It flew off the tracks with such speed and force that all but two of its eight passenger carriages were completely derailed. When the dust had settled, the engine lay on its side with two carriages also overturned. Amazingly, of the thirty-four passengers, only eight were seriously injured, two of whom later died. The kink had been caused by a combination of the previous day's frost and today's unseasonably hot weather, causing the metal to contract and expand too quickly. (www.railwaysarchive.co.uk)

———— •◆• ————

1934: Also on this day, J.B. Priestley's *English Journey* was published. What has this travel book, written by a Yorkshireman and published in London, got to do with Gateshead? Merely that its description of Gateshead has long since dogged the town. After visiting, Priestley suggested that the town was 'designed by an enemy of the human race … no true civilisation could have produced such a town'. History has not recorded the critical response of Priestley's Gateshead's readership to his newest work, nor whether Priestley was ever invited back! (Priestley, J.B., *English Journey*, 1934)

MARCH 27TH

1933: On this day, a massive explosion shook the Sunderland Road area. Six people were killed in the disaster, which took place in Carrville Street where a steam navvy and a gang of workmen were constructing a new road. To quote the *Journal*, 'two houses of flats collapsed like a pack of cards, burying the occupants in the debris. The air was filled with brick dust and flying glass, and the screams of women and children were heard as far away as Allhusen's works, from which men poured to assist in the rescue.' This being the time of the Great Depression it seems that many of the injured were not in the flats at all, but were simply men standing around, hoping for paid employment on the road-works. One of the victims, John George Thompson of Low Fell, had just started his first full week's work for two years. It was found that a hidden gas pipe had been accidentally breached during the work and had somehow ignited. Pathé News reported one extraordinary act of heroism and self-sacrifice: William Devenport, 67, used his body to shelter his baby grandson from heavy rubble for over an hour. Once the pair were found and dug out, Devenport handed the child to safety before finally succumbing to his own injuries. (www.britishpathe.com / *Newcastle Daily Journal*)

MARCH 28TH

1944: On this day, the Tyneside Apprentices Strike began. It is often forgotten that the Second World War saw relatively high levels of industrial action. The government was running short of coal, and while coal owners grew richer, safety grew worse. To increase production, the unpopular Bevin scheme aimed to conscript 10 per cent of apprentices to the coalface. Tyneside apprentices had been working hard, for very low pay, to achieve a skilled status, and were deeply unhappy about being pushed into the pits with no guarantee that they would be able to return to their trade after the war. In the absence of an official trade union, they formed a new organisation, the Tyne Apprentices' Guild – 'the government of the apprentices, by the apprentices, for the apprentices'. They demanded the nationalisation of the miners and exemption from the 'pit compulsion plot', linking up with apprentices in other areas and securing support wherever they could. Over the last week of March, 26,000 apprentices – firstly in Tyneside, then in Glasgow, Huddersfield and Teesside – came out on strike, calling 'Bevin won't climb down, so we'll pull him down'. In the end the strike lasted only two weeks. Three men and one woman from the Communist Party were charged with inciting and furthering of an illegal dispute, and went to jail. Nonetheless, in the end no more Tyneside apprentices were in fact sent to the pits. (Dabb, T., 'Official Secrets', *Socialist Review*: April 1995)

MARCH 29TH

1973: On this day, the *Gateshead Post* reported on a peeping Tom. Police alleged that on March 3rd, Edward Lidden 'did peep at a window for the purpose of spying on persons who might be undressing and that he did spy on Mrs Jennifer Margaret Smith.' Bizarrely, he was also accused of stealing a half-pint tumbler, valued at 5p. But the Felling man's defence complicated matters: Lidden claimed that, far from spying on Mrs Smith, he was in fact spying on his sister-in-law who lived nearby. This was not, he claimed, for his own lascivious ends. Apparently, he suspected her of 'having it off with other men' whilst his brother Arthur – her husband – was serving time in prison. Whilst taking part in his fraternal reconnaissance mission, Lidden claimed he spotted two policemen. Owing to previous convictions – the nature of which are not mentioned – he believed that the policemen would jump to unfortunate conclusions. Naturally, he ran away and simply hid on the veranda of Mrs Smith's ground-floor flat. The fact that the policemen had observed him for four or five minutes, crouched down with his eye to the gap in the curtains was explained as 'coincidental'. Lidden was bound over for a year in the sum of £20 for his offence. He was discharged conditionally for the theft of the tumbler (which he had 'just picked up' from a doorstep!). (*Gateshead Post*)

MARCH 30TH

1759: On this day, a 'terrible affray' took place at Swalwell between a Royal Navy press gang and 'Crowley's crew' – men from the local ironworks. According to Thomas Haswell, with the wars against the French gaining momentum, Royal Navy press gangs were sent out along the length of the Tyne, searching for new recruits to lure into service, by fair means or foul. He reports that 'a press-gang went to Swalwell in quest of men, but the inhabitants [Crowley's crew] making head against them, they came off with a severe drubbing.' The men returned with reinforcements and weaponry, leading to an escalation of violence: 'Part of them laid hold of one William Moffat, a barber, and Mr. Bell, one of the chief inhabitants, interfering, received five stabs with a sword in different parts of the body, in consequence of which he died and others were dangerously wounded.' Sykes takes up the story, informing us that Moffat escaped, but on April 7th, Bell's widow issued a reward of £20 for his apprehension. He was eventually arrested at Whitehaven by a man named Mr Osbourne, also known as Captain Death. Moffat was brought to Durham, where he was tried at the assizes in August 1759 but acquitted. (Haswell, G., *The Maistor, Being some account of the life and work and times of Thomas Haswell*, Walter Scott: 1895 / Sykes, J., *Local Records*, i, 1833)

MARCH 31ST

1974: On this day, Gateshead's County Borough merged with former Urban District areas Blaydon, Whickham, Ryton and Felling, as well as with a large part of the Rural District of Chester-le-Street (including Birtley), in order to form the Metropolitan Borough of Gateshead. This represented a massive overnight growth – the new Borough was roughly eight times larger than the old, and its population about doubled. To commemorate this, every schoolchild in Gateshead's County Borough was officially presented with their very own copy of *A Short History of Gateshead* by Ian Clark Carlton. Carlton's book was designed for use in schools and by schoolchildren. Although subtitled as an adaptation of Frank Manders' book *A History of Gateshead*, published a short time before, it is not simply an abridgement, but contains information not found within Manders' weightier publication. Both books are incredible achievements, considering the time given. In the Foreword to Manders' book, Alderman William Collins reveals that it was only in 1972 that it was suggested to him that 'Gateshead Corporation should publish a comprehensive history of the town.' To write a book relating to all major events, personalities, civic leaders, industry, technology, religion, health, education, politics, leisure, transport and localities – and covering over 1,000 years of Gateshead's history – is an achievement. To do it in less than two years is astounding. (Manders, F., *A History of Gateshead*, Gateshead Corporation: 1973)

APRIL 1ST

1933: On this day, Mayor J.H. Ritson and members of Gateshead Corporation took part in a ceremony laying ten new boundary stones, to mark out the newly extended 'Greater Gateshead'. The Gateshead Extension Act of 1932 swelled the town's populace from 122,379 to 124,575 and increased its acreage from 3,128 to 4,461, including parts of Whickham and Chester-le-Street. Each boundary stone stood 3ft high and held an inscribed bronze plaque. They stood on Chow Dene Road, Great North Road (south of Peggy's Bank), Long Bank (Wrekenton), Springwell Road, Windy Nook Road, Split Crow Road, Sunderland Road, Derwentwater Road, Whickham Road and Consett Road. (*Evening Chronicle / Gateshead Post*)

◆

1966: Also on this day, Sharon Hodgson, Gateshead East and Washington West's last MP, was born. Hodgson was not the first female MP to represent part of Gateshead in Parliament – her predecessor in Gateshead East was Joyce Quin, who first won the seat in 1987. When Quin announced her retirement before the 2005 election, Hodgson was controversially selected as Labour's new candidate from an all-women short-list. But the Gateshead East seat was abolished in 2010, making way for a newly revived and unified Gateshead seat. This time Hodgson's chief opponent in the selection process was male, and David Clelland won the closely fought contest. Hodgson went on to represent Washington and Sunderland West. (*Evening Chronicle*)

APRIL 2ND

1836: On this day, gardener William Falla 'destroyed himself during a period of temporary insanity'. His suicide followed a period of depression caused by his failing horticulture business. Living up to the high standards of his grandfather and father, great businessmen and respected horticulturalists, proved too much for William Falla III, who was unable to pay off his creditors. The night before his death, his brother-in-law had noticed that he seemed 'in bad spirits, dull and little disposed to conversation.' Then he walked into Ravensworth Woods and used a penknife to cut his own throat. Intriguingly, when his body was found weeks later, the bloodied penknife was folded shut and had somehow found its way into his waistcoat pocket ... (*Newcastle Courant*)

1861: Also on this day, over 100 men and boys took part in 'riotous proceedings' in Windmill Hills, as the Gateshead mob let their collective feelings be known. In the past few months, much common land had been enclosed by local land owners, apparently illegally. Two men, Robinson and Freeman, responded by partially breaking down a wall which partitioned public land for private use. Their acquittal at court led the way to today's scenes 'of a serious and disgraceful nature ...' Aiming to 'assert their rights to the full and free enjoyment' of the common land, the mob destroyed not only the wall in question, but all partitioning walls in Windmill Hills. (*Newcastle Courant*)

APRIL 3RD

1939: On this day, the North East Trading Estate (NETE) at Team Valley won a strange bet … On March 3rd, Miroslav Sigmund had instructed the NETE to build a 23,000 sq. ft factory within one calendar month. Sigmund recognised that international affairs were leading the country towards war and knew that mass-produced air-raid precaution equipment would rapidly be needed to meet increased demands. Spotting an opportunity, the entrepreneur wagered that the NETE could not meet his deadline. The NETE accepted, on condition that Sigmund paid extra rent of up to £60 per year if they were successful. The statistics that followed are staggering: two shifts of up to sixty bricklayers laid 156,000 bricks in seventeen days, eighty-three tons of steel was erected in four days, and the flooring and roofing was completed in just a week. All of this was despite the terrible Gateshead weather – over an inch of rain fell on one particular day! The Team Valley works produced water pumps for ships and engines, and quickly became the leading stirrup pump manufacturer in the country, equipping air-raid wardens and fire-fighters throughout the war. Sigmund also imported refugees from his native Czechoslovakia to work in the factory, making Bren gun parts using designs smuggled from under the nose of the country's Nazi occupiers. Local press reported today's completion of this important Gateshead factory as a massive PR coup: 'if industrialists want a factory quickly, the place to come is Team Valley!' (*Evening Chronicle*)

APRIL 4TH

1923: On this day, the *Illustrated Chronicle* gave its readers advance notice of the unveiling of the memorial to those soldiers from Blaydon and District who fell in the First World War. The statue itself – a soldier with head bowed – still stands in Blaydon cemetery and was unveiled on April 7th by local heroine Jane Cowen. As well as providing £200 towards the monument, Miss Cowen did much for local soldiers. The daughter of newspaper owner and radical politician Joseph Cowen, she gained an OBE in 1918 for services with local war relief agencies. She also established the Joseph and Jane Cowen Training School for Maimed Soldiers and Sailors in Benwell. During the Second World War, she presented two ambulances to the Northumberland and Durham War Needs Fund. (www. newmp.org.uk)

———•◆•———

1989: Also on this day, police began investigating a series of pet poisonings in Chopwell. In early April there were two isolated cases of family dogs dying after fits and convulsions. By July the number of deceased dogs had reached double figures, including seven in one day. After a vet conducted autopsies on the canine corpses it was found that strychnine was the cause of death. It was likely to have been left in chunks of meat in order to kill foxes. (*Gateshead Post*)

APRIL 5TH

1853: On this day, the Lunatic Asylum Inspectors' report on Dunston Asylum was presented to magistrates. The report made for shocking reading, and recommended that the proprietor John Etridge Wilkinson, who had run the place since its opening in 1831, should not retain his licence because of his mistreatment of the inmates. According to the report, one 'charge against Mr W. was that of having horsewhipped a lunatic who had attacked him.' But Wilkinson's draconian treatment of this particular inmate – a Mr Gibson – did not stop there. He not only ordered 'some of his teeth to be extracted' but stood by and watched while this punishment was enacted. The report acknowledges that Wilkinson claimed that the horsewhipping was in self-defence against a violent man, and that the extraction of his incisors was to prevent biting. One witness, however, testified that Wilkinson only sent for the horsewhip once Gibson had already been overpowered! The magistrates agreed that Wilkinson had acted with 'undue severity' and 'flagrant cruelty', and the asylum passed into the control of Cornelius Garbutt. But Wilkinson must have still been on the scene – his daughter married Garbutt's son, who was also the next proprietor of Dunston Asylum! (*Newcastle Courant*)

APRIL 6TH

1926: On this day, Gateshead's Central Library was opened. A direct replacement for the library on Swinburne Street (which became a specialist children's library), the new library offered the town not just a new, bigger building, but also a new, better system! In the past, borrowers would have to check to see whether certain books were available by consulting the huge Cotgreave Indicator Board. This board showed whether the book requested was 'in' or 'out', which enabled the visitor to request a librarian to collect it for their perusal. The new library was one of the first to adopt an open access system, where borrowers could browse shelves themselves and see what was available. This resulted in a huge increase in book issues – over 33 per cent – and a doubling of the number of borrowers! One thing was unchanged – from 1906 to 1939, the council insisted the library would not support gambling. As one poet put it, the council:

> ... reads the papers through and through,
> And with a censor's pen,
> It scratches out the betting news
> – Oh! Good and Holy men!

(www.localhistorygateshead.com)

APRIL 7TH

1851: On this day, the Mayor of Gateshead was presented with a mayoral chain of office by the ladies of the borough. As Mrs George Hawks (wife of the first mayor) placed the gold chain around Joseph Robson's neck, three cheers echoed around the Town Hall, followed by another three for the ladies' committee she represented. The chain, valued at £130 at the time, is still worn by the present Mayors of Gateshead. (*Newcastle Courant*)

———•◆•———

1806: Also on this day, two Gateshead shipyard workers made an interesting discovery while sawing an ancient elm tree. 'They were suddenly stopped in the middle of their work by a harder body than the wood, which, on further examination proved to be a horseshoe, in good preservation, and which there was no reason to doubt, had been there since the first growth of the timber. It was found in the very core of the tree, where a fine impression of the shoe was made on the surrounding surface. No visible injury appeared to have been sustained by the timber in consequence of this strange companion.' (Sykes, J., *Local Records*, i, 1833)

APRIL 8TH

2012: On this day, a former Mayor of Gateshead fell foul of a very modern political *faux pas*. Councillor John Eagle issued an apology to the borough after joining a Facebook group entitled 'Margaret Thatcher doesn't have to be dead before we give her a funeral'. The social networking website allows users to show approval for groups by pressing a 'like' button. According to a report, this particular group included violent comments about former Prime Minister Thatcher. Apparently, in the mistaken belief that his Facebook privacy settings prevented the public from viewing the groups that he had endorsed, Councillor Eagle also 'liked' a group entitled 'Nobody likes a Tory'. The apology he made included the words 'as a Councillor I recognize I have a responsible position and local residents have the right to expect me to conduct myself in the correct way … I am sorry if my actions have caused any offence.' He also added 'I can't support Thatcher, but I can't remember "liking" that group.' Eagle is not alone in accidentally endorsing ill-advised Facebook groups. Earlier in the year Florence Henderson of Sunderland Council was suspended for being a member of the same group, whilst later the same month Lib-Dem councillor for Gateshead John McClurey was found to have accidentally 'liked' a group entitled 'Chavs are freaks, throw rocks at them'. (*Sunday Sun*)

APRIL 9TH

2004: On this day, Gateshead grandmother Marion Richardson was counting her lucky stars. Fifty-four-year-old Richardson lived alone and had recently been forced to retire from her job as a postal worker due to ill health. She felt at the end of her tether – but continued to buy a Euro lottery ticket each week because to her it represented a 'glimmer of hope'. And on this day, Richardson's numbers – inspired by the ages of her five children – came up, bringing with them almost £17 million. She remembers, 'I thought my son had done something to the telly. I was in shock – in a bubble. I couldn't eat or think … The ticket stayed in my knickers that whole weekend. The lottery operator said it had to stay somewhere no one could get to it. So I thought, "Where better than my Bridget Jones knickers?".' Richardson made millionaires of nine members of her family, before settling back to a life of travel and shopping. Richardson was the first Britain to win the Euro Lottery – around two months after it began – and was its highest British winner for three years. (*Daily Mirror*)

April 10th

1969: On this day, the newly built St Cuthbert's Village was given official approval as the mayor, the mayoress and many councillors paid a ceremonial visit to its show house. According to a local newspaper report, improbably entitled, 'Where Slums Stood – a Small Paradise!', the country's 'most up-to-date Council houses' would be ideal accommodation for Gateshead residents, with rents being from £4 13s to £5 for a three-bedroomed concrete 'unit' with a rooftop garden. Residents would enjoy 'covered streets' and a proposed shopping precinct. Special provisions would be made for elderly residents. Little did today's dignitaries know that, less than eighteen months later, the same newspaper would be reporting a different story. The list of issues provided by the Tenants' Association included: debris and building materials left by workmen, infestations of rats, beetles and other insects, poor drainage, inadequate lighting, lack of public telephones, non-burglar-proof locks on doorways, and noise pollution from echoing footsteps. One resident said 'the noise is absolutely unbearable' while another stated that her child found a big brown rat and 'ran after it, thinking it was a puppy ...' The flats for the elderly also had their own problems; kitchens designed without ventilation or windows meant that doors to the (adjoining) toilets had to be left open while cooking to allow steam to leave the room. The 'village' was demolished after less than twenty-five years. A 'small paradise' indeed ... (*Gateshead Post*)

APRIL 11TH

1907: On this day, Gateshead's police were given their very own gymnasium, and in return put on a spectacular show of their fitness. The gymnasium, which was donated by magistrate Walter de Lancey Willson, was in a large room above the recently erected fire station at Swinburne Place. Described as 'excellent and commodious', the room contained all mod cons: 'a first class vaulting horse, and spring board, the climbing rope, climbing ladder and suspended rings, horizontal bars, Indian clubs, dumb-bells and bar bells; Sandow's exercises and anything that could be of use to the modern gymnasium athlete.' Its main purpose, however, seems to have been to accommodate the Gateshead Police's love of … wrestling! It seems that the constabulary were enthusiastic and adept wrestlers, particularly in the Cumberland 'catch-as-catch-can' style. This variation on the sport has a much looser interpretation on traditional wrestling moves, allowing combatants to grab a hold of any part of their anatomy – including below the belt – hence catching wherever they can. A win was recorded when one competitor managed to force a verbal submission or pin his opponent down. Willson himself was given the pleasure of declaring the gymnasium open. To honour their benefactor, the men put on a fine show of their prowess on the new equipment as well as a few rounds of their beloved sport. (*Daily Chronicle*)

APRIL 12TH

1871: On this day, Mr Thomas Ironsides of Kibblesworth celebrated his 100th birthday. Described as 'hale and hearty' (albeit with impaired hearing), Ironsides was the oldest tenant on the Ravensworth estate and appears to have been still active. Indeed, he led the dancing during the party that the village held in his honour! He spent the day happily in the company 'of children, grandchildren, great-grandchildren ... whose ages ranged from over 70 down to half a dozen years.' Ironsides was reported as occupying 'the same room that he was born in and [having] slept only about two nights out of his own house.' (*Dundee Courier and Argus*)

◆

1921: Also on this day, the people of Gateshead saw their brand new, state-of-the-art motor ambulance for the first time. Bought to attend the victims of street accidents, the ambulance was equipped with 'two stretchers, one of which is on wheels, and is fitted with a special arrangement for maintaining the patient in a horizontal position whilst a steep incline is being negotiated. There is also a heating apparatus, tip-up wash basin, etc.' One of the biggest attractions of the car was its self-starter motor. This enabled quicker response times than the crank-handles that were usual in cars at the time. It also boasted a powerful four-cylinder engine and even had electric lighting! (*Evening Chronicle*)

April 13th

1989: On this day, car-thieves dumped a Ford Sierra 4 x 4 in Gateshead. The £16,000 car was stolen from Darlington railway station the previous day and had been left near Springwell village, minus its wheels. The owner of the car? Tory MP for Richmond, and future leader of the Conservative Party, William Hague. (*Gateshead Post*)

———— • ◆ • ————

2012: Also on this day, an 8-year-old leukaemia patient from Rowlands Gill had a day to remember. Ben Charlton was guest of honour for Sir Ian 'Beefy' Botham's Great British Walk, fund-raising for leukaemia research. The former England international cricketer (and Scunthorpe United football player) was on day two of his fourteenth charity walk-a-thon in twenty-seven years. Botham started the Tyneside leg of his ten-town and 150-mile journey across the country at Newcastle's Quayside earlier in the day. Every town or city that he visited nominated one child to represent leukaemia sufferers in the area. Ben, who was diagnosed aged just 6, was chosen as this region's Local Hero because of his positive attitude to coping with cancer. He walked alongside Botham for much of the distance, despite the impressive average pace of 4½ miles per hour. Today's walk ended with a 4-mile walk through beautiful countryside, across the National Trust's Gibside Estate. Ben and his family have raised over £3,000 for Leukaemia and Lymphoma Research. (leukaemialymphomaresearch.org.uk)

APRIL 14TH

1912: On this day, the *Titanic* hit an iceberg and took over 1,500 people – including Alfred King of Gateshead – to their deaths. King was only 19, and working as a first-class lift attendant on board the ship. His body, in a blue steward's uniform, was one of very few which were recovered from the sea, along with a range of personal items, including his pipe and keys, and a silver watch that had stopped at 2.20 a.m. on the 15th, when the ship is known to have hit the water. One hundred years later his story was turned into a musical by his great-great niece, and performed by children at Gateshead Reavley Theatre School. (*Northern Echo*)

———— ◆ ————

1961: On this day, Charles Parker interviewed the folk-singing Elliott family of Birtley for *The Big Hewer*, a radio programme which introduced the culture and music of the mining villages of the North East to a public largely unfamiliar with it. The Big Hewer was part of the Radio Ballads series, which combined drama, folk music and oral history in a new way. The Elliotts were key figures in bridging the gap between the traditions of nineteenth-century Durham, and the folk revival of the 1950s, and helped form the genre of the industrial folk song. In 1962 they also helped found the Birtley Folk Club, which is still going strong. (Wood, P., *The Elliotts of Birtley*, Heron Publishing: 2008)

APRIL 15TH

1786: On this day, the search was on for a wonderfully described criminal. 'Escaped from justice, charged with diverse felonies, petty larcenies and various other misdemeanours. Robert Thompson, his size 5ft 10ins, raw-boned of a sallow complexion, stoops much and has a shamble or slouch in his gait, with a downcast eye and is of a most suspicious appearance. When speaking he turns his head from the person he addresses, conscious of the guilt he in vain endeavours to conceal: he is about 40 years old … and was lately head gardener at Gibside. Whoever apprehends the offender … shall be entitled to a reward of 5 guineas by applying to Gibside.' This remarkable description may not have been entirely trustworthy! Its evident bias may be due to Thompson's continued support for Mary Eleanor Bowes – his original employer at Gibside – after she escaped and fled from her abusive husband (*see* March 7th). Andrew Robinson Stoney Bowes had been known to mistreat the loyal staff she left behind, including Thompson. Thompson, for his part, had never liked his new master and had subverted his orders whenever possible. He continued to write to his mistress in secret, even after her escape, providing updates about her garden, and was sacked for refusing to submit these letters to his master. Thompson was caught and tried in August the same year. He was sentenced to seven years' transportation for grand larceny. (*Newcastle Courant*)

April 16th

1831: On this day, the old Scotswood Bridge – known locally as the Chain Bridge – was opened. Originally it was to be the Tyne's first combined rail and road crossing – a precursor to the High Level Bridge – but the railway company involved withdrew from the venture. Instead, the Chain Bridge formed an important pedestrian and carriageway crossing, linking the turnpike road to the west of Gateshead with the north side of the Tyne. Designed by local architect John Green, the attractive bridge consisted of a long roadway which was suspended – as its nickname suggests – from wrought-iron chains, hanging from cables. The chains were supported by two stone towers in the middle of the river, and affixed to points on the north and south riverbanks. During its official opening, dignitaries walked along Scotswood Road to the new bridge. After crossing and visiting Swalwell and Blaydon, the party then re-crossed the bridge and returned to Newcastle for further celebrations. The bridge made back its own cost through tolls, and became a part of the Tyne's cultural heritage until its closure in 1967. Indeed, not only was it used as the finishing line for rowing races from the High Level Bridge, it was also immortalised in Geordie Ridley's famous song 'The Blaydon Races' – 'We flew across the Chain Bridge reet into Blaydon toon, The bellman he was callin' there, they call him Jackie Broon'. (www.bridgesonthetyne.co.uk)

APRIL 17TH

1812: On this day, engraver Thomas Bewick, who had lived for many years in Newcastle, bought a house over the river. The area had recently been a part of the wild common land of the Fell, but after an Enclosure Act of 1809, housing and nursery gardens moved in. Here, Bewick saw a house being built on Mirk Lane, bought it, and began to build an extra back kitchen. But immediately, his plans were shattered as he fell seriously ill. He was lucky to survive and was out of action for months, first at his old home, then with friends in Carr's Hill. He did not move into his new home until November 1812. At this point he was 59 years old and had recently brought his son into the business as a partner; his move can be seen as coinciding with a semi-retirement. Certainly his most famous works – often considered to be the pinnacle of the art of wood engraving – were behind him, but he did continue to work on new versions of familiar themes – fables and the natural world – as well as overseeing the workshop and writing his memoirs. He died in his house in 1828. (Uglow, J., *Nature's Engraver*, Faber and Faber: 2006)

APRIL 18TH

1969: On this day, St Mark's Methodist church on Durham Road hosted its annual Industrial Festival. A local newspaper was perhaps guilty of overstating the case when it ran the headline, 'The explosion of change; new step in human evolution,' but the festival was nonetheless an important and enjoyable celebration of local industry. This year's theme was communications, and the church welcomed 'exhibits from industry, commerce, the Church, the Police, British Rail and a number of other firms whose success depends to a great measure on communications.' The festival opened with a mannequin parade – or catwalk fashion show – of 'summer fashions for the trendy young miss'. It also featured a parade of transport through the ages, cookery demonstrations, and even an 'introduction to decimal currency' hosted by the Trustee Savings Bank. Naturally enough for a festival held within a church, events closed with a sermon. Reverend Roy Collins, in his own way, entered into the spirit of the 'carnival atmosphere' by writing these words in the festival programme: 'This century we have had two World Wars – not because man has become more evil, but because of the powers of communication … and the weapons which technology provides.' He added that, 'technological invention has created a world population explosion which leaves half the world hungry, given birth to new nations, created racial problems of a new kind and increased the possibility of international strife.' (*Gateshead Post*)

APRIL 19TH

1829: On this day, in St Paul's church, Winlaton, Thomas and Margery Oliver baptised their (possibly adopted) son and christened him John. This marks the first public record of the man that was to become known locally as Coffee Johnny. Many who sing the words of 'The Blaydon Races' do not realise that Coffee Johnny – who 'had a white hat on' – was a real person. A blacksmith, John was a bare-knuckle fighter of much repute. Over 6ft tall, and with the strength of a man of his trade, his already imposing physique was often embellished with the addition of a tall white top hat. In 1850, aged 22, he fought an epic battle with champion Will Renwick, an older, more experienced boxer. Lasting for thirty-six rounds, the fight ended with John victorious and Renwick being taken home in a cart. Another opponent of note was a pub landlord named Kirksopp who, it is said, never again walked with a straight neck! When Coffee Johnny died of pneumonia in 1900, aged 72, he was buried in the cemetery of the same church in which he was baptised. It is said he once joked with Lord Ravensworth that one day he would be a bigger landowner than him – 'because when I die it will take 7ft of land bury me but less to bury you, so I'll be a bigger landowner.' His burial plot was indeed 7ft long! (Winlaton and District Local History Society)

APRIL 20TH

1872: On this day, Archdeacon Edward Prest of Gateshead was unable to perform his scheduled services at St Mary's church, owing to the unfortunate death of his son, Walter. It appears that Walter's death was sudden, as the *Gateshead Observer* commented that 'The boy, who was eight years of age, had been ill but a few days, having been at school as recently as last Monday.' What makes this death even more shocking is the tragedy that followed. Another of the Rector's sons, Herbert, died just 6 days later. According to his memorial stone: 'Herbert Prest ... fell asleep at Durham School, April 26th 1872, aged 12 years.' It is currently unknown what caused the two deaths, or even whether they were linked. This double tragedy may have destroyed the beliefs or religious enthusiasm of some men, but not so the energetic Edward Prest. Indeed, for the next decade, Prest dedicated his life to his work with aplomb. According to his obituary, 'his addresses were full of Gospel teaching and his fervent exhortations found entrance into many hearts.' During his service as rector in Gateshead and Ryton, he set up a series of missionary ventures, built an iron church at his own expense in Windmill Hills, ran the Temperance Society and led religious education in local board schools. He died in 1882, aged 56 years, ten years after his boys. (*Gateshead Observer*)

APRIL 21ST

1739: On this day, the Gateshead populace was given notice that they were to be treated to a show of strength from London's premier strongman! Thomas Topham, hailing from Islington, was known for his spectacular feats, having performed for the Royal Society. According to his billing, 'He bends an iron poker, three inches in circumference, over his arm; and one of two inches and a quarter around his neck; he breaks a rope that will bear two thousand weight, and with his fingers rolls up a pewter dish of seven pounds hard metal; he lays the back part of his head on one chair, and his heels on another, and suffering four men to stand on his body, he moves them up and down at pleasure; he lifts a table six feet in length by his teeth, with half a hundredweight hanging at the further end of it; and lastly, to oblige the publick [sic], he will lift a butt full of water.' The venue for these displays was the Nagg's Head public house. As a footnote, although Topham was master of his physical strength, he proved unable to control his emotional strength. Ten years after his Gateshead appearance, he killed his wife in a London pub, in a fit of jealous rage, before cutting his own throat and stabbing himself. It took him two days to die. (Sykes, J., *Local Records*, i, 1833)

APRIL 22ND

1841: On this day, Thomas Wilson laid the foundation stone for the new public reading and literary rooms in his beloved Low Fell. Wilson was an immensely popular man and local celebrity, becoming well known for his works as the Pitman Poet. As this epithet suggests, Wilson came from a poor background in Low Fell itself, and worked underground for much of his early life. Keen on self-improvement, he educated himself until he managed to achieve the qualifications to become a schoolmaster. By the 1820s, Wilson had put his love of literature and reading to good use, writing poetry to be published in local newspapers. His most famous works – *The Pitman's Pay, The Weshin' Day* and *The Market Day* – were not only written with first-hand knowledge of north-east working class life, they were proudly written using Wilson's local dialect:

> I sing the Pitman's plagues and cares,
> Their labour hard and lowly lot,
> Their homely joys and humble fares,
> Their pay-night o'er a foaming pot.

(*See* also July 18th and November 9th.) (Walton, C., *Gateshead Personalia*)

APRIL 23RD

1866: On this day, a school concert descended into a riot. The Barrington School of Eighton Banks was established in 1832 and named after the then Bishop of Durham, Revd Shute Barrington. By the 1860s the school building – two converted cottages – needed replacing. The new building's opening ceremony consisted of a concert and optional tea laid on for the local populace. Tickets were on sale at 1s for both concert and tea, and 6d for concert only. The pricing may seem insignificant, but it led directly to riotous behaviour before and during the inaugural concert! It seems that people who had paid 6d (mainly miners) had rapidly filled the building, leaving no room for the (mainly middle-class trades) people who had paid 1s. A mini class-war broke out, with accusations of rudeness and violent pushing and shoving from both sides. The press placed the blame squarely on the mining community. One miner, James Bell, was so incensed that he wrote a lengthy defence of his comrades, stating that miners were not wholly to blame; in fact the 'mechanics were the most violent and rudest'! He added that, 'As regards the tea party: who boiled the kettle? – the miner. Who baked the bread? – the miner. Who lighted the room with gas? – the miner. And if it had not been for the miner and the miner's wife, it would have been a poor affair.' (*Newcastle Courant*)

APRIL 24TH

1856: On this day, a terrible explosion occurred at Kibblesworth Colliery, killing two men. Edmund Cuft and Thomas Leadbitter were both firemen; their job was to maintain the fire in the colliery boilers to create steam used to work underground machinery and pump water out of the mine. In this case there were actually five boilers, linked in a series, for four men to supervise. As the valve of one boiler was opened, it was necessary that the valve to the next boiler was closed so that the boilers did not spew high-pressured boiling water and steam into each other. On this fateful day the water gauge – called a float – may have become stuck, leading to a misreading of water level by one of the firemen. Both valves were opened, causing water to pour into a red-hot boiler, sending scalding water and burning iron through the roof, killing both men outright and sending the top of the boiler 2ft into the hillside. The incident pointed to massive inadequacy in training and safety procedures for the firemen, especially as only a few months before an even more spectacular explosion had happened in exactly the same place, caused by identical circumstances! On September 19th 1855, John Bewley was 'blown an immense height into the air, his body making a deep indentation in the earth when it fell, nearly 200 yards from the pit.' (www.dmm.org.uk)

APRIL 25TH

1981: On this day, Whickham Football Club won the FA Vase Final at Wembley. The match was notable for being the first final to be played at Wembley as an all-seater ground. Not that Whickham and their opponents Willenhall Town had a hope of filling the seats in the English national stadium. Nonetheless, 12,000 fans turned up to watch their teams bid for silverware. The Whickham contingent must have felt that their train fares to London had been wasted when, only ten minutes into the game, the side had already conceded two goals with no reply. Twenty-five years on, Whickham's then manager Colin Richardson recalled the part that the loyal fans played in turning the match around: 'There may only have been 12,000 but the noise from the tunnel was unbelievable ... if that doesn't get you going, I don't know what ever will.' Spurred on, Alan Scott and Ronnie Williamson scored a goal each to force the match into extra time. Willenhall had lost their goalkeeper after a collision with a Whickham player – their star centre-forward donned gloves as his replacement. Whickham took advantage and Billy Cawthra scored the winner after twelve minutes of added time. After collecting the trophy from the legendary Sir Matt Busby, Whickham FC returned to the warm welcome of 5,000 fans. As a strange footnote, eight of the winning side left the club almost immediately afterwards, all signing for comparative giants, Newcastle Blue Star. (*Northern Echo*)

APRIL 26TH

2006: On this day, a Gateshead school was controversially given Ofsted's highest report rating for the third time in a row. The lead inspector called Emmanuel School 'remarkable' and commented that 'excellent behaviour and very high levels of attendance emphasise [the students'] desire to make the most of what the college offers them.' The controversy lay not with the glowing report, but with the reputation of the school itself. Backed by local businessman Sir Peter Vardy, Emmanuel College has attracted accusations of teaching Biblical creationism as fact alongside evolutionary theory. Back in 2004 the school published a document entitled 'Christianity and the Curriculum', which seemed to recommend that fundamentalist beliefs should be taught across the curriculum. The National Union of Teachers leader Steve Sinnott argued that Christian philanthropists should not be able to have 'undue influence' on educational matters – 'What we will continue to oppose is people being able to peddle, in our education system, their narrow beliefs and prejudices because they are prepared to put £2m into a school.' But Sir Peter told BBC Radio 4 that whilst he believed in 'a Creator God' who could have made the earth in six days if he had wanted to, this had no bearing on the curriculum taught in his schools. Meanwhile, the school still attracts both controversy and success in equal measures. The outstanding rating was repeated for a fourth time in 2009. (www.bbc.co.uk)

APRIL 27TH

1989: On this day, a Labour councillor was 'gagged'. Left-wing Councillor Neil Waite had been very public in his condemnation of the Conservative introduction of the Poll Tax or Community Charge. As a councillor for Felling he encouraged people not to register for the upcoming tax, and ultimately to refuse to pay it. It seems that his comments caused quite a stir amongst Labour Party colleagues – at a meeting Waite was informed of an unwritten rule that before going to press with outspoken views, party leadership should be consulted first. Eventually, he did sign an agreement to that effect, but deftly side-stepped the issue of commenting on the Poll Tax, saying 'I can't do it *as a councillor* – only as Secretary of Gateshead against the Poll Tax.' The Poll Tax did not only create controversy amongst politicians. In August 1990, when the first Community Charge payments should have been paid, two members of Christians Against the Poll Tax staged a twenty-four-hour fast outside Gateshead magistrates' court. Franciscan friar Father Martyn Jeffs and Sister Pat Devlin from the Little Sisters of the Assumption, fasted in order to show 'the injustice of this tax which takes from the poor to subsidise the rich in our society.' In total about 16,000 people in Gateshead had been issued with liability orders for non-payment. Ironically, because of their religious vows, both Jeffs and Devlin were exempt from the Poll Tax. (*Gateshead Post and Times / Catholic Herald*)

APRIL 28TH

1846: On this day 'a massive silver tureen and salver, value £130, were presented to Mr Alderman William Henry Brockett, of Gateshead, by the merchants and ship-owners of Newcastle and neighbourhood, to mark their thanks for his services in connection with the removal of the passing toll levied on shipping by the Corporation of Scarborough.' As honorary Secretary of the Newcastle and Gateshead Shipowners' Society, Brockett had successfully negotiated an exclusive deal where Tyne and Wear merchants could move coal and other goods past Scarborough harbour without paying any toll, thus stimulating the local economy. Local historians have called him 'one of the borough's unsung heroes' and a plaque was erected in his honour in 2011. His influence on early Victorian Gateshead should not be underestimated. Apart from beginning the town's first newspaper (*see* November 18th), Brockett also served as mayor from 1839–40, helped establish the town's West Street dispensary after the cholera outbreak of 1831, and began writing a history of Gateshead, which he regrettably never completed. Upon his death on January 15th 1867, he left behind a wealth of documents of local importance. Gateshead Libraries Service holds a collection of letters, tracts, legal and financial records, newspaper cuttings and personal recollections that have yet to be fully mined for information. Quite what happened to his 'massive tureen' is, however, unknown. (www.gateshead.gov.uk / Fordyce, T., *Local Records*, 1867)

APRIL 29TH

1939: On this day, the young patients of Gateshead's Children's Hospital received a very special treat. According to a press report from the time, 'as a pleasant sequel to the Royal visit to Tyneside in February, when the Queen, during the inspection of Gateshead's Children's Hospital, expressed herself pleased with what she saw, a large piece of Princess Elizabeth's birthday cake has been sent to the Matron, Miss Dawson, for the children in the hospital.' (Local press)

2010: Also on this day, the Rose Garden in Saltwell Park hosted a commemoration event for the annual Workers' Memorial Day. A new stone plaque was unveiled, reading 'In memory of everyone in Gateshead who has died either at work or through a work-related illness. Remember the dead, fight for the living.' The significance of the event would not be lost on the councillors present – missing from their number was Maureen Chaplin, Gateshead's mayor until 2009 when she died of cancer, believed to be caused by exposure to asbestos while working as a nursing auxiliary. In 2012, the day was used to launch the Northern Asbestos Support and Campaign Group, which operates under the Trades Union Congress. Asbestos fibres, which had been freely used in Gateshead industries in the twentieth century, had by 2012 become the biggest single cause of work-related deaths. (www.mkmrf.org)

APRIL 30TH

1781: On this day, the Tyne Bridge was opened – this being the Georgian Tyne Bridge, not, of course, to be confused with either the earlier medieval Tyne Bridge or the later New Tyne Bridge! After the terrible flood of 1771 (*see* November 16th) washed away the medieval bridge – and every crossing point to the east of Corbridge – there was an urgent need for a replacement. To have two major towns such as Newcastle and Gateshead disconnected from each other by the Tyne was damaging for most trades and businesses on both sides of the river. Indeed, the only businesses to thrive as a result of the flood were those of ferryboat owners who suddenly found themselves able to charge extortionate fees for their services, with customers having no alternative! A temporary wooden bridge was erected as a stopgap – both literally and figuratively. It had weight restrictions, however, and was far too narrow for long-term usage, and its replacement was designed as a permanent solution. Designed by Robert Milne, it comprised of nine stone arches, the southern three being the responsibility of Gateshead. Its cost was recovered over the next forty years through tolls. Not without its problems (*see* June 15th), it nonetheless served its purpose until being replaced by the Swing Bridge in 1876. (www.bridgesonthetyne.co.uk)

MAY 1ST

1934: On this day, Oswald Mosley's British Union of Fascists (BUF) ran into trouble. They wanted to gain support in depression-stricken working class districts, but were up against Tyneside's strong Labour movement. They began to recruit among young men attracted to the Blackshirt uniform, the part-time work, and quite probably the chance to smash windows and get into fights. BUF meetings often descended into chaos as opponents sought to disrupt proceedings – but the traffic was two-way. Outside the Labour Exchange on Windmill Hills on this day, the Independent Labour Party were staging their traditional May Day meeting. Suddenly a group of Blackshirts headed for the rostrum chanting 'M-O-S-L-E-Y'. Perhaps they expected the support of the men in the dole queue – but they were mistaken. Instead, a thousand men charged at them! They fled, but not before one was knocked unconscious and another lost teeth. This was a turning point for the anti-Fascist campaigners. They would no longer just react; they would smash the Tyneside BUF. The Anti-Fascist League was formed, and on the 13th they besieged the BUF headquarters in Newcastle. On the 14th the Blackshirts had booked Gateshead Town Hall for a meeting, but found it surrounded by thousands of demonstrators. When speaker Beckett finally got in, he found that the audience contained three times as many hecklers as supporters. Beckett needed police help to leave before spending another night under siege in the BUF headquarters. (Todd, N., *In Excited Times*, Bewick Press: 1995)

MAY 2ND

1823: On this day, Gateshead formally joined the anti-slavery movement. In the Anchorage building adjoining St Mary's church, Revd John Collinson took the chair in a meeting with other town dignitaries. Together they created a petition to be signed by all supporting townsfolk and delivered to the House of Commons. Their resolve and righteousness is evident in their words to Parliament: 'Your petitioners, feeling as Christians, most deeply and sincerely deplore the debased, degraded and miserable condition of the numerous Human Beings who are held in a State of Slavery, by Subject of His Majesty in Colonies belonging to the British Empire, a State in direct Opposition to the Principles of Christianity, and highly aggravated by the Cruelties, Deprivation and manifold but, unhappily, too well known Evils, revolting to Humanity, to which those unfortunate creatures are, by their treatment, subjected.' They went on to ask that 'Slaves be alleviated, and their Condition be so far ameliorated as that they may be encouraged in their Efforts to obtain their Freedom, and that when obtained, they may afterward securely enjoy the Benefits resulting from it.' The petition lay awaiting signatures at the Goat Inn and several Gateshead shops before joining the many others from similar, liberally minded towns and contributing to the eventual abolition of slavery. (Charlton, J., *Hidden Chains*, Tynebridge Publishing: 2008)

MAY 3RD

1975: On this day, Whickham Bank lost one of its most notable landmarks – Axwell Colliery's pit head building. The earliest record of the name Axwell Colliery seems to be from the 1830s, when a shaft was sunk, but there had been coal mines in the vicinity since the fourteenth century. Located at the top of Whickham Bank, it linked to Swalwell's drift mine at the bottom of the bank. According to Whellan's 1894 *Directory of Coalmines*, Axwell employed 250 men and boys and produced 360 tons of coal per day, with a further 120 miners digging 100 tons of coal and 70 tons of clay from Swalwell daily. The colliery served as an unlikely venue for an unusual event, early in the twentieth century. On April 6th 1900, an underground party was held there in the richly and gaily decorated Five Quarter coal seam! It was in aid of fundraising to refurbish the chancel of the church of St Mary the Virgin in Whickham – the church that most of the miners attended and where many were christened, married and buried. From 1898 to 1906 modernisation led to the winding gear being placed high above the shaft in an enclosed brick building. The enclosure of the winding gear in a building was very unusual and, according to local historians, an unsuccessful attempt was made to preserve it as a listed building after the mine closed in 1953. Instead, the building stood empty until being demolished. (www.webwanderers.org)

MAY 4TH

1832: On this day, the Battle of Friars' Goose reached its ugly climax! In 1831, Thomas Hepburn had started the Northern Union of Pitmen. Not only did his union negotiate better pay and conditions, it did so without violence. The following year, mine owners resolved to smash unionism by refusing to hire union members. The union again favoured industrial action, but the strike of 1832 did not go according to plan. Mine owners employed men to eject miners' families from their pit-cottages. Over forty lead miners came from Cumberland to replace the workforce. On their arrival on May 1st, they were pelted with stones by the Gateshead miners, eager to keep their homes. The violence soon escalated – special constables were sworn in on May 2nd, but were attacked during their investiture by 'several hundred' pitmen. On May 4th, Thomas Forsythe, Newcastle's Marshall, armed reinforcement constables with firearms and cutlasses with the aim of ejecting the Gateshead miners. They marched to Friar's Goose near Felling, and there met the pitmen, who gave three defiant cheers. After a tense stand-off, violence erupted, with Forsythe and many of his men being injured during their savage attack on the miners. The miners defended themselves with guns purloined from the town's guardhouse. By the time the military arrived, the crowds had dispersed, leaving many wounded but – amazingly – none dead. During subsequent police searches of houses, over forty people were arrested, twenty of whom were sent to the county gaol. (Sykes, J., *Local Records*, 1833)

MAY 5TH

1822: On this day, the newly built St Mary's church in Heworth (then part of the parish of Jarrow) was formally opened for divine service. The Revd John Hodgson played a huge part in this achievement – it was through his hard work that the new building was created, much to his own design, and it was his aim to see Heworth become a distinct parish in its own right. Built at quite a reasonable cost of around £2,200, St Mary's was a labour of love for the whole family. Apart from Hodgson's own architectural input, the church benefitted from stone and masonry skills provided by Mrs Hodgson's family, the Kells, who owned the local quarry. Hodgson was clearly torn between the love of his old chapel and his vision of a new, sizeable and important place of worship. In a letter to his wife he said that, 'It will give me pain to see the workmen begin to pull down a place which I have now been familiar with for thirteen years.' It was, however, necessary. Above those reserved for notable families, the old building had only sixty-seven seats free to general church-goers, whereas the new design had 687. Heworth did eventually become a separate parish in 1843, two years before Hodgson's death in Hartburn. (Raine, J., *Memoir of the Rev. John Hodgson*, 1858)

May 6th

1949: On this day, Gateshead welcomed an esteemed, if controversial, singer and actor. Paul Robeson was invited to perform in the borough by its far-left Labour MP Konni Zilliacus, just six days before a local election. Robeson, best remembered for his recording of 'Ol' Man River' and for a staggering stage interpretation of *Othello*, had already been blacklisted in his native America for his outspoken civil rights speeches against racial segregation. He arrived in Gateshead amid accusations back home of Communist Party membership. To Labour's opponents, Zilliacus' invitation appeared to be a publicity stunt, whilst Labour maintained that there was 'no political significance'. The performances went ahead as planned, and Gateshead was treated to a world first – Robeson waived his fee and played to the audience for free! If the reports are to be believed, onlookers at Bensham Cinema and then later in the day at St John's church, Sheriff Hill, were spellbound by the 6ft 3in singer's resonating bass voice. The audiences included specially invited elderly people, twenty blind people with guides and even (apparently) some of Labour's opponents! Rent and Ratepayers' Candidate S.A. Heppell voiced his suspicions – 'whilst admiring Paul Robeson as a great singer … I deplore the fact that he has been brought to Gateshead to give free concerts under the aegis of a political group,' before cheekily adding, 'there is no truth in the report that the Rent and Ratepayers' Association are bringing in Danny Kaye.' (*Gateshead Post*)

May 7th

1902: On this day, Gateshead received its current mayoral mace, presented by Alderman Gillies. The Mace Bearer on that day was Town Hall Caretaker, Ralph Teasdale, who retained that honour for twenty-eight years, though tragically he died only a week before retirement in 1929. The metre-long mace he protected is made of silver, covered with a thin layer of gold. On its top, an orb and cross represents the Church of England. It is also embellished with a crown and royal coat of arms and has engraved symbols to recognise the contribution of industry, education, commerce, science and the sea to Gateshead's prosperity. (*Newcastle Evening Chronicle*)

———◆———

1939: Also on this day, Gateshead had a pre-war blackout! Between the hours of 1 and 3 a.m., the whole of Gateshead's Air Raid Precautions services were told to take part in a practise blackout. Every electric light, sign and car headlamp was switched off, kerbs were painted reflective white, police were instructed to knock on the doors of any house that had light visible, and RAF planes flew overhead. The aim of the exercise was mainly to observe from the air how visible Gateshead's targets were to enemy planes without light. Unfortunately, heavy fog descended, rendering that part of the test impractical! A week later, the intended test was repeated, with added fires and explosions for the services to deal with. (*Newcastle Evening Chronicle*)

MAY 8TH

1945: On this day, VE day celebrations in Gateshead were captured on film. Apparently taken by an unknown off-duty police officer from the Gateshead Police Photographic Unit – who would presumably have had greater access to film and equipment than most amateurs – the footage is astonishingly rare, being shot in full colour! It begins with a panning shot along the Tyne, filmed from St Mary's church, showing some of the sailing vessels that had made it back to Blighty. This is followed by jubilant scenes of street parties in Gateshead, including highly decorated streets, packed with revellers. Doorways and windows are decorated red, white and blue. Each street is festooned with flags, streamers and bunting, and the long tables are laid with an impressive spread, considering the rationing of the time. Teapots and teacups are poised at the ready as children and adults are to be seen giving the victory sign. Most poignantly, a group of people are holding a huge, homemade banner which reads 'VICTORY – There will always be an England'. A truly fascinating glimpse into Gateshead life on what was, after all, a life-changing day. As a footnote, on April 15th 2010 the BBC launched a campaign to find out who the party-goers were in the video footage. It is not known how successful they were at putting names to the smiling faces. (www.movinghistory.ac.uk)

May 9th

1876: On this day, a tragic boiler explosion occurred in Felling Shore. For once, this is not a tale of a coal mine – instead, the setting for this catastrophe was a paper works. Quite what caused the number-one boiler at the works to explode in the early hours of that morning is unknown, but the scale of the blast was phenomenal, and the effects of the disaster on one family in particular would be indelible. Six men were working late that night. Of the five killed, three shared the surname Abbot; 38-year-old engineer Patrick and his sons, Patrick Jnr, 17 and John, 14. Their grave in St Mary's church, Heworth, makes for chilling reading:

> Take warning by our sudden call;
> That you for death prepare,
> For it will come, you know not when,
> The manner, how nor where.

Alfred Smith, son of the works manager, and machine man Robert Smart were also killed. The sixth man, George Clark, had a very narrow escape. He had ended his shift but waited behind inside the mill to see a friend. When the friend did not arrive, he left – barely ten minutes before the explosion. (*Newcastle Courant*)

MAY 10TH

1934: On this day, any early morning commuters across the River Tyne were treated to an unusual dawn chorus from above. This was not the customary calls of kittiwakes, however. Being Ascension Day in the Christian calendar, Canon Stephenson arranged for the St Mary's Gateshead Choir to ascend to the roof of the church and perform several hymns, including the appropriately chosen *Hail the Day that sees Him Rise*. The *Evening Chronicle* reported that 'Glorious sunshine enhanced the novel scene, the surplices of 20 odd choristers, men and boys, contrasting sharply with the time-worn grey of the old church tower. Hymns mingled with the roar of traffic on the bridge. Despite the hour – 7 am – a fair-sized crowd, mainly women, gathered round the foot of the church tower and joined in the singing, while many others watched from the windows of houses in the neighbourhood.' Canon Stephenson's idea was to revive at St Mary's the ancient custom of many old churches to sing on the roof to celebrate Ascension Day. The choir were congratulated on their performance by Stephenson and the choirmaster before enjoying a well-earned breakfast – presumably at ground level. (*Evening Chronicle*)

MAY IITH

1861: On this day, a heart-breaking tale unfolded in Eighton Banks. A miner by the name of Stoker left his wife and four children in Galloping Green, while he visited Newcastle. With four children to feed – the youngest only seven months old – bad times had hit the family hard, especially as Stoker had been absent from work in Springwell Pit through illness. Little did he know how much it had affected his wife. Just after three o'clock, Mrs Stoker called in her second-youngest child. She drew the blinds and locked the door behind her. The house remained silent for a few hours until Mr Stoker arrived to find his eldest two children crying on the doorstep, locked out of the house. Fearing a terrible accident, Stoker managed to break through a wooden ventilation cover on one window and sent one of the two children through to unlock the door. Inside was a terrible scene. The bodies of Mrs Stoker and the two youngest children were lying on the bed, covered in blood, their throats cut. Immediately Stoker sent for a doctor from Wrekenton. Incredibly, Mrs Stoker was not yet dead, and once her neck was sewn, was able to confess to double infanticide, saying that 'I was out of my head', before succumbing to her own injuries. It emerged that since the birth of their last child, Mrs Stoker had been 'depressed in spirits' – something which is now recognised as post-natal depression, but was tragically less understood in Victorian times. (*Manchester Times*)

MAY 12TH

1984: On or around this day, Mrs Jane Snowball of Leam Lane became the world's first online shopper! The 72-year-old used a ground-breaking new Gateshead Council Shopping and Information Service (SiS), to purchase her weekly groceries from Tesco. This service allowed elderly Gateshead residents to order shopping using their television and remote control, connected electronically to the supermarket's own computers. A forerunner of later internet-based grocery shopping services, the SiS was partially developed by ICT wizard Michael Aldrich. After retiring to Arizona, Aldrich began a worldwide search for Mrs Snowball, and stumbled upon local news footage of her using the system. He contacted Gateshead Council who then located the Snowballs. On May 12th 2009, although Mrs Snowball had long-since passed away, Gateshead Council recognised her significance by presenting her family with an engraved paperweight. Her son Derek said, 'I'm delighted to come to Gateshead today to accept this gift on behalf of my mother. I know she would have been incredibly proud to receive it. My mother was devoted to her home shopping system and demonstrated it to everyone who came to the house. It helped tremendously when my father needed round-the-clock care … If others had seen the system in operation in Gateshead, the take-up of home shopping may have been more rapid, but my Mam certainly thought it was smashing.' (www. aldricharchive.com)

MAY 13TH

1831: On this day, the Black Bull Inn echoed with harsh words. The event was a dinner thrown by the Friends of Parliamentary Reform, including Durham MP William Russell and Cuthbert Rippon, later Gateshead's first MP. In a rabble-rousing speech, Rippon voiced his support for religious reform. He compared the upper echelons of the Church to 'vampires [living] off the life blood of the Constitution.' Russell went a step further, comparing 'an unfortunate Curate working hard for 50, 100, or, at most, 150 [pounds] a year' to 'Bishops, with ten, twenty-five and thirty thousand pounds a year, who really do nothing … They talked about a strike among the pitmen. Why should there not be a strike among the Curates?' (*Newcastle Courant*)

1908: Also on this day, five local boys got a nasty shock. It seems that they had found a rusty tin can just inside the graveyard at St Mary's. Inside the tin was a black substance, somewhat resembling coal. Boys being boys, they threw stones at it and kicked it around. It was discovered that when the can hit water, the substance inside reacted. One boy, by the unfortunate name of Burns, decided to apply a match and see if it was flammable … A massive explosion erupted, injuring ten people (including the boys) and a passing horse. Amazingly, nobody lost their lives – and no one ever did explain what the mystery black explosive was. (*Durham Chronicle*)

MAY 14TH

1080: On this day, the people of Gateshead took bloody revenge! Shortly after the Normans conquered England in 1066, William the Conqueror invited trusted Normans to fill positions of power. William Walcher, a priest from Liège, was soon elevated to Earl and Bishop of Durham. He was fairly popular – for a Norman – but an incompetent leader, too easily influenced by others and too weak to prevent unrest. He did nothing to prevent Scottish forces from raiding Northumberland. His household knights plundered and destroyed property, even murdering natives without punishment. Local leaders began criticising Walcher's leadership, which angered his Norman henchmen. One fateful night, a popular Northumbrian called Ligulf of Lumley – an outspoken critic of Walcher – was murdered by Walcher's kinsman, Gilbert. Enraged, the Northumbrians rioted. In an effort to prevent a full-blown rebellion, Walcher agreed to meet them, choosing the parish church of Gateshead, probably near to the current St Mary's, as the venue. Negotiation was obviously not Walcher's strong-point; the crowd ignored his pleas for peace and called for Gilbert's blood, forcing him, and hundreds of his men, to seek refuge inside the church. The enraged mob now had a captive enemy. They set fire to the building, forcing those inside to choose whether to burn to death inside or run outside to be hacked to pieces. In the massacre, Walcher, Gilbert, and most of the Normans met their grisly end. (trans. Stevenson, J., *The Historical works of Simeon of Durham*: 1855)

MAY 15TH

1657: On this day, George Fox, the founder of Quakerism, visited Gateshead. His visit prompted a snub to Newcastle in his journal! Having visited Newcastle earlier, 'but meeting with no encouragement ... we got a little meeting among friends in Gateside (Gateshead); where a meeting is continued at this day in the name of Jesus.' (Sykes, J., *Local Records*, i, 1833)

———•◆•———

1998: Also today, a Gateshead resident was denied permission to wear a Newcastle United shirt. Not newsworthy, perhaps, except that the resident in question was the Angel of the North! Newcastle United were due to play in the FA Cup Final against Arsenal. At some point in the previous week (sources differ), ingenious Magpie fan Ian Waugh and his friends managed to catapult ropes over the statue's wings. They hoisted up a 30ft shirt, emblazoned with the name of Newcastle's talismanic captain Alan Shearer, and his famous number 9. Police ordered the shirt to be taken down within minutes, but the idea prompted an official request from fans to reinstate it. Unfortunately, Gateshead's authorities rejected the plea, quoting stipulations from Antony Gormley, the Angel's artist. It was also quipped that, should the Angel wear a black and white shirt for the cup, it would have to wear a red and white one should Sunderland gain promotion later in the year! In the event, Newcastle lost 2-0 in a poor performance. (*Newcastle Evening Chronicle*)

MAY 16TH

1884: On this day, thousands of locals flocked to the North Countrie Fayre, held in Gateshead Town Hall. Although this should have been their last chance, the events popularity led organisers to extend the fair by another day. The plan was to raise funds for the renovation of Gateshead Fell parish church, by transforming the town hall into a village green deep in Merry England. Volunteers had only a few days to work their magic, working late into the night to bring stone, wood and thatch into the main hall. There were other more illusory effects, including transparent images of rural beauty in the windows, and a huge wall painting of a woodland glade. The 'modern ghastliness of the gallery' was transformed with ivy, a maypole placed in the middle, and a series of stalls, each with a medieval-style signboard, displayed a range of crafts. These stalls covered a range of articles 'useful and ornamental', including dolls, bouquets, cutlery, sweets, china, glass, and a wide range of needlework. The Old Cannon hostelry, opened in a side room, claimed to serve 'manne and beaste' (leading the *Tyneside Echo* to jokingly query why, then, no dogs were allowed in?) The event was a huge success, leading the Echo to comment on 'the ready response Charity receives to her calls when she dons the old English attire'. (*Tyneside Echo*)

MAY 17TH

1926: On and around this day, the miners of Gateshead took a further step in confirming their commitment to strike action. Their campaign had already suffered a massive blow – the General Strike had been called across the nation at the start of the month, but on May 11th the TUC folded and the railwaymen, ironworkers and others returned to work. The miners had no intention of following suit. In fact, a few days on they began to bring the pit ponies up into the fresh air. Charles Lambert recalls that at this time, 'lads and men who had handled these pit Galloways in the past collected at the Whickham pit gates to welcome their favourites to bank. There was Doctor, Dragon, Saxon and Sweep, Duller, and Freddie, Daskie and Tip and so on. Now some of these ponies had been underground for weeks, some years. They were hard working, docile and very friendly. Now in bright sunlight after two weeks rest, they took some handling. There was prancing, neighing, squealing, kicking, all round. It was quite exciting. All assembled they left the pit yard, to a field near the Whaggs Pit. Each handler had his work cut out to keep control. Crowds gathered to see these little mites, whose heights ranged between three and four feet.' The ponies are said to have leaped around happily throughout their summer vacation – even when local lads jumped up on them for rides. (Oral history transcript, Gateshead Library)

MAY 18TH

1997: On this day, the first Northumbrian University Boat Race was contested between Newcastle and Durham Universities. Setting off from Dunston Staithes and covering the 1,800m to the Gateshead Millennium Bridge, the race was actually four races, each named after one of Tyneside's most accomplished figures from the sport's Victorian heyday. The men's Senior Eights competed for the Clasper Trophy (named after Harry Clasper), whilst the women competed for the Chambers Trophy ('Honest Bob' Chambers, Clasper's rowing partner). The younger, less experienced Freshmen and Freshwomen competed for trophies named after James Renforth and Matthew Taylor, respectively. Sponsored by Northumbrian Water, the winners of the overall race were to be decided by totalling the victories across the four events. On this occasion, the winners were Durham, who won every race. Durham went on to win or draw the next ten meetings, with Newcastle waiting until 2009 for their first overall victory! By 2011, however, the advantage had truly swung towards Newcastle. In the preceding British Universities and Colleges Sport Regatta in Nottingham, Newcastle beat Durham so comprehensively that Durham conceded all future races that year, leading to the annual Tyne race being forfeited! (www.nwl.co.uk)

MAY 19TH

1879: On this day, an all-night prayer meeting led to some surreal scenes. An exhausted journalist had been following the Salvation Army for the week, culminating in an all-night meeting at Handyside's Hall. He wrote: 'Pleasure has denigrated into toil … I assured myself that the leaders of the Salvation Army would be as tired as I was, and that if they were resolved not to go home till morning, they would at least make up their minds to be off at the first glimmer of sunrise. But the energy of these people is wonderful. The same faces have been visible, and the same voices have been heard, at all the meetings which have been held since Saturday; yet here again the "Hallelujahs" were as full of spirit and determination, and far more overpoweringly noisy, than ever. If ever I go to an all night prayer meeting again, I shall take something to steady the nerves. Such a terrifying gathering as that which was held last night has, I should think, never been seen before – not in the wildest excesses of Primitive Methodism.' He went on to describe the religious fervour he observed as 'Pandemonium on a *fete* day; Bedlam let loose; the madness and noise of a Bacchanalian orgie [*sic*] without the wine.' But for all that, the correspondent concluded that the movement was for the greater good, as many of the attendees were of formerly questionable social morals, and whilst in the throes of religious passion, were at least not on the streets committing harm! (*Newcastle Daily Chronicle*)

MAY 20TH

1937: On this day, Joicey Road School was finally opened. First considered as early as 1925, the financial crises of the early 1930s slowed things down. When finally built, the school catered for 150 of 'the physically handicapped and delicate' children of Gateshead aged between 6 and 14. The Council's School Medical Officer selected suitable children – not only those with permanent disabilities, but also those suffering or recovering from long term diseases like polio, tuberculosis, or respiratory problems. Joicey Road school was unusual – it was an Open Air school, part of an open air education movement begun in the early twentieth century. By 1939 there were a total of 127 open air schools across the country. In all but the worst weather, classes were conducted in the open air. Even the classrooms had large folding windows on three sides. Diet was also carefully controlled. Pupils would get milk and a biscuit at 9.30 a.m., a two-course meal at 12.15 p.m. followed by a nap in a 'rest shed', a room open to the west. School finished at 4.15 p.m., then the children got milk, bread and butter, and fruit. After the Cedars Day and Residential School for Physically Handicapped Children was opened in 1952, the Joicey Road School's intake shifted accordingly. It closed in 1970, but the buildings still stand, and are Grade II listed. (www. britishlistedbuildings.co.uk)

MAY 21ST

1871: On this day, thousands of men across Tyneside went home from work – and did not return until October 7th! In Gateshead alone, a thousand men walked away from John Abbott's ironworks. They were joined by five hundred from Hawks and Crawshay's ironworks, five hundred from Black and Hawthorn's engineering works, and another three hundred from Clarke, Watson and Gurney's engineering works. At issue was the right to work a mere nine-hour day. From the start, it was a bitter dispute, and employers refused to negotiate with the men directly. Additionally they brought in foreign workers, many from Belgium. Magistrates were soon seeing a succession of prosecutions of men and boys for throwing bricks, bottles and stones at the blacklegs. There was some sympathy for the strikers, even amongst the magistrates. One told the accused: 'the bench are not satisfied that there is sufficient evidence to convict the defendants, and they are dismissed. And now, my men, take care and don't do it again!' When the Belgian workers realised they were being used against their fellow workers, many were willing to return home, and money was raised across the country to pay for their return fares. Labour was scarce and demand for engineering work booming, which favoured the strikers. When the men went back to work, they had indeed won a nine-hour day. (Allen, E., *North-East Engineers' Strikes of 1871*, Frank Graham: 1971)

MAY 22ND

1753: On this day, Swalwell enjoyed its annual hoppings fair. And an interesting glimpse into the entertainments and pastimes of eighteenth-century life it makes! A notice proclaims that 'On this day the annual diversions at Swalwell will take place, which will consist of dancing for ribands, grinning for tobacco, women running for smocks, ass races, foot courses by men, with an odd whim of a man eating a cock alive, feathers, entrails and all.' (White, W., and Parson, W., *History, Directory and Gazetteer of the Counties of Durham and Northumberland*, 1827)

———◆———

1838: Also on this day, Robert Forbister and John Brown fought a bare-knuckle boxing match on Hedley Common in Ryton parish, with tragic consequences. Forbister was 4in taller and 20lb heavier than the 5ft 6in Brown, but perhaps the less skilled. The match took place at the county border, and when a Durham magistrate arrived, the fight moved to the Northumberland side. Ropes were strung for a 24ft ring, with spectators at 30 yards distance. Brown scored first blood and first knockdown, but tired after the twelfth round. After 37 rounds and an hour and a half, Brown was knocked down by a blow to the neck and he did not get up. He was carried to a nearby public house, where he died that evening. The local clergyman refused to allow Brown to be buried in the churchyard, and Forbister was sentenced to four months at hard labour. (T. Fordyce, *Local Records*, 1867)

MAY 23RD

1944: On this day, two young people – George Marshall of Newcastle and Joyce Sharpless of Gateshead – met for the first time. George was a stoker in the navy, who had had a narrow escape in 1941, when he was on board the HMS *Barham* when it was sunk with loss of over 850 lives. Joyce was employed at Parsons engineering works. They had been set up as pen-pals two years earlier – Joyce's friend Mary was writing to a sailor, and suggested that he might have a friend to whom Joyce could write. They wrote to each other more and more, and eventually – though they had never met – George proposed, and Joyce said yes! Finally in 1944, George had shore leave and headed to Gateshead, which had been his home as a child. On this day, there was a knock on Joyce's front door – and there George was. He said, 'you're just as I expected'. Five days later, they were married by special license at the church of the Venerable Bede, Gateshead, with Mary as maid of honour. Even at the time, their story was very unusual, so much so that they were interviewed by the Sunday Sun and the Daily Mirror (to whom Joyce said 'I know we will be very happy, we are so well suited.') They were married until Joyce's death in 1982. (*Evening Chronicle*)

MAY 24TH

1966: On this day, Princess Margaret arrived in Gateshead during which she formally opened the luxurious, brand new £750,000 Five Bridges Hotel. Having Royalty open the Five Bridges was quite a coup, given the difficulties that Gateshead had in building it. The Council faced opposition from residents in the area, objecting to a two-year building programme, but also quoting an obscure 1877 covenant. This document stated that the site should only be used as a garden or pleasure ground for the benefits of residents of Bewick Road. It prevented the selling of intoxicating liquor, which would severely hamper the hotel's proposed three public bars. Perhaps less relevant were the covenant's stipulations that prevented the drying of washing, the keeping of poultry, or the building of a summerhouse and vinery more than 8ft high! Reporting on the Royal visit, *The Journal* waxed lyrical about the 'Sunshine Princess's' attire and make up. 'It was springlike in every way – the dress and jacket pale apple green overlaid with a raised yellow check … Her hat was lime green corded silk with a bluey straw crown. Most unusual was Princess Margaret's tan make up worn with orange lipstick and a soft grey eye-shadow.' Such a colourful spectacle was certainly at odds with the grey skies and heavy downpour of rain that accompanied the Princess during her visit. Less fashionable people were not quite so favourably welcomed by the new hotel: bar staff were instructed not to serve men wearing flat caps! (*The Journal*)

MAY 25TH

1812: On this day, Felling was rocked by one of the worst explosions in British mining history. The blast was heard several miles away, and pieces of wood and coal rained down. In Heworth blown coal dust noticeably darkened the air, and fell so heavily that footprints could be clearly seen on the ground. Locals ran to the pit head to find out what had befallen their neighbours and relatives, and attempts were made to reach the workings. Thirty-two men were brought up alive from outlying tunnels, though three died later. The pit had been full, because it was shift's end, and one set of men had gone down before the first had come up. That left almost ninety men unaccounted for, but further rescue attempts proved too difficult – the shaft frames and pulley systems had been shattered and burned, and in any case the coal itself was burning strongly. In the end the mine was made airtight, and left for six weeks, before anyone entered. Over the course of the summer, the bodies were slowly recovered, and buried in Heworth chapel yard, two coffins deep in a long trench. By September, it was confirmed that Felling pit had claimed the lives of 92 men and boys. The cause of the explosion was never fully known, though the disaster was a major spur to the invention of the safety lamp. (Richardson, M., *Local Historian's Table Book*: 1844)

MAY 26TH

1983: On this day, as the *Gateshead Post* reported, conservation volunteers in Windy Nook 'got well and truly stoned'. They had made an appeal for loose stone, to help them build a dry stone wall to border Windy Nook Nature Reserve, but were surprised by the response – five lorries full of loose stone that builders in Whickham had unearthed while making house foundations. Volunteers were then taught the art of dry stone walling in a series of workshops. Yet more stone was brought to the Nature Park to form Richard Cole's *Windy Nook*, a massive piece of landscaping which was officially opened in Gateshead's Sculpture Festival in 1986. It transformed a former colliery spoil heap into something occasionally mistaken for an ancient hill fort, comprising a series of terraces in concentric circles, made from turfed earthworks and stone walls. At 160m high, covering over 5,000m, and incorporating 2,500 tons of granite which was once part of the pillars of the old Scotswood Bridge, it remains one of the largest environmental sculptures in Europe. The labourers were, surprisingly, paid for by the Manpower Services Commission. Fittingly, the nature reserve is on Stone Street! (*Gateshead Post* / www.gateshead.gov.uk)

MAY 27TH

1859: On this day, Catherine Booth – wife of evangelist and founder of the Salvation Army, William Booth – preached for the first time. William and Catherine had come to Gateshead in 1858, and by January 1859 William had begun a series of revival meetings at the Bethesda Chapel, Melbourne Street. He was a fiery and popular preacher, and even though he preached seven times most weeks, the chapel was packed out every time, often with up to 2000 people squeezing in to the small chapel. The local ironworkers even named the place 'the converting shop', so many of their workmates were finding God. Catherine had always left the preaching to William, concentrating on working with the poor in the town, but on this day, Pentecost, she felt inspired by the Holy Spirit to go to the front of a church 'crowded to the doors, with people sat on the very window-sills' and begin to speak, confessing that she had wronged her Saviour by refusing to speak in the past. Increasingly in the years to come she would share the preaching work with her husband, and the novelty of a woman preacher was such that she was invited to speak across the region. The couple remained in Gateshead until 1861. (www. vision.pwp.blueyonder.co.uk/revival)

MAY 28TH

1960: On this day, to almost universal dismay, Gateshead Football Club was voted out of the Fourth Division of the Football League. The Fourth Division had only been created in 1958, and the system was that the bottom four teams had to face re-election on an annual basis. Gateshead were convinced they would be all right – after all, two teams had finished below them, and competitors Southport were facing their third successive fight for survival. But in the event, Gateshead was the first team to be voted out from the division, with only 18 votes (Southport were the next lowest at 29). They were replaced by Peterborough United, in their twenty-first attempt to gain entry into the league. There was a great feeling of injustice about this, and many believed that the southern teams had voted against Gateshead simply because they didn't like having to travel so far north. Certainly of the five teams which were relegated from the league over the next twenty years, all were replaced by a team from further south! Gateshead FC next applied to join the Scottish League, without success; they went on to join the Northern Counties League and in 1968 became founder members of the Northern Premier League.

MAY 29TH

1986: On this day, the Gateshead Post reported on the previous week's Sport Aid, and how Gateshead 'ran the world'. Locals had risen to the occasion, with an estimated 23,000 taking to the streets and running 10km to raise money to combat famine in Africa. Impressively, though only a tiny fraction of the nearly 20 million who ran worldwide, this was the largest British gathering for Sport Aid outside of London. (*Gateshead Post*)

2012: On this day, the *Evening Chronicle* reported on a remarkable local find. Ten-year-old Harriet Marshall was helping her mum in their Winlaton garden when she came across a smooth, bullet-shaped fossil. Thinking that it might be a dinosaur tooth, Harriet took her find to the Great North Museum. Here, experts identified the fossil as a belemnite, the hard insides of a squid-like creature that lived 160 million years ago. If Harriet had lived in the south of England, this would not have been a terribly unusual find – in some places on the south coast the belemnite, known in folklore as a thunderbolt, is not uncommon. But in England, the belemnite had not previously been found north of the cliffs around Whitby, which – unlike the rock of Gateshead – date to the same period as the belemnite itself. How this specimen ended up in Winlaton remains a mystery. (*Evening Chronicle*)

MAY 30TH

1825: On this day, Stargate Pit exploded. Dug from 1800, it was one of the deepest in the region, as the coal seam began 152m down. Transport was via a straight shaft – corves (wicker baskets) would be attached to a circular rope, and then filled with coal or men. It was an advanced pit for its time, with the first-ever underground self-acting incline (where the momentum of the full tubs moving down a slope was used to also take empty tubs up the slope). Nonetheless, ventilation relied simply on a furnace to move air through, and most miners used candles, rather than lamps. But while the furnace had kept burning, at some point a rock fall must have blocked the air flow, and the miners were taking naked flames into a lethal mix of flammable gas. At 3 a.m. a shift was starting, and men were walking through the main tunnels when the gas exploded. The blast carried towards the shaft, collapsing workings and erupting from the pit's mouth, travelling up the pit shaft so hard that it literally blew one man from the bottom to the top. Of fifty workers, thirty were dead, and most of the rest seriously injured and lying in poisonous gases. Those who survived were either near the entrance, or in two cases able to creep down an almost-forgotten drainage channel. In the end, thirty-eight men and boys died, leaving behind nineteen widows and sixty-two children. (www.dmm.org.uk)

MAY 31ST

1636: On or around this day, the bubonic plague claimed its first local victim of the year. The St Mary's church register was not kept precisely over that nightmarish summer; plague deaths are merely recorded as a long list of names, beginning at this point. By the end of September, the list had on it 200 names (this is sometimes confused with the 515 recorded as dying in 'Garth-side in Newcastle' over the same period, but this probably relates to somewhere else, perhaps Castle Garth). We can see something of the concerns of the dying by reading surviving wills. For example, Gateshead man Thomas Swan rewrote his will, 'by reason his children were all dead but one, and that he was greatly indebted, and knew not which way it should be paid but that he was likely to leave his wife in much care and trouble'. He ordered the sale of his house (with so many dying, no one could afford to be squeamish about that!), and ordered that enough cash be set aside to pay to complete his son's apprenticeship. Unusually, he also ordered that all the goods which his wife had brought to the marriage, should revert back to her intact, as 'he would be sorry to leave her in a worse estate than he found her'. (Wrightson, K., *Ralph Tailor's Summer*, Yale University Press: 2011 / eds. Newton, D., and Pollard, A., *Newcastle and Gateshead before 1700*, The History Press: 2009)

JUNE 1ST

1829: On this day, Whit Monday, 'the ancient custom of holding an annual merry meeting' on Windmill Hills was revived. An advertising handbill gives an insight into the rich variety of prizes on offer for achievements in the field of making-merry: 'The following prizes will be awarded: A hat to be run for by men; another hat to be run for by boys; a cheese to be run for by men tied up in sacks; a pound of tobacco to be grinned for through a horse collar, and another pound of tobacco to be wrestled for.' 'Grinning' here is not smiling; it is gurning, pulling hideous or amusing faces for the entertainment of judges. Truly worth the prize … (Original handbill)

1908: Also on this day, *Scout* magazine reported that, 'Gateshead is taking an active part in the Boy Scout Movement. Two troops have been formed under the titles of 1st Gateshead Troop and 2nd Gateshead Troop.' This was the first recorded mention of a scouting presence in Gateshead. The local troops were probably inspired by the publication of the first part of *Scouting for Boys,* six months earlier. By 1910 there were already 599 members in Gateshead, many of whom had the honour of being inspected by Lord Baden Powell himself at North Durham Cricket Ground later that year. (Telford, W., *A Tale of Shorts,* Telford: 1988)

JUNE 2ND

1917: On this day, the commanding officer of the 9th Battalion, Durham Light Infantry (DLI) – also known as the Gateshead Gurkhas – was awarded the Victoria Cross. Raised in Gateshead in August 1914, the 9th Battalion was always in the forefront of First World War combat, serving in the second battle of Ypres, at the Somme, Arras and Passchendaele. In May 1916 they were joined by Lieutenant Colonel Roland Boys Bradford. By October he had already began to turn the Gateshead battalion into one of the British Army's most respected units. After his commanding officer was injured, he took control of both his own battalion and the 6th DLI and spearheaded a successful attack on the German front line. His exemplary leadership shone, with clear, precise orders issued fearlessly under heavy machine-gun fire. Bradford's citation was for 'most conspicuous bravery and good leadership in attack'. Tragically, less than six months after receiving his VC from George V, Bradford was killed in battle at Cambrais. (Durham Light Infantry Museum)

* * *

1953: Also on this day, Canon H. Stephenson of Gateshead attended the coronation of Queen Elizabeth II. This hugely influential man had been a King's Chaplain since 1938, and he was one of only eight chaplains representing England during the ceremony. The last time a rector of Gateshead was present at a coronation had been in 1689, when William of Orange was crowned William III. (*Gateshead Post*)

JUNE 3RD

1657: On this day, the people of Gateshead vented their frustrations at Thomas Weld, Gateshead's least popular rector. Originally from Essex, Weld's life took an interesting route to Gateshead. He moved to New England in 1632, where he was one of the chief prosecutors in the Boston trial of Anne Hutchinson, a woman who had dared to suggest that women were as able to interpret the Bible as any man! Hutchinson was publicly humiliated and banished from the Church. Returning to England, and installed during the ascendency of Oliver Cromwell, Puritan Weld set about alienating the people of Gateshead. He displaced seventeen of the town's 'Four and Twenty' leaders whom he saw as 'not fit to be entrusted in that employment', then excommunicated all but ten of his own parish. Today's petition pleaded that 'since Mr. Weld hath had the incumbency of Gateshead, the greatest part of his parishioners have, by him, been denied the comfort and benefit of both sacraments, to which being intitled as Christians ... have induced us ... to endeavour our restauration to those priviledges.' Weld died in 1661 and normalcy was soon restored. To this day a plaque to all of Gateshead's rectors, displayed in St Mary's church, lists Weld's name alongside the epithet of 'The Intruder'. (Lang. A., *The St Mary's Story*, Gateshead Council: 2009 / Barnes, A., *Memoirs of the Life of Ambrose Barnes*, 1867)

JUNE 4TH

1868: On this day, the laying ceremony of the foundation stone of Gateshead Town Hall was marred by tragedy. The building had already been built to a height of around 15ft, and it was at this height that the 'foundation' stone was going to be added. So that people could get a good view, two 25ft-tall wooden platforms had been built – one for ladies next to West Street, and a larger one for gentlemen, adjoining Swinburne Place. Hundreds of respectable citizens reserved their seats, and got into position on the stands. As the *Newcastle Courant* put it, 'had they been – which they were not – substantial erections, all would have gone well'. At first things went according to plan, and the stone was laid without issue. One lad fell off the back of the stand, but was not hurt. But then part of the gentlemen's stand gave way. The ends stayed firm, but the middle collapsed in a ruin of timber into which hundreds of people were tipped. Seven people were taken to the Dispensary for treatment, including three with broken bones; many more were bruised. Most were men, but a few women had sneaked onto the men's stand. One man, James Barnett, died later that night from injuries to his feet. The inquest determined that a lack of care lay both with the architect, and with the sub-committee who altered his plan without consulting him. (*Newcastle Courant*)

JUNE 5TH

1743: On this day, Charles Wesley preached in Gateshead during the course of one of his tours. Like his brother John, Charles Wesley came to the North East on several occasions. During this particular visit to Gateshead, he records in his diary, 'My soul was revived by the poor people at Chowden'. The following week he was in Chowdene again, and says, 'I preached ... at seven to the poor people in Chowden.' He also preached more than once on Ryton village green – the first recorded time being a year earlier in 1742, when he preached on the subject of 'The Great Supper'. He was still coming back fourteen years later – on December 28th 1756, he writes, 'I hastened through the snow to Gateshead, and preached out to many, who promised fair for making hardy soldiers of Christ.' The idea of preaching outside of a church building was an unusual but effective means of spreading the word. Charles Wesley wrote many hymns, including 'Hark! The Herald Angels Sing'. One of his less well-known hymns, 'Ye neighbours and friends of Jesus draw near', was written after preaching to the colliers of Tyneside. (www. biblicalstudies.org.uk)

JUNE 6TH

2011: On this day Google revealed the winners of its competition to find the best streets in Britain, after collating over 20,000 votes. One of its categories was for the 'hippest' street, and – probably much to the annoyance of London – this was won by South Shore Road, Gateshead. South Shore Road runs near the riverside, alongside the Sage Gateshead music centre and the Baltic Centre for Arts, and overlooks the Gateshead Millennium Bridge. Call Lane in Leeds came second, and Whitecross Street in Islington third. Claire Byers, deputy director of Baltic, said the skyline of South Shore Road was known the world over. 'It not only offers fantastic views of the River Tyne, but boasts some of the best contemporary art in the world, superb live music, festivals, events and delicious places to eat, drink and meet friends. No wonder it has come to symbolize NewcastleGateshead as one of the best locations in the country.' Unsurprisingly it was the scene for the launch of Gateshead's 2012 campaign for city status – which ultimately failed, but was still said to have had benefits for the profile of the town. Not bad for a street that less than 100 years before had been filled with the grime, smells and sights of a fat-rendering plant, chemical works, flour mills, roperies, coal staithes and many other industrial buildings! (*Guardian*)

JUNE 7TH

1849: On this day the Mayor of Gateshead, George Hawks, ceremonially hammered in the last key to tension the chain of the final arch of the new High Level Bridge. Designers had long suggested a high-level crossing, but it became more important after 1837, when the railway line from London could reach Gateshead, but no further. The design is Robert Stephenson's, although William Martin previously published a very similar design (with added giant sculptures!), and claimed Stephenson had stolen his ideas. In total, around 800 families were displaced as their homes were knocked down during construction. Work began in April 1846, helped by a newly patented pile driver which replaced much of the manual work. Originally the whole thing was painted stone-coloured, but after smoke pollution made it black, it was repainted in black, and later dark grey. Although in theory the two-level system benefited walkers, in practice the ceiling of their layer leaked badly, in spite of its asphalt roof. That didn't put everyone off – in 1859 the *Illustrated London News* reported that this quarter-mile of straight covered track, which could easily be blocked at both ends, was proving popular for dog racing! (Manders, F., and Potts, R., *Crossing the Tyne*, Tynebridge Publishing: 2001)

JUNE 8TH

1931: On this day, Gateshead held a by-election in unusual circumstances. The Labour Party had always enjoyed strong support in Gateshead and could usually rely on a positive result in any election. Labour MP James Melville was immensely popular and had won the general election in 1929 with over 50 per cent of the votes. The year 1931 was to see another general election and the stage was set for yet another successful if uneventful victory for Labour. Unfortunately Melville died on May 1st 1931, leading to an urgent by-election to choose his replacement before October's general election. Without a solid and respected candidate to step into Melville's shoes, Labour were in danger of losing their seat in Gateshead. Luckily for them their next choice of candidate, Herbert Evans, retained the seat on this day – just! Labour's majority had dropped from over 30 per to only 3 per cent. Still, on the bright side, Evans had four months to prepare his campaign for the general election. Unluckily for Evans – and indeed Labour – the replacement MP himself died on the 7th October. After not one but *two* unexpected deaths, the replacement (replacement) Labour candidate, Ernest Bevin, had only twenty days to prepare his election campaign! Unsurprisingly, Bevin lost the seat to Thomas Magnay, the National Liberal candidate. This represents the only occasion to date since 1924 when a Labour candidate has not represented the people of Gateshead in Parliament. (Craig, F., *British Parliamentary Election Results 1918-1949*, Macmillan: 1977)

JUNE 9TH

1862: On this day, one of the most famous accidents in Gateshead's history probably did not happen! 'The Blaydon Races', one of the region's most famous songs, colourfully celebrates the accidental crashing of an omnibus, heavy-laden with horseracing spectators. According to the song the crash happened 'on the ninth of Joon, eiteen hundred an' sixty-two, on a summer's efternoon.' While Geordie Ridley, the song's author, certainly performed his song on June 9th 1862, it is likely that he either created a fictional crash or was inspired by one from a previous year. So vivid were his words, however, that many today believe the events to be true. The races themselves had humble beginnings: horse races were held on Stella Haugh in the early nineteenth century but were stopped in 1835, when a railway station was built on the former track. When the races were revived as a huge-scale event in 1859, ironically the railway station proved a blessing. For the 1861 event, the races were moved to Blaydon Island, a perfect racecourse – flat, oval, and around a mile in circumference. They were held in conjunction with the Blaydon Hoppings, and passengers came by train, bus, and river steamer. Whilst Ridley's song may not be based in reality, with its 'spice stalls an' munkey shows an' aud wives selling ciders', it does vividly capture the buoyant mood of those travelling to the races. (Winlaton and District Local History Society, *A History of Blaydon*, Gateshead Council: 1975)

JUNE 10TH

1725: On this day, two men attempted to murder Gateshead mine owner William Cotesworth (also spelled Coatsworth) in his home at Park House. The two would-be assassins were his trusted butler, John Brown, and his gardener Christopher Richardson. Brown dosed Cotesworth's morning cup of hot chocolate with a substantial quantity of arsenic, which he had talked Richardson into supplying. Arsenic was easy to get hold of from any apothecary's shop, as it was the standard method of poisoning rats. It was also relatively cheap and virtually tasteless. Doctors remarked that Cotesworth was lucky to survive. The motive was seemingly entangled in the complicated rivalries of local coal owners. Cotesworth was an energetic, self-made man who had made enemies through aggressive legal suits. One of those entangled in complex legal wrangles with Cotesworth was Richard Ridley – intriguingly, Brown's previous employer! He also supported the two men during their imprisonment. Although Ridley's direct involvement was never proven, the Durham judge argued that the men must have been coerced or prompted into action from a more powerful source, as 'so great and so vile an attempt was not the produce of the fellows' own brains'. As punishment, both men were jailed only to be taken out and 'whipped ten times around the market place', on June 10th 1726 – the anniversary of their crime. (Ellis, J., 'The poisoning of William Cotesworth, 1725', *History Today*, November 1978)

JUNE 11TH

1880: On this day, 19-year-old heiress Alice Purvis Buddle found herself before the Gateshead Police Court. Her crime was a strange theft. She had gone to jeweller John Dove Caris, and persuaded him to let her borrow three golden Albert guard chains, saying that her uncle Jacob Atkinson was interested in buying more. She took the chains to three different pawn shops, and ended up with £3, perhaps a quarter of the chains' true value. She then went to her current home, a lodging house in Corbridge. In court she said, 'it is quite true. It seems as if I cannot help but do this sort of thing'. While a modern court might order psychiatric assessment for kleptomania – Buddle certainly didn't need the cash – the Victorian court merely committed the heiress for trial. The defence argued that she could not help herself and was a respectable woman who would be 'taken care of' in future. The judge said that this was 'a painful thing to see', but nonetheless sentenced her to three months' hard labour. (*Daily Gazette / Carlisle Patriot*)

———— • ◆ • ————

2006: Also on this day, Jamaican sprinter Asafa Powell equalled his own world record while competing at Gateshead International Stadium. He ran 100m in 9.77 seconds (actually 9.763, beating his previous record by 0.003 of a second!). He later managed 9.72, which held until the rise of Usain Bolt in 2008. (www.bbc.co.uk)

JUNE 12TH

1937: On this day, Edith Dawson of Springwell sat down to describe her day. She was one of 500 volunteers who had been recruited in May for the Mass Observation Survey. This phase involved a monthly 'day survey' and questionnaires. Fifty-year-old housewife Dawson was the survey's most prolific respondent! On this day, she described her routine on a relatively easy Saturday, as well as ruminating on everything from free education to euthanasia. She got up at eight, and had breakfast over the newspaper and discussion about Wallace Simpson. At eleven she was washing 'woollen and silk underwear, stockings etc, knowing full well how shocked the natives are to find washing out in the garden on Saturday!' After preparing dinner, she helped her 15-year-old daughter with dressmaking homework, and discussed the 'nice young man she likes to smile on'. This got her to thinking about her 19-year-old girl, who had worried that 'when I go out for a walk with a boy, I might have a baby'. Edith had settled for talking about 'bees and pollen, and left out the rest ... How the heck can any mother tell the plain unvarnished truth. No nice girl wants to hear it!' In the afternoon she cooked, while her husband built a 'scientific' wheelbarrow for the garden; and then in the evening they headed to Washington Cinema, for crime drama *The Man who Lived Twice*. (Mass Observation Survey)

JUNE 13TH

1833: On this day, a massive salmon catch was pulled from the Tyne, the largest for many years. Over 500 were taken to market. This was, of course, before the mounting industrial pollution began to take its toll! Salmon travel out to sea and back inland again every year, so they can only thrive if the river is unpolluted all the way up. Salmon fishing on the Tyne goes back a very long way – records of catches exist from the twelfth century. On June 12th 1755, more than 2,400 salmon were caught by a single net fishery, just above the bridges. And in 1759, the river's largest ever individual fish was recorded, weighing in at 54lbs. In Victorian times, over 100,000 might be taken in a single year. But numbers were starting to decline. The river was being dredged, disturbing habitats, and huge fishing nets at the river mouth took their toll. As the first flushing toilets were brought in around the 1920s, thousands of gallons of untreated sewage poured into the river. This added to the products of expanding industries – the riverside was crowded with tanneries, alkali works, soap works, breweries, gas works, and abattoirs, and oxygen levels plummeted. In the 1930s, what few fish were caught tasted of tar! By the 1950s, the Tyne salmon was almost extinct. Since the 1970s numerous cleaning processes, together with restocking schemes, have ensured that Tyne is again one of the best salmon rivers in the country. (*Independent*)

JUNE 14TH

1931: On this day the first premises of the Gateshead Yeshiva were officially opened. The Yeshiva – a Jewish Talmudical college – was started by Rabbi Dovid Dryan, who arrived in Gateshead in 1927. In the town he found a community of traditional Jews, seemingly unaffected by external and modern influences. His idea was to found a college to teach an extremely Orthodox interpretation of Jewish beliefs. There was considerable opposition from the Jewish community, in particular those more liberallyminded Jews who did not support Dryan's rigid stance. Nonetheless, Dryan opened a (very) small-scale teaching college in October 1929, when two boys from Leeds attended lessons in a corrugated iron synagogue in Corbett Street. As the reputation of the college grew, so did its numbers. Initially, scholars were accommodated by private families but soon the demand for lodgings rocketed. In order to spread the burden, students operated on a rota, staying with different families on different nights of the week and even having their meals with other families! So, in 1931 the Yeshiva took over 179 Bewick Road, a double-fronted terraced house in Bensham, which became the college's first premises. The conversion was paid for by a collection of *6d* per week from every Jewish family in the community. It lasted for thirty years until being demolished to make way for purpose-built dormitories. The Yeshiva was only the UK's third, and still enjoys an excellent worldwide reputation. (Olsover. L., *The Jewish Communities of North-East England*, Ashley Mark: 1980)

JUNE 15TH

1965: On this day, Councillor J. Foster criticised his fellow Gateshead councillors, accusing them of mumbling and speaking too quietly. During a meeting in the Town Hall he exclaimed that 'You miss far too many important points, and to make matters worse the acoustics in this building leave much to be desired … stop mumbling and speak up!' One newspaper ran a humorous poem concerning the dispute, including the lines:

> Full many a gem that crowns the spoken word
> These murky, muttering vaults of discourse crush;
> And flowers of wit and wisdom wilt unheard,
> Amidst an almost incoherent hush.

The opposition to Foster's motion to improve soundproofing in the Town Hall stated that it was unnecessary and costs would be too high. Ironically, this argument was made by councillors shouting over the sound of a pneumatic drill outside! And in a further irony, when the unsuccessful Foster then asked why one of his earlier motions had not been discussed, the reply was that 'no-one heard the motion being raised'. (*Newcastle Journal*)

JUNE 16TH

1826: On this day, the first mail coach made its way to Gateshead using the new road over Gateshead Fell (*see* July 18th). Thomas Wilson described it as, 'the road through the fields', referring to the mile or so of farmland still in existence between Gateshead and Low Fell. The new route, while straight, was not necessarily easy, including a long steep uphill section and then another steep downhill. Some complained that this was too hard on the horses pulling wagons, but others joked that horses actually enjoyed the variety and the fresh air on top of a hill. The new mail coach might have gained by the route, but times were about to get tough for them with the advance of the steam train. Still, taking the road had some advantages. The magistrates had granted licenses for four new inns along the new stretch of road – The Ship, The New Cannon Inn, The Engine and The Sovereign. Once a year The New Cannon Inn was extremely busy – it was where the assize judges (travelling north to hold court in Newcastle) met with the High Sheriff of Northumberland and his men. Many of the local gentlemen treated this as an excuse for a get-together, and at this period a popular sheriff could have as many as 500 gentlemen's carriages following him to The Cannon. However, this tradition also died as railway travel became more popular. (www.gateshead-history.com)

JUNE 17TH

1876: On this day, the newly built Swing Bridge opened for river traffic for the first time, although road traffic had been crossing since the 15th June. Its unusual swing design allowed large ships to reach the Armstrong works, Elswick. Other plans had been suggested for the site. Some wanted another higher level bridge; others favoured one with a single section that tilted up. Alternatives included a new ferry network and plans were even drawn up for a tunnel. The first planned swing bridge was discarded when someone realised it would, at the extreme of its turn, hit the High Level Bridge! Eventually the current design was settled on. When the previous bridge was being dismantled, it was found that on one pier the foundations of previous bridges – Roman, medieval and Georgian – could be seen on the same site. Apparently the Roman carpentry was the best! The machinery was made at Armstrong's, and although it needed forty-five minutes' notice to get up to steam, it took only ninety seconds for the bridge to rotate through ninety degrees. It had room for ships 31.7m wide, which at the time made it the largest swing bridge in the world. Though it is now powered by electricity rather than steam, much of its machinery is original. (Manders, F., and Potts, R., *Crossing the Tyne*, Tynebridge Publishing: 2001)

JUNE 18TH

1964: On this day, two Wrekenton puppies settled into a new home in Norfolk after being bought by a mysterious new owner. Bill Davidson of Biteabout on Moss Bank received a letter from William Meldrum, enquiring whether Spring and Sherry – two black Labrador puppies – were for sale. After agreeing the sale, a specially made transportation box arrived with the new owner's name and address printed on it: HM The Queen, The Kennels, Sandringham! Meldrum was chief dog trainer for Queen Elizabeth II. Sherry and Spring departed for the Queen's country residence on June 17th, looking forward to a bright future in trials and eventually being put out to stud. (*Evening Chronicle*)

———— • ◆ • ————

1890: Also on this day, Gateshead's first swimming baths were opened at the foot of Windmill Hills by Mayor Lucas. Lucas said, 'In a maritime nation such as this, where so many earn their living by pursuits on the water, it naturally follows that their avocations [are] dangerous … if the art of swimming was more in vogue, thousands of valuable lives would be saved.' The heated swimming pool proved especially popular with schools. This being a Victorian venture, men and women were only allowed to use the pool separately – women from 7 a.m. to 3 p.m. on Mondays and on Friday mornings, and men during the rest of the week! (*Newcastle Weekly Courant*)

JUNE 19TH

1844: On this day, the first continuous train journey from Gateshead to London, via Darlington and York, arrived at its destination. The train had arrived in the small hours of the 18th at the brand new Gateshead railway station, Greenesfield. It set off again soon after, and reached Euston Square, at about half past midnight on the 19th. This was possible following the opening of the Newcastle and Darlington line – but the line didn't actually reach Newcastle because there was no rail bridge, although senior engineers were being consulted for their plans (*see* February 19th). Gateshead station was an impressive building, over 100m long with a façade of Ionic columns and an ornate wrought-iron roof. At one end was a new hotel. But passenger traffic only stopped at the station for six years. After the High Level Bridge took traffic to Newcastle, Central station took over and Greenesfield was left for railway workshops and goods traffic. In the meanwhile, the trouble was that Gateshead was not well known to those of Newcastle, let alone further afield. As an anecdote of the time has it, a Gateshead belle wrote to a Newcastle lawyer, 'I hope that you will come to our Gateshead Dispensary Ball'. The response: 'And pray, madam, where is Gateshead?' (Watson, R., *The Literary and Philosophical Society of Newcastle upon Tyne*, Walter Scott: 1897)

JUNE 20TH

2008: On this day, Gateshead invested Toru Nishimura as an Honorary Freeman of the town. Nishimura was Mayor of Komatsu City in Japan, with which Gateshead has been twinned since 1991. He is the only non-British person to have received the honour, which he accepted during a ceremonial visit. During the visit, Nishimura enjoyed a tour of the borough and inspected its amenities, paying close attention to education: during a stop at Lord Lawson of Beamish School, the mayor was fascinated by the students studying vocational qualifications in hairdressing and food technology! The Japanese link has been cultivated further since his visit. In 2011, to commemorate the twentieth anniversary of the partnership, Saltwell Park opened a Japanese friendship garden, specially designed by Hiro Kitamura and Susumu Kitayama. This was a reciprocal gesture, as Gateshead had designed a friendship garden for Komatsu in 2001 to mark the tenth anniversary. Other projects have included art installations such as the Japanese tapestry that hangs in the Civic Centre, emblazoned with the phrase 'It is very far from England to Japan but it is the same sky.' Gateshead is also twinned with St Etienne de Rouvray in Normandy, although this came by default after Felling (which had been twinned with the town since 1963) became part of the Gateshead Borough in 1974! (www.gateshead.gov.uk)

JUNE 21ST

1820: On this day, a dangerous man was returned to Gateshead Asylum. Jonathan Martin was from a very unusual family. One of twelve children, he was born in Hexham in 1782, where he was raised by his staunchly Protestant grandmother. Amongst his siblings were William Martin (inventor and known eccentric), John Martin (controversial artist) and a sister who was murdered by a female neighbour (in front of the young Jonathan). He was press-ganged into the Navy in 1804, serving six arduous years against his will. It is perhaps no surprise that Jonathan Martin turned out a little unstable … Having absorbed his grandmother's religious ideals, he became an outspoken critic of the established Church and in 1817 he threatened the Bishop of Oxford Edward Legge with assassination. As a result of this he was tried and eventually committed to Gateshead Asylum. Clearly the asylum was not as security conscious as necessary, as he somehow escaped on June 17th 1820, only to be recaptured four days later. Jonathan Martin then went on hunger strike before escaping once again on July 1st! His most notorious 'achievement', however, was an act of arson nine years later. On February 1st 1829, during an evening service at York Minster, Martin became irritated at a buzzing sound coming from the organ, prompting him to return to set fire to the offending instrument! He was returned to asylums after that, eventually dying in the (more secure) Bethlehem Hospital (Bedlam) in London. (*Oxford Dictionary of National Biography*)

JUNE 22ND

1925: On this day, Chopwell's miners' strike began – eleven months before the General Strike of 1926. Like the General Strike, Chopwell's dispute was over reduced pay, changes to shifts and unsafe working conditions. The village's far-left political leanings were not new – in 1913 Chopwell was one of only three places in the country to have a Communist Club. It had a Socialist Sunday School and a library full of Socialist literature. By 1924, the village's mining banner had been changed to include images of Marx, Lenin and Keir Hardie, whilst its streets were named after the residents' socialist heroes. All of this helped the village attain the unofficial title of Little Moscow! In 1925, the local members of the Durham Miners' Association refused to accept new, unfavourable conditions of employment and organised a lockout. The pit closed. As a community, Chopwell closed its doors on mining officials and harangued any workers who tried to break strike. Policemen were enlisted to deal with the crowds of 200–300 people that assembled around the colliery, many of whom were women and children. It wasn't until May 1926 that the miners of Chopwell were joined by the country as a whole, by which time the community was close to starvation and desperate for the deadlock to break. Ultimately, it was deprivation that forced an end to the strike, with miners forced to accept a much worse deal in December 1926 than they had rejected in June 1925 ... (www.chroniclelive.co.uk)

JUNE 23RD

1753: On this day, the *Newcastle Journal* reported on 'the great cricket match that has been for some time depending, between the Gentlemen of Gateshead, and those of Newcastle'. It was played the previous week, on the Haughs near Redheugh, 'and won with great ease' by Gateshead. At this time the laws of cricket were barely codified, the first known code of cricket having been drawn up for London teams in 1744. Most aspects of the mid-eighteenth-century game are still recognisable today, but others were quite different. The ball would have been rolled along the ground, to a man wielding a bat shaped a little like a hockey stick. To complete a run, the batsman had to touch his bat to another held by the umpire. The middle wicket, a maximum bat width, and the leg-before-wicket rule were not introduced until the 1770s. Gateshead did not have a permanent cricket team for another eighty years, and even when Gateshead Borough Club was formed in 1834, cricket was still very much a game for gentlemen. Rivalry with Newcastle continued, though, and the teams were not above a little gamesmanship. When the club was accused of fielding twelve men against Newcastle Standard Club in 1838, the chairman admitted that this was true, but contended that four of those twelve were not club members (as if that made a difference!)

JUNE 24TH

1528: On this day, an early experiment in lead smelting was under way in Gateshead. Cardinal Wolsey owned mines in the north, including lead mines in Weardale and Hexhamshire. In 1528, he sent Dr Strangeways and Richard Bellasis to survey all his coal and lead mines, and find ways to make them more profitable. One idea was to try to maximise the value of these mines by melting the lead, and extracting silver from it. The novel part was to be the use of sea coal instead of wood, and Gateshead was chosen as a suitable place to build a house and furnace for the experiment. Wolsey agreed, and told them to proceed as soon as possible. On this day, Strangeways and Bellasis reported: 'The finers sent for smelting the lead ore at Gateshead have not yet done it, but have changed many and divers points of their works in devising new devices. They have promised to set to work in a fortnight.' By August, the coining works built on the same site was having some success, but the metal kept running out of the lead furnace. Bellasis asked for another, made of whole stone – and advised they would give up if this did not work. It seems not to have done – in December we see the chancellor in the North, William Franklin, excusing the size of his remittances by saying that he had to provide lead, and specialist refiners. No mention is made of any profits. (Welford, R., *History of Newcastle and Gateshead*, 1836)

JUNE 25TH

1702: On this day several of Gateshead's populace were nursing sore legs, and probably sore heads! The previous day had been the annual perambulation of Gateshead's boundaries. An ancient custom, perambulations involve the leaders of parishes and towns walking around the entire boundaries in order to ensure that their territory has not been encroached upon by neighbouring parishes. In some extreme cases, officials carried weapons and tools for destroying property and walls found to have strayed over the bounds. This day in 1702 was the first recorded boundary walk in Gateshead, though it is likely that they were nothing new. Three weeks earlier, the Four and Twenty, who controlled Gateshead at the time, had granted £6 towards refreshments, entertainment and food for the annual walk. The few surviving receipts paint an interesting picture of the proportion of money spent on liquid refreshment: whilst meat for the day cost 3s 4d and bread cost tuppence, one receipt states that 'Received then of Mr Cotesworth the sum of Fourteen Shilling and Seven Pence for Drink ...' As most of the Four and Twenty took part in the walk, perhaps they weren't too dismayed by this! As a footnote, the perambulation of 1704 suffered an unfortunate extra expense. Over-zealous Gateshead officials destroyed the property of William Bradley – incorrectly! On November 4th of that year, the Four and Twenty reimbursed him £24 14s 6d for their error ... (Oxberry, J., *Notes and News*, *Gateshead Library Record*)

JUNE 26TH

1971: On this day, a 13-year-old boy caught a 5lb pike in Saltwell Park's boating lake. Tony Rutherford was a keen angler, going sea-fishing every week, but – in his own words – catching 'nothing but a tiddler' for his time and effort. But today he decided to abandon the sea in favour of much calmer waters. Going for a fun day out with a friend, Tony casually dangled an un-baited nylon line behind his hire-boat. He wasn't even using a rod. To their amazement, the line violently pulled, and the boys dragged their struggling catch to the shore! It was not the first occurrence of pike in the lake – in 1968 by a strange coincidence another 13-year-old called Tony had also reeled in a 7.5lb pike, prompting a local press investigation about how the pike ended up in the land-locked lake. The *Journal* reported afterwards that a lad called Bob Brownless had put some 3lb pike in the lake in around 1963. Rumours about giant pike lurking in the Saltwell lake have circulated ever since … (*Newcastle Journal*)

JUNE 27TH

1727: On this day, three of the biggest coal mine and landowners of Tyneside – George Bowes of Gibside, Sidney Wortley and Sir Henry Liddell of Ravensworth – signed an agreement to work together, forming a cartel known as the Grand Alliance. The aim was to control the coal trade from the River Tyne to London, trumping rival families such as the Claverings of Axwell. Making profits from coal depended on being able to cheaply transport it to a river. Unfortunately, most mine owners also possessed patches of land in Gateshead and Newcastle, and they were reluctant to let competitors cross their land without paying extortionate tolls, known as wayleaves. The Grand Alliance agreed to share way leave rights and to cooperate over the development of collieries for mutual benefit. By 1736, the three signatories had over 140,000 wagons of coal crossing through Gateshead from pits in Tanfield, Hutton and Teams. (www.mininginstitute.org.uk)

———— ◆ ————

2004: On this day, Yelena Isinbayeva of Russia bettered her own pole vaulting world record of 4.86m by one centimetre, much to the delight of the fans watching in Gateshead Stadium. Her first world record was achieved there too, the previous year. Unfortunately, Isinbayeva's new record stood for less than a fortnight before being improved upon – by another centimetre – by a fellow Russian, Svetlana Feofanova. Isinbayeva won back her title three weeks later and went on to dominate the sport, reaching 5.06m in 2009. (www.bbc.co.uk)

JUNE 28TH

1981: On this day, the first Great North Run was under starter's orders. The brainchild of middle-distance runner Brendan Foster, the half-marathon was originally billed as a small, local event. Born in Hebburn, Foster had already enjoyed a great deal of affinity with the neighbouring town (*see* August 3rd), and later became President of Gateshead Harriers and a Freeman of Gateshead. The Great North Run proved popular beyond all expectations. About 5,000 entrants were expected, but in all over 12,500 people ran on the day! Local runner Mike MacLeod, who later won a 10,000m silver medal for Britain in the 1984 Olympics, was victorious with a time of 1:03:23. The route started in Newcastle, but crossed the Tyne bridge immediately and continued south of the river all the way to the coast, passing through Gateshead Quays, along the Felling Bypass, past the Gateshead International Stadium and then along to Heworth Interchange and onwards to South Shields. Now a truly international affair, it is one of the largest athletic events staged in the country each year, and one of the most popular in the world, with over 54,000 entrants from more than forty countries. (www.greatrun.org)

JUNE 29TH

1989: On this day, local press reported preparations for the upcoming Europa Cup athletics meeting in Gateshead Stadium … and the statistics are staggering! The Swallow Hotel listed the food required for the athletes that would be staying there. In one breakfast sitting during the two-day event, the hotel chef reckoned on needing 500lb of sausages, 30 boxes of cereal, 200 eggs and a barrel of beans. He remembered a previous event where one American shot-putter had eaten two whole boxes of cereal in one sitting. Meanwhile, it was not just the 600 athletes themselves that needed to be catered for. The Council's Head of Parks and Recreation commented that he would have to provide facilities, sustenance and accommodation for 200 games officials, staff from twenty-five TV companies and twelve radio companies, plus 300 journalists and 100 photographers. To become Europa Cup hosts, Gateshead, a town with a population then of around 200,000, had managed to beat off stern competition from German city Frankfurt, with a population of over 600,000. The event itself proved a huge success: the British men's team were victorious, ending a long domination of track events by the soon-to-be-disbanded Soviet Union and East Germany, and turning successful athletes such as Kriss Akabusi and Linford Christie into household names. Quite how much of that success was due to the catering is not clear! (*Gateshead Post and Times*)

June 30th

1918: On this day, Private Thomas Young of High Spen was honoured by the people of Gateshead for the Victoria Cross he had been awarded by King George the previous day. A crowd of 10-15,000 gathered in Saltwell Park to watch the ceremony, making it the largest gathering in the park since Queen Victoria's Diamond Jubilee twenty years earlier. A guard of honour was made up from the 1st Durham County Volunteers, Boys Scouts and Church Lads Brigade, along with two local military bands. The Earl of Durham presented Young with a watch, cigarette case, and war bonds. Young's response was recorded: 'I am not much of a speaker. There's not a man of the Durham's who wouldn't have done what I did; it was just what any one of them would have done if he could. The thing happened to come my way and I did it. That's all.' Young had been born Thomas Morrell, at Boldon Colliery. When he signed up with the 9th Battalion of the Durham Light Infantry, in 1914, he was 19, going by his step-mother's name, and working as a hewer in High Spen pit. In March 1918, English forces were overrun near Bucquoy. They formed a new line, but many men were trapped in no man's land. Nine times, Young ventured into the crater-filled landscape, found an injured man, and brought him back to the English trenches, all the while risking death from gunfire. He wasn't even armed. (www.lightinfantry.me.uk)

JULY 1ST

1841: On this day, 15-year-old Charles Gibb started what was to prove an illustrious medical career. Anxious to follow in his father's footsteps, Gibb signed on as apprentice to Thomas Common, the resident 'surgeon and apothecary' at Gateshead Dispensary. The building itself was still quite new, having been built in West Street in 1832, a response to the previous year's terrible visitation of cholera. Here, Gibb was to spend five years learning his craft – and, in theory, not doing much else; the apprenticeship papers he signed forbade him from card playing, fornication, matrimony, or even absenting himself without Dr Common's permission! At the same time, Gibb gained a more theoretical education from the Newcastle School of Medicine and Surgery, where one of his tutors recorded that he was a 'diligent and attentive student'. After three years abroad, Gibb returned to the Tyne, spending time in the Newcastle Infirmary at a time characterised by great acrimony amongst the medical men of the town. Ten years later, he set up a private practice in Newcastle, working from the same house for over fifty years. And yet his name is forever associated with Gateshead, if only because of his name-check within the song 'The Blaydon Races' (the races fittingly ended in the same year as Dr Gibb himself). (Pickard, B., *Charles John Gibb, MD*, www.blaydonraces150.co.uk)

July 2nd

1788: On this day, curate Jonathan Mirehouse wrote down some interesting figures concerning the make-up of the population of Ryton Parish. In total, he believed that there were 1,210 families in the parish, around half in Winlaton, a quarter in Ryton itself, and the rest in and around Crawcrook and Chopwell. As well as those who attended his church, he reckoned that there were 56 members of the Church of Scotland, 3 Anabaptists, 100 Methodists, and as many as 350 Catholics. This number was on the rise – eight years previously, he had counted 324 of them. Interestingly, many of them would have attended a place with a long history of worship. As early as 1143, a nunnery stood on the Blaydon site (*see* January 3rd). In the Reformation it was sold to the Tempest family, who demolished it and built Stella Hall, complete with its own domestic chapel. Many members of the Tempest family were Catholic – as far as they could be, in troubled times – and willing to shelter other Catholics. In 1700, Stella Hall passed by marriage to another Catholic, Lord Widdrington, a Jacobite who set off from it in 1715 to join the rebellion of the Earl of Derwentwater. For his part in the rising he was very lucky to be reprieved and regain his estate. In Mirehouse's time, therefore, the chapel had long served as a focal point for local Catholics, who continued to use it until a church was built in 1831. (Bourne, W., *History of the Parish of Ryton*, 1896)

JULY 3RD

1820: On this day, John Bowes, 10th Earl of Strathmore, died. He had spent most of his life in Gibside, and made major alterations to the buildings, notably hiring John Dobson to remove the third storey and add a parapet to the south front. But he is best remembered for his rather complicated private life. His first love was Lady Tyrconnel, his close companion for ten years with the apparent acceptance of her husband. But she died of consumption while staying at Gibside. In 1809 he fell for a servant girl named Mary Milner, only 22 years old to his 40. As the daughter of a gardener, she was thought to be a completely unsuitable match – but he set her up in London and lived there with her for years. They had a son, John Milner Bowes, to whom John Bowes gave a large sum of money, and a good education. By 1820, Bowes knew that he had not long to live, so he decided to marry his long-standing mistress, in spite of the class divisions that had so far kept them apart. They married in London on the July 2nd, and the following day, he died. John Milner Bowes was now a legitimate heir – but the earl's brother Thomas disputed his claim, and lengthy legal proceedings followed. In the end, Thomas got the earlship and the Scottish property, but John Milner Bowes kept the English property. (Chapman, C., *John & Josephine*, The Bowes Museum: 2010)

JULY 4TH

1912: On this day an inquest began into a most peculiar series of events. A few days earlier, bailiff Thomas Dixon had arrived at the house of two elderly sisters, Elizabeth and Christina Neil, to collect seven weeks of unpaid rent. Met at the door by Christina, they barged past into the house, ignoring her ramblings and curses. Reports vary as to whether it was they, or the police, who searched the house – and found in a bed in the attic, wrapped in a white tablecloth and under the covers, the body of Elizabeth Neil. That would be shocking enough – but Elizabeth was desiccated and dark brown, mummified! The examining doctor said that she must have been dead for over a year. Elizabeth was known to have been ill for some years, probably following a stroke, and her sister had cared for her. But no one had seen Elizabeth for a couple of years – the rare visitor was met by Christina at the door, and not allowed in. There was no obvious cause of death, and the coroner decided that she had probably died through an inability to eat. On some level, Christina must have known that she was sharing the house with a corpse, but could not face the truth of it. She was unable to speak coherently on the subject, and was sent to Gateshead Workhouse Hospital. (*Daily Chronicle*)

JULY 5TH

1812: On this day, Henry (Harry) Clasper was born in Dunston. There's no evidence he had any kind of schooling; instead we first find him as a young teenager engaged in a series of manual labour jobs close to the Tyne. Eventually he became a publican – but his true passion was rowing. Despite being only 5ft 8ins tall, and weighing only ten stone, Clasper had natural talent, and was one of the first of a wave of Geordie oarsman who took the region by storm. Yet, after a series of successes, it was a beating at the hands of a Thames team of four in 1842 that really spurred him into action. Blaming the weight of his team's boat, Clasper began to design a whole new rowing boat, with a smooth shell. It was the prototype of the modern racing boat, and helped Clasper gain his revenge in a rematch a couple of years later. He was part of teams that won the professional fours championship seven times in the next seventeen years. He also created a successful boat building business. Clasper was a genuine Gateshead folk hero, and when he died in 1870, a huge crowd gathered to line the route of his funeral procession. (*Oxford Dictionary of National Biography*)

JULY 6TH

1814: On this day, antiquarian John Hodgson passed a remarkable find on to the Society of Antiquaries – or so he thought. The collection of twenty-three tiny copper coins, in a clay pot, had been found by workmen in the graveyard of Heworth's parish church. Some were legible, and could be identified as 'stycas' from the reign of Ecgfrith (AD 675–685). Hodgson became convinced that this was a dedicatory offering for a new church, showing a direct link with the nearby seventh-century monastery of Jarrow. Not everyone believed it – Robert Surtees noted he was 'sceptical' of the find, 'as it precedes any other known issue of the Northumbrian mint by nearly 150 years.' But in 1822 when a new church, St Mary's Heworth, was dedicated, the foundation stone credited its first foundation to Ecgfrith. However, when the church had the coins scientifically tested in 1984, the reply was unequivocal – the copper was Georgian, scarcely older than its 'discovery'. This of course leaves the question of who put the coins there, and why. Hodgson himself is generally thought too genuine in his researches to play such a trick – so was someone playing a trick on him, or even wanting to give him proof of his theories? Whoever it was must have had an excellent knowledge of both metalworking and history, which rather narrows the field! (www.stmaryschurchheworth.com)

JULY 7TH

1938: On this day, the Inspector-General of the ARP (Air Raid Precautions), Wing-Commander Hodsoll, was in Gateshead inspecting the facilities and opening the ARP's Gateshead headquarters inside South Dene Towers, in Saltwell Park. The Mayor of Gateshead pointed out a problem, however, when comparing Gateshead to Newcastle, where Hodsoll had opened another headquarters the day before. He said, 'we could not hope to give a display similar to what we saw in Newcastle yesterday, because we have not got the resources.' Newcastle had five times the budget (since it had five times the rateable value) – but only twice the population. Hodsoll's reply – that 'I have quite enough problems without that one!' – was not terribly encouraging. Hodsoll also visited a huge warehouse in the Team Valley Trading Estate – then new – where the plan was to store gas masks for emergency distribution to the populations of Northumberland and Durham – all 3 million of them! And he handed out badges to hundreds of new ARP wardens, praising the town for the encouraging progress made over the past six months. More than half the volunteers were women (the mayoress herself was an ARP volunteer) and were given their badge in 'brooch' form. (Local press)

JULY 8TH

1854: On this day, printer William Douglas committed suicide. He had begun the day normally, attending to his duties as Gateshead's postmaster. But at around eleven, he went into his private office at the printing works and shot himself in the head. He died a few hours later. It would appear that he had been depressed for some months, due to financial worries. A year previously, he'd gained an order for a large quantity of printing relating to the burgeoning railways. Accordingly, he'd bought new machinery, so he could produce high quality work quickly. But when renewal came up, he was undercut by another printer. Although he remained solvent at the time of his death, the loss of the contract seems to have weighed heavily upon his mind. (*Gateshead Observer*)

———◆———

1933: On this day, Saltwell Towers, within Saltwell Park, was opened as a museum, housing items of local social and industrial history, and also a natural history collection. It remained open until 1968, when dry rot forced the removal of the roof and a closure of several years.

JULY 9TH

2010: On this day, after a massive manhunt, killer Raoul Moat was cornered by police on the riverside near Rothbury. He had gone on the run on July 3rd, after shooting a man dead. Prison officers had warned the police force that on his release, following a two month sentence for assault, Moat might target Samantha Stobbart, the mother of his child. Sadly they were right. When he found that Stobbart had left him, and was now seeing another man, Chris Brown, he went to her Birtley home and killed Brown outside, then shot Stobbart herself through the front window. Moat also maintained a grudge against the police, believing they had ruined his life, and early the next morning, he shot policeman David Rathband. He left a long message for the police, writing 'the public need not fear me but the police should as I won't stop till I'm dead'. Firearms officers were brought in from across the north to track down the armed and dangerous Moat. On this day, he was cornered, leading to a long and tense stand-off during which, controversially, unauthorised high-powered tasers were fired. Six hours later, in the early hours of July 10th, Moat shot himself. Three other men were found guilty of offences related to helping him commit his crimes, or covering evidence on his behalf. (www. bbc.co.uk)

July 10th

1842: On this day, a group of men were ordained as clergy at Auckland Castle, County Durham. One of them was a remarkable man from Winlaton. Blythe Hurst was a blacksmith by trade, who had left school at seven with some knowledge of scripture, and the basics of reading. His reading improved at Sunday school, but he still had to teach himself to write. Even more impressively he single-handedly gained a basic acquaintance of Greek, Latin, Hebrew, Arabic, Syriac, and French! He was now able to read the Bible in its earliest forms, as well as lecturing on hieroglyphics at the Blaydon Literary Institute. In response to the arguments of Alexander Campbell, who was in the village to try to convert the local workforce to socialism, he wrote a pamphlet, 'Christianity no priestcraft'. This reached the rector of Winlaton, who sent a copy to the Bishop of Durham. The bishop in turn sent the Rector of Whickham to visit Hurst. He found that Hurst learned as he worked, chalking words on his 'flame stone'. The Church rallied round to help Hurst prepare for his ordination, despite the fact that he was completely the wrong class to aspire to the position, and had dallied with Methodist thinking in his youth. Hurst moved on to a curacy near Alston, then to the parish of Collierly, just south of Gateshead. He also gained a PhD by examination from a German University! (Sykes, J., *Local Records*, ii, 1833 / *Hampshire Telegraph*)

JULY 11TH

1916: On this day an unknown person sealed the day's local newspaper behind a wall underneath the stairs of a house in Rectory Road, Bensham. It is possible that the culprit may have been a workman or builder doing renovations or plasterwork to the building. The covering over of the *Evening Chronicle*, which included reports on the Battle of the Somme, might well have been accidental. None of this is remarkable, except …

———◆———

Also on this day, in 2010, a man in Rectory Road, Bensham was busy doing some DIY in his mother's house when he uncovered an *Evening Chronicle* that had lain undisturbed for ninety-four years – to the day! Graham Mitcheson discovered the document quite by accident whilst installing some new plumbing. Seeing the brittle and rodent-nibbled condition of the paper, Mitcheson realised that it was old and decided to investigate further. Naturally, he received a shock when he looked at the date next to the heading! He found himself reading advertisements for the latest Charlie Chaplin movie, stories about acts of bravery and heroism in the First World War, and some horrifying wartime casualty statistics. Mitcheson and his mother reported their find to the modern *Evening Chronicle*, which ran a report about it. It concludes with the revelation that Mitcheson had decided to return the newspaper to its resting place – along with one from 2010 – for future residents to discover! (*Evening Chronicle*)

July 12th

1856: On this day, the anniversary of the Battle of the Boyne, Protestant and Catholic clashed violently on the streets of Felling. A group of Orangemen – supporters of British rule in Ireland – had gathered around Newcastle's Black Swan public house and were marching, with two bands, to meet their Gateshead brethren. But they had chosen a route which can only be seen as inflammatory, right through the heart of Felling. This tight-knit community was populated by Irish labourers who undertook hard and dangerous work in nearby chemical works – and who were almost all Catholic. These Ribbonmen responded to the march with force, and before long the scene degenerated into beatings, stabbings and even gunfire. It was sheer luck that no serious injuries or deaths followed. The newspapers tended to place the blame with the Catholics of Felling. The *Gateshead Observer* praised the willingness of the Irish Catholics to work in the factories, but was unhappy about the Irishman's tendency to carry his 'natural quarrels' wherever he went. The *Newcastle Chronicle* characterised the Orangemen as full of 'the folly of ignorance', but blamed the Catholics for the violence, 'for they seem to have lain in wait overnight … for the purpose of assaulting the Orangemen.' The *Illustrated Times* went so far as to say that the Orangemen had tried to retreat when faced with a Catholic mob, but were attacked anyway. (MacReild, D., *Faith, Fraternity and Fighting*, Liverpool University Press: 2005)

JULY 13TH

2002: On this day, the £46 million Baltic Centre for Contemporary Art opened its doors for the first time. Building work had been going on since 1998 to create a new structure incorporating elements of the original 1950s Baltic Flour Mill. The north and south facades were retained, and between them a new structure was built, with six floors and three mezzanines amounting to 3,000 sq. m of arts space. A notable architectural feature is the glass lift with stunning views over the Tyne. The first exhibition featured work by five contemporary artists. Key exhibits included a 15m-long model of the Tyne Bridge made from Meccano by Chris Burden, and Carstan Holler's labyrinth of fluorescent lights. Outside the gallery, the scene was illuminated by a brilliant shaft of white light pointing skyward. The gallery was opened at midnight, and thousands of people formed a queue over the Millennium Bridge and along Newcastle Quayside during the evening to be amongst the first to get in. In spite of sceptics who argued that there was no audience for modern art in the North East, visitor figures exceeded the most optimistic expectations, with over 35,000 people visiting the Baltic in the first week alone. (*Guardian*)

JULY 14TH

1936: On this day, the last – and most controversial – military tattoo was held at Ravensworth Castle. The problems began when members of the council objected to the use of council road and land for an event which might glorify war to the youth of the town. The Labour Party called it, 'a deliberate policy to prepare the public for warlike operations'. The opposition argued that as people had a right to go to the display if they wished, so the council needed to provide enough new access routes and avoid a dangerous crush. But a strong campaign continued to promote the view that the re-enactments were in poor taste, and that children, for whom the First World War was ancient history, would be dangerously enchanted by military spectacle. The council, therefore, was urged to refuse to grant permission for children to miss school, to attend with their Boys' Brigade or other youth groups. The mayor reluctantly allowed the tattoo the use of the additional road – and for this he was expelled from the Gateshead branch of the Labour party! At the time, the event was the largest tattoo ever held outside Aldershot. It featured around 3,000 troops, with military bands, staged combat scenes from history, and displays of pageantry and horsemanship, as well as a mock fire-drill displaying use of fire-fighting and rescue equipment. (*Evening Chronicle / Newcastle Journal / Hansard*)

JULY 15TH

1850: On this day, the Tyne Improvement Commission was formed – and not before time. Over the previous centuries, the River Tyne had been so abused that it was rapidly losing its viability as a major waterway. As early as 1774, Captain Phipps, a parliamentary candidate for Newcastle, said that ignorance, inattention and avarice had turned the Tyne into a 'cursed horse-pond'. It was supposed to be cared for by Newcastle Corporation, but they maintained only a small channel to their own quays, and put up taxes on anything landed further downstream. By 1850, there were 800 acres of sandbanks between Newcastle and the sea, and some places in the channel were, at low tide, barely more than 2ft deep! On this day, Royal Assent was given for the formation of a new organisation. From this point on, all communities along the river would have a voice, with representatives from the corporations of Newcastle, Gateshead, South Shields, Tynemouth, and Jarrow, as well as the various industries which relied upon the Tyne traffic. It took them a few years to work out a plan of campaign, but by 1854 the programme of improvement was under way, deepening the river by removing millions of tonnes of earth from sandbanks and islands, and building various new docks, piers and other structures, including the staithes at Dunston. (*Tyne Improvement Commission Centenary, 1850-1950*, 1950)

JULY 16TH

1833: On this day, a group gathered at the alkali works of Anthony Clapham, Friar's Goose, to celebrate the completion of his new architectural venture. The whole complex had been around since 1827, producing chemicals like alum, soda, and Epsom salts. But the new addition was the most impressive feature – it was a 263ft-tall brick chimney, and as the party gathered and enjoyed their meal at its base, they are said to have 'expressed their surprise and astonishment at this stupendous work of art'. They had good reason. At the time, it was the tallest chimney in England, 38ft taller than 'Muspratt's famous chimney at Liverpool', and also 69ft taller than the steeple of St Nicholas' church, Newcastle. Its height was needed to try to reduce the damage caused by the works' emissions of hydrochloric acid. It was also extremely narrow, being only 27ft wide at the base, and 7ft wide at the top. But it still contained more than half a million bricks, and weighed nearly 2,000 tons. It was still in use until 1932, by which time the alkali works had produced 2 million tons of spoil. (Fordyce, J., *Local Records*, 1867)

JULY 17TH

2005: On this day, at 4 a.m., around 1,700 men and women gathered together and stripped off, in the name of art. The artist was New York photographer Spencer Tunick, who had already orchestrated large-scale nude photo shoots in New York, Barcelona, Belgium and Brazil. This was his first large-scale British installation, sponsored by the Baltic Centre of Contemporary Art and titled 'Naked City'. The men and women, given white plastic ponchos for use when not being photographed, moved to four locations in Newcastle and Gateshead. The artist, and those involved, maintain that there was no sexual element to the images. Instead, as the Baltic put it, 'the sculptural mass of bodies transforms the familiar landscapes, creating a poetic whole which challenges traditionally held views on nudity and privacy as well as social and political issues surrounding art in the public sphere.' That could be said of several of Tunick's works, but in this case an added layer was created by the theme of Apocalypse. Tunick took photographs of people 'falling dead', quietly standing up again for the Last Judgement, and bowing in prayer. Other shots showed figures clinging to the architecture of the Baltic and the Sage, and 'corpses' stacked in rows on the Millennium Bridge. Tunick exhibited the images at the Baltic early the following year. (www.bbc.co.uk / *Guardian*)

July 18th

1826: On this day, the *Tyne Mercury* published 'The Oiling of Dicky's Wig', a new poem by Thomas Wilson. Wilson was a prolific poet who favoured songs and monologues, often comedic and in Geordie dialect. His most famous poem, 'The Pitman's Pay', was published in the same year, and features the discussion of a group of miners at the end of a long week's work. 'The Oiling of Dicky's Wig' has a more celebratory tone – it was written to commemorate the agreement to build a new road over Low Fell. It praises the Fell and the road, and says that those of Newcastle will no longer be able to look down their noses at the people of Low Fell. And obviously, the alehouse was by far the best place to celebrate the news. The road was clearly very important to Wilson, who was born in Low Fell as two years earlier he wrote another poem, 'Stanzas on the intended new line of road from Potticar Lane to Leyburn Hole', in which a group of people put forward arguments for different routes. The Low Fell route, favoured by the character Dicky, is the one that won out – hence Dicky could return for the sequel. (www.indigogroup.co.uk/durhamdialect)

July 19th

1819: On this day, disaster struck at Sheriff Hill Colliery. Firedamp (methane gas) built up in the tunnels, and then exploded, killing thirty-three men and boys who were working nearby. One man was 70, but most were in their teens. Fourteen were under 13, and the youngest was only 7. Three were brothers from Whitehaven, whose mother had applied to management to have them reinstated after they were all dismissed from the pit. Another twenty men and boys were far enough away from the explosion to suffer only slight injuries from the blast concussion and from 'afterdamp', a noxious mix of gases left behind after a firedamp explosion. The loss of life would have been even greater, but the hewers had just knocked off for the day, indeed the whole place was about to shut down for the night. *The Times* put the accident down to 'neglect or mismanagement regarding the safety lamps', but given the technology of the time that is not necessarily a fair comment. Still, even after this accident basic safety was often neglected. In June 1824, two pitmen were 'committed to hard labour in the House of Correction in Durham' for removing the tops of their Davy lamps while working in Sheriff Hill Colliery. The management seems to have been cracking down – but too late. (www.dmm.org.uk / *The Times*)

July 20th

1919: On this day, Gateshead's radicals met to demonstrate against the war in Russia. Around 40,000 British soldiers had gone to war in Russia, bolstering the tsarist regime, but public support was never great. Ruth Dodds, who had joined the Independent Labour Party earlier in the year and was deeply committed to socialist politics, was three days before at 'an amusing Thursday meeting at the ILP discussing the Sunday "Hands off Russia" Demonstration & other things'. On this day, she wrote in her diary: 'Of course it poured for the Russia Demonstration & our last garden tea for the Play-centre children. It was annoying especially for us as one of the National speakers actually turned up – most unusual for us … As it was coming down whole water the meeting was held in the Westfield Hall'. This star lecturer was one Mr Warne, a firebrand speaker, 'very Bolshevick & extremely good looking, with just the sort of square-cut ruddy determined face that a labour leader should have; he had also a flashing dark eye & curls, & his clothes were of a fascinating individuality. He was quite young and shouted rather too much, but he made a very clever use of his dialect.' (Dodds, R., *A Pilgrimage of Grace*, Bewick Press: 1996)

JULY 21ST

1955: On and around this date, the Five Smith Brothers were celebrating their greatest hit. Unlike some other bands of the day which claimed to be related, the Smith Brothers really were brothers. By this date though, only four – Alfred, Harold, Royston and Stanley – were the real deal. Martin Smith had been killed in a road accident in 1946, so a non-Smith was brought in to fill the gap. All five of the original line-up had been born in Newcastle in the 1910s, but grew up in Gateshead, where they first performed professionally in 1932. Military service interrupted the group's career, but they returned to music after the Second World War. They all also had regular professions before getting into showbiz – as engineers, professional footballers, or both! In the window between the end of the war, and the birth of full-on rock and roll, they carved a moderately successful career as close-harmony singers, performing on the radio and in summer seasons at Blackpool. They mixed songs from Tyneside and elsewhere with their own material, releasing titles like the sentimental 'A Kiss for Every Candle', the up-tempo skiffle 'ABC Boogie', and their own version of 'Muffin the Mule'. Their biggest hit, 'I'm in Favour of Friendship', made it to number 20 in July 1955. This blithely optimistic ditty on the subject of friendship 'all over the world', complete with honky-tonk piano, obviously struck a chord in post-war Britain. The group's popularity declined in the late '50s, but they continued to tour, especially in Scotland. (whirlygig-tv.co.uk)

July 22ND

1336: On this day, the High Sheriff of Durham held a meeting to investigate complaints that Newcastle had been riding roughshod over the (alleged!) rights of the people of Gateshead (and perhaps more importantly, the rights of the Bishop of Durham). Generally, the people of County Durham were able to travel in the mid-stream of the Tyne, and take cargo up and down the river so long as they were loaded and unloaded on the south bank. Twice a week they held markets on the Tyne Bridge, which reached to its mid-point; so did the annual St Peter's Day fair. But, it was argued today, Newcastle men had come across the river and 'with force and arms' taken the fish which had been caught in the river and brought to Gateshead's market – and carried it to sell (and tax) in Newcastle. They were repeatedly forced to load and unload in Newcastle, rather than anywhere else on the riverside. Fishermen who sold their fish elsewhere were being fined and imprisoned. Newcastle had even begun building at the very southern end of the bridge (*see* January 28th). Worst of all, witnesses complained, when a Gateshead man working on the bridge fell in and drowned, he was 'dragged' over to Newcastle (although he was later returned to St Mary's, Gateshead). All of these complaints were forwarded on to the king. (Welford, R., *History of Newcastle and Gateshead*, i, 1886)

JULY 23RD

1965: On this day, the *Gateshead Post* was full of articles reflecting on the poor state of housing in the town. Headlining was an inquiry into the poor condition of 100 seventy-year-old houses on Redheugh Road. Their sagging ceilings, bulging walls and rising damp led to a condemnation by the Medical Officer of Health, and a compulsory purchase order covering the whole area. But some residents objected, citing the money they had put in to keeping their own homes in good shape. Meanwhile, two Gateshead MPs were taking to Parliament the issue of houses being converted from single-use to multiple occupation, leading to overcrowded buildings without enough amenities. And one of Gateshead's Aldermen was worrying about flat names. Hearing someone say they lived in B-Block, he said, 'I thought he was living in a hospital, but it turned out he lived at Barn Close'. He resolved to give the four blocks of flats – only ten years old, and themselves built over the site of the worst of the area's slums – individual names! A more positive note, perhaps, came in the *Post*'s announcement the same day of plans to hold a large-scale modern-living exhibition in Saltwell Park the next year. (*Gateshead Post*)

JULY 24TH

1916: On this day, the *Illustrated Chronicle* reported on the opening of Saltwell Towers as a St John Ambulance Brigade Hospital. Two cars had been converted for use as motor ambulances and presented to the hospital. Another donation came from a rather unusual source. The Premier of Newfoundland, Mr Lloyd, had once taught in a Gateshead secondary school, and provided a bed for the hospital. Saltwell Towers remained in use as a hospital until early in 1919. By this point over 1,000 soldiers and sailors had passed through its walls as part of their convalescence. Many of them were missing limbs. In January, the Order of St John of Jerusalem presented Gateshead Town Council with a certificate of thanks, in recognition of their loan of Saltwell Towers for hospital use – the only such certificate granted to a corporation. They, along with the British Red Cross, had worked together to administer the work of the Voluntary Aid Detachments or VADs, such as those working within the Towers. Two hospital quartermasters were awarded the MBE, and two commandants of the Royal Red Cross 2nd Class. (www.newmp.org.uk)

JULY 25TH

1594: On this day, Catholic priest John Ingram was in Gateshead preparing for death. Born in Herefordshire, Ingram had converted to Catholicism while studying at Oxford, and then left the country to train for the priesthood at a Jesuit College. After ordination and time in Europe, he set off for England – but storms pushed his ship northward, and he eventually landed in Dunbar. He began to minister in the Borders of Scotland, but was forced to enter England when things became harder for Catholics in Scotland. He was trying to return to Scotland when he was arrested. He was sent to the Tower of London, and tortured, but did not reveal the whereabouts of his colleagues. From there, he was taken back northward to Durham, where he was tried along with two others, on the 24th. All three were found guilty, even though there was no evidence that Ingram had ever acted as a Catholic priest in England – the mere fact of his being one, on English soil, was high treason and punishable by death. One of the three, Boste, was executed that day; the other two began their final journeys, Swallowell to Darlington, and Ingram to Gateshead. On the 26th, he was hanged, drawn and quartered, probably near the site of the modern church of the Holy Trinity. He was only 29. (rcdhn.org.uk)

JULY 26TH

1891: On this day, a terrible accident took place at United Alkali Chemical Works. This was a huge factory, formed earlier the same year from the combination of the Jarrow Alkali Works and Friar's Goose Chemical Works, and the accident is frequently referred to as the Friar's Goose disaster. The initial problem – coke heating up dramatically inside a huge condenser used for making hydrochloric acid – was bad enough. When three men struggled to put out the fire, two of them went to fetch a hosepipe. While they were gone, the condenser collapsed, trapping the remaining man, Heslop, up to his waist in debris. But worse was to come. Men were gathering around to try to free Heslop when three other condensers, their structure weakened, also fell. Heslop and another six men were buried in hundreds of tons of equipment. All but one died instantly. The last was only trapped to the knees, but his feet were completely stuck. Men worked around him in acid fumes for several hours, but he died before they could free him. Rather than risk the sequence of events ever recurring, the remaining two condensers were destroyed in controlled explosions a few days later. (Local press)

JULY 27TH

2008: On this day, aged ship, the *Tuxedo Princess*, was towed away for the last time. The *Princess* first arrived in Gateshead in 1983 as a twenty-year-old former car ferry, and was refitted as a nightclub, called The Boat. She remained in situ for another twenty-five years, bar a brief visit to Glasgow (during which time she was replaced by another ex-car ferry, the *Tuxedo Royale*). The *Princess* would have been on the Newcastle side, but failed to get planning permission, and was forced to find a permanent mooring on the southern bank. In the early days, The Boat had a strict dress code, and all the staff wore naval uniforms. The nightclub was infamous for its revolving dance floor, created from the ferry's car turntable, which, combined with booze, certainly left many dancers with their heads spinning! There were several bars and dance floors though, each with its own theme. Twenty-five years on, some locals regretted the loss of the *Tuxedo Princess*, seeing it as the end of an era. Others considered that the ship had become something of an eyesore compared to the new vistas of the regenerated Gateshead Quays. While it was initially hoped that the *Tuxedo Princess* could begin a new life in Greece, she was scrapped soon after arrival. The *Tuxedo Royale*, meanwhile, was a Middlesbrough nightclub for a while but is now semi-submerged in the shallows of the Tees. (www.bbc.co.uk)

JULY 28TH

1858: On this day, the Bishop of Hexham laid the foundation stone for St Joseph's Catholic church. It was much needed. There had been no formal church to serve the Catholics of Gateshead for over 100 years, since the sacking of the chapel on the Riddell estate in 1746. In 1850, work began on creating a parish in Gateshead. With the bishop's approval, Father Betham, a Newcastle curate, asked the Catholics of Gateshead to start raising money for the building of a church. The following year, he started ministering from a temporary chapel, Our Lady and St Wilfred's, on the top storey of a Hillgate warehouse. But Betham left in 1853, and Gateshead was only served by Newcastle priests. Worse yet, the Hillgate warehouse was a casualty of the great fire of 1854 (*see* October 6th). All the congregation could manage for the next few years was the Long Room of the Queen's Head Hotel, on Bottle Bank (*see* August 6th). Maybe that's why the new building was first used after less than a year, before all the work was finished (for instance the tower and spire were not built). Still, the organ was working and the altar covered in flowers, as was the focal point statue of St Joseph and child. The church soon became known as St Joseph's, even though it was originally intended to be another Our Lady and St Wilfred's. At this time, there were about 3,000 Catholics in Gateshead. (stjosephsgateshead.co.uk)

JULY 29TH

1999: On this day, the XIII World Veterans Track & Field Championships opened at Gateshead International Stadium. This event has been held every two years since 1975. It is limited to athletes of over 35 years old, with different races open to competitors within five-year age brackets. Events also took place at stadia in Chester-le-Street and Jarrow, but Gateshead was the centre of the event. The existence of different categories means more competitors – with around 6,000 competitors from seventy-four countries, this was the largest single track and field championships ever staged in the British Isles. One notable figure at the 1999 games was local man Ted Joynson, one of the three men who carried the torch in the opening ceremony. He joined Gateshead Harriers in 1948 and never looked back, consistently competing at club level for many years. But as his peers slowed down, Joynson just kept on going. In 1974 he was the British 50-54 years 1,500m champion, the first of a string of veterans' titles. He was still competing well into his eighties. The 1999 event was not without controversy – the gender of 56-year-old Kathy Jaeger was called into question after her record-breaking performance. Then she tested positive for steroids – though the probable cause was her hormone replacement medication. The debate about acceptable drug use for older athletes continues unabated. (www.webwanderers.org / *Guardian*)

July 30th

1832: On this day in 1832, the Three Tuns pub, Sheriff Hill, played host to a lavish public dinner to celebrate the passing of the Great Reform Bill. Tickets were 2s each, and a handbill was posted announcing the names of the various gentlemen who had tickets for sale. Dinner, it also said, was to be served 'at 2 o'clock precisely'. Tables were set up in the adjoining field for the 200 guests, and the Felling Band were there 'in full blast'. The crowd wanted to hear 'The Bonny Pit Laddie' played – but every time it was requested, the band came out with something else. Eventually as the crowd grew more insistent, the band leader admitted that they hadn't got the music. The chairman replied, 'well, play it without – any daft lad can play that tune on a tin whistle!'

2004: Also on this day, Baltic Square was the scene for the filming of a special *Top of the Pops*, to celebrate the show's fortieth birthday. Short segments had been filmed this way in the past, but this was the first time in almost 2,000 episodes that the whole show was filmed live and outdoors. The extended one-hour show featured Will Young, Busted, Jamelia, Sugababes, The Streets and Girls Aloud, and was presented by Tim Kash, Reggie Yates and Fearne Cotton. (www. brandrepublic.com)

July 31st

1982: On this day, the second – and last – Rock on the Tyne festival was held in the Gateshead International Stadium. Headlining were locals The Police. Singer Sting said, 'seven years ago I left this town and I said I would make it. It's nice to come back and make you part of the success'. Oddly, some reviewers reported him relaxed and in good form, while others noted his snide comments about Virgin Records, and his surprisingly blue language. Apparently the band's dry ice smoke was also largely wasted because the stage had no back and it simply blew away! U2 had second billing. Also performing were The Beat, Gang of Four and Lords of the New Church. The festival wasn't a complete success – the crowd that gathered on this dull and windy day was somewhere between 6,000 and 15,000, though the venue could accommodate 25,000. Perhaps this was due to the ticket cost; £8.30 doesn't sound like a lot today, but for a young person in a town suffering from a string of industrial closures, it was a substantial outlay. The first Rock on the Tyne Festival had also undersold, despite a two-day programme including Elvis Costello, Ian Drury, Lindisfarne – and U2 (again), who had not yet troubled the charts. (www.ukrockfestivals.com)

AUGUST 1ST

1858: On this day, John Hewison flung himself to his death from the High Level Bridge. This caused a particular stir because Hewison, a former clerk, had been admitted to Bensham Lunatic Asylum the previous week. He was 'in a melancholy state, his mind having been deranged by religious matters.' Nonetheless the doctors considered it beneficial for him go out with the convalescent patients, and he'd been out every day without showing particular distress. But as 'keeper' Rankin Duff and two other inmates were walking along West Street, Hewison hit Duff in the chest and ran for it. Duff and the two patients followed him along Wellington Street, and saw Hewison dive past the High Level Bridge toll keeper, shouting that he would be back shortly, and would pay him then! What he actually did, though, was climb the railings and jump, landing on a patch of ground owned by the North Eastern Railway Company, in Pipewellgate. An inquest decided that Hewison had destroyed himself while in a state of insanity. (*Manchester Times*)

August 2nd

1948: This day was the last day of the Dunston Carnival. Twenty-seven organisations brought together hundreds of local men, women and children 'in their Sunday best'. Curiously, the central figures of the carnival procession – the 'King and Queen of Dunstonia' – were Jack Walker and … William Hewitt. No explanation for this is given! The parade of decorated carnival floats and fancy dress started on Wellington Road and went around the town in a loop. The *Gateshead Post* gives us a great insight into the range of fancy dress outfits which were attempted by the people of Dunston. There were Swiss yodellers and Hawaiian girls, a bathing belle, a Robin Redbreast and a Tarzan (complete with monkey). Real life figures were represented, including 'Mr and Mrs Shinwell' (presumably Manny Shinwell, the Secretary of State for War) and cricketer Don Bradman, with some model Ashes. Prize money was given to the Child Safety Campaign for the best tableaux (*see* September 24th), and to 'Family Allowances' for the most original display. Dunston Carnival was first held in the early 1920s, when it was called 'Dunston Shopping and Carnival Week' and featured competitions from vegetable growing to climbing the greasy pole. It has recently been revived. (*Gateshead Times*)

AUGUST 3RD

1974: On this sunny Saturday, the inaugural race meet was held at Gateshead International Stadium, which was being reopened with a new and improved track. Only a year before, Gateshead athlete Brendan Foster had been forced to travel to Edinburgh to train for the European. He won gold in his race – in Britain, only Edinburgh and London had top-notch tracks. On his return, 500 people turned out to watch his next training session! At the same time, Foster left his job as a chemistry teacher and took up a post for Gateshead council, and began working on putting the new improved stadium on the map. As a statement of intent, Foster promised that, on the opening day at the first event, an invitation-only international athletics competition known as the 'Gateshead Games', he would run a world record. Amazingly, he succeeded, running the 3,000m in 7:35.2, beating the previous record by almost 2.5 seconds. He says that he was buoyed up by the roar of the 13,500-strong crowd (the highest attendance for any British athletic event that year). Foster was later named BBC Sports Personality of the Year. (*Sports Illustrated*)

AUGUST 4TH

1914: On this day, the first shot of the First World War was fired, by a twenty-three-year-old Gateshead man. The war would not begin on land for another two weeks, but Britain declared war on Germany on the 4th, and as it happened, both countries' ships were already manoeuvring. The German ship *Konigen Luise* was laying mines off the Thames estuary on this day. Overnight, she ran into the British Light Cruiser *Amphion*. Private John Brown-King of the Royal Marines, who came from Windy Nook, was on board the *Amphion*, and fired at the *Konigen Luise*. She was sunk – but only a few hours later the *Amphion* fell foul of the mines already laid and 149 men were drowned. Browning was rescued, but he was very badly wounded in trying to put out the flames engulfing one of his fellows, and died in Harwich Hospital a fortnight later. Brown-King is buried nearby, but there is a memorial to him in Windy Nook church. He was one of almost 700 men who left Windy Nook for the armed forces in the First World War. Another was verger Joseph Askew. When a bomb landed in his trench, he picked it up and threw it back just before it exploded, saving several lives – for this action he was awarded the Military Medal. (Walton, C., *Gateshead Memories and Portraits*, Northumberland Press: 1940)

AUGUST 5TH

1856: On this day, John 'Whisky Jack' Cane was acquitted of murder. Young doctor Robert Stirling had been stabbed, battered and shot by a quiet road in Gibside, only ten days after he arrived in the area, perhaps in a case of mistaken identity. The story has it that Stirling's mother had, unprompted, travelled from Scotland because she had had a dream of her son being murdered. And John Cane was tried partly because she identified him as the man she saw in her dream! In any case, Cane was already known to the police as an illegal distiller and trader of whisky. He was identified as having been seen near the crime scene, and a button that matched his was found by the body. But in court, for each point, a counter argument was made, and Cane and his co-defendant, blacksmith Bill Rayne, were found not guilty. The murder trial was the end of his illicit career – the police were watching him too closely – but oddly this was the making of him. Given another chance by radical industrialist Joseph Cowen, Cane became a gardener at Stella Hall, married a maid, got involved in the early Co-operative movement, and settled down to a whole new life. (www.bpears. org.uk / ferryhilllocalhistory.com)

AUGUST 6TH

1849: On this day, Sir Robert Peel – baronet, Conservative politician and twice Prime Minister, most recently in 1846 – visited Gateshead, accompanied by his family. He was on his way to a holiday in the Scottish Highlands, but could not do it privately. Crowds gathered as he walked through Gateshead and Newcastle, admiring the new structures of the Victorian townscape, before catching a train northward. Notably, Peel chose to stay at the Queen's Head, Bottle Bank, possibly the poshest hotel in Gateshead. Built in the eighteenth century, it had already served as a bar, coaching inn, and post house. By the time Peel arrived, Bottle Bank had several good quality inns. But shortly afterwards, the building of the High Level Bridge marked the start of a gradual decline of the area. Over the next generation, rooms within the Queen's Head would still be the site of lavish balls and celebrations – like that for the opening of the Ragged and Industrial School (*see* October 17th). It would also function as a Catholic chapel (after the fire of 1854), a courtroom, a temporary town hall (1867), a billiard room and a Harmony Hall. But Peel had seen the best, and the Queen's Head increasingly stood alone as other pubs in the area went into decline. (www.gateshead-history.com / isee. gateshead.gov.uk)

AUGUST 7TH

1901: On this day, Gateshead Council met to discuss the business of the day. On the agenda were the proposed new cemetery, and the possibility of electric lighting in the Town Hall. One hot topic was the tramways, still less than a year old. Responding to a petition, the council had been examining the fare structure, and announced a series of routes which would only cost a halfpenny. In June they had also considered the risk of fatality should a falling trolley wire hit anyone, and the children who for some reason were endangering their lives running after tram cars 'to obtain tickets from the passengers'. Today's business also involved the position of lady sanitary inspector. The worry was that only one candidate so far had the credentials, and she had previously been associated with 'co-operators, trades unionists, and members of the Labour party', a fact which caused 'a perceptible wave of feeling' in the committee. Rather than hire her, it was decided to re-advertise, the excuse being that the committee wanted a greater variety of choice! Another strange report centred around the testing of a sample of drinking water, which was notable for an 'offensive smell' and 'fishy taste' due to a 'particular organism'. The report concluded that this was probably living in the reservoir, 'and should be permanently remedied' – but the company replied that it had had no other complaints. It makes you wonder what the people of Gateshead thought normal water tasted like! (*Newcastle Leader*)

AUGUST 8TH

1836: On this day, work began on building the stretch of railway which later became known as Brandling Junction. Several companies had been vying to secure support for their own proposals for railway routes across north Durham. One of the front runners was the Brandling Junction Railway Company (named for the Brandling brothers who formed it), which was granted permission to build a line from Gateshead to South Shields and Monkwearmouth. This made it much easier to get coal to the sea from the collieries of Felling, avoiding the need to use the keelmen of the Tyne. Another section connected the route to that of the Newcastle to Carlisle Railway Company, using a viaduct over Oakwellgate (though some favoured a tunnel). Some sections of the railway were on inclines, which needed the power of a stationary engine (or later, several locomotives together) to move the loads of four coal wagons. This work went on day and night. No wonder the owners of the Redheugh Estate were paid not only £6,000 for the land used for the track, but a further £2,000 as compensation for the loss of value due to noise disturbance. In 1842 the route also led to the building of Gateshead's first railway station, Brandling station – one of the oldest passenger stations in the country. It cost 1s (or 1s 6d, first class) to get from Gateshead to Monkwearmouth. (Manders, F., *A History of Gateshead*, Gateshead Corporation: 1973 / Carlton, I., *A Short History of Gateshead*, Gateshead Metropolitan Borough Council: 1998)

AUGUST 9TH

1886: On this day, John Lennon (no relation) died on Gateshead's South Shore. Nine-year-old Lennon was playing with two friends nearby to Allhusen's Chemical Works, when he fell 15ft down the ventilation shaft of a drain. A rescuer went down the shaft, but was overcome by the fumes coming from the sewer. Another man then tried the same thing, but only made it halfway down the steps when he, too, was overcome. By this point Edward Scullion had fetched a protective mask. He attached ropes to the stricken three, and hauled them up – but Lennon and his first rescuer were dead. The second man died the following night. Scullion was awarded the Albert Medal for Bravery. Sadly accidents in and around Alhusens, and the other chemical works on the banks of the Tyne, were not uncommon, though they usually involved employees. In Lennon's time, the main plants were Jarrow Alkali works, featuring the largest chimney in Tyneside; and the Newcastle Chemical Works Company, otherwise known as Alhusens, employing 1,200 men. This was dangerous work – in the 1880s the Gateshead Poor Law Union tried to make the chemical companies answer to the Factories Inspectorate for the damage to young women's lungs. But the production of soap, soda, Epsom salts and other chemicals was a cornerstone of Gateshead's economy until the early twentieth century. (*Gateshead Observer* / Manders, F., *A History of Gateshead,* Gateshead Corporation: 1973)

AUGUST 10TH

1984: On this day, a valuable brass lectern from St Mary's church, Gateshead, was found on board a ship halfway across the Atlantic to America. It was taken from Borough Road Church Hall, where it had been stored since the fire the previous month. The Hall had been raided several times – in late July 1984, thieves also took a set of church bells dating from 1788. These, too, had been moved following fire, in this case that of 1979. Fortunately they too were found not long after the theft, in a scrapyard in Sunderland.

———— • ◆ • ————

2010: On this day, the police opened a new branch – in the Metro Centre. Not content with simply conducting occasional patrols, the police wanted to take an opportunity to be more accessible to the local community. Here people could meet their local police, report crime, raise concerns and get advice. More curiously, they could also look at a range of police uniforms and equipment from times past. Certainly the Metro Centre provided a convenient place for police to meet a cross section of locals – it was, and remains by some measures, the largest shopping centre in Europe. (*Evening Chronicle*)

AUGUST 11TH

1970: On this evening, Gateshead Police received a message to hurry to the car park of Trinity Square Shopping Precinct, to attend a crime scene. A witness reported seeing two men brazenly stuffing the body of a third into the boot of a car! But when the police arrived they soon found out what was really going on – the witness had seen the film crew of *Get Carter* (*see* September 3rd) in the last stages of packing up for the day, and the 'body' was a dummy that had been used in some stunt shooting. According to car park attendant Joseph Thompson, the dummy had stood in for one of the film's villains, Cliff Brumby, in his dramatic fall from a second-storey window. Director Mike Hodges later recalled the scene: 'This part we could safely shoot at the lowest level of the car park, with mattresses out of sight, so that Caine could actually tip Bryan Mosley, the actor playing Brumby, over the parapet. Later we'd shoot a dummy falling and a crushed car with Brumby's corpse on top. Three shots and the illusion was complete.' The police visit was just an added extra – but what the law thought of this waste of their time is not recorded. (Local press / The *Independent*)

AUGUST 12TH

1644: On this day, the Scottish army came into Gateshead in force. The town itself had fallen a few weeks earlier, stormed by the men of James Livingstone, Earl of Callendar. It seems to have been relatively easy to drive the small Royalist force off the high ground of Windmill Hills, and hold the town. Lithgow reports that Callendar's men, 'fiercely facing the enemy, beat them from the hill, chased them down the Gatesyde and rushing them along the bridge, closed them within the town.' The next day Scots forces took most of the bridge, built earth ramparts on it and in the town, and put artillery behind them. On this day, the large remainder of the army arrived, under the command of the Earl of Leven. The vice was tightening on Newcastle. A Parliamentary writer reported: 'The enemy from the castle doth mightily annoy us with their great artillery, but the Scots are casting up with incessant labour what works they can both by day and night to defend themselves. In the meanwhile, our pioneers are as busie at works underground as our canons are playing above it. The endeavors of both sides are indefatigable and in the thick clouds of smoke the thunder of the canon perpetually disputing.' The Gateshead guns made most of the people of the lower town of Newcastle flee towards the northern end of town. This situation lasted for over two months, until the Scots finally broke the siege and moved into Newcastle itself.

August 13th

1975: On this day, adventure film *The Land that Time Forgot* was released across Britain and America. The Gateshead connection was James Cawthorn, a Teams-born writer and illustrator who co-wrote the screenplay with fantasy author Michael Moorcock. Cawthorn was also the first person to illustrate an edition of *The Lord of the Rings* after Tolkien himself.

———— • ◆ • ————

2011: Also on this day, the Gateshead Quays hosted the opening of the first NewcastleGateshead Bridges Festival, a free festival aiming to celebrate the distinctive architecture on both sides of, and spanning, the Tyne. The opening event was centred on the Swing and Millennium Bridges, which were the launch pads for a huge firework display. Other attractions included an illuminated 'showboat' pontoon, fire effects, and a musical score featuring sounds sampled from the Port of Tyne. Then there was 'Banks of the Seen', an art installation depicting the river's industrial past and the lives of those who were part of it. The Swing Bridge was transformed into a temporary formal garden. Add a charity rubber duck race for children, music, boats (full size and model), street theatre, and a stretch of real beach, with imported sand and deckchairs, and no wonder the event was a massive success. Part of the inspiration for the event was a desire to celebrate the tenth birthday of the Millennium Bridge (*see* November 20th) – the party was a month early, but the thought was there. (www.newcastlegateshead.com)

August 14th

1770: On this day, Robert Hazlett was tried for robbing a mail coach as it crossed Gateshead Fell a week earlier. The area was notorious as a haunt of highway robbers, and it was not uncommon to wait for a group to build up before travelling across it. But on the 6th, Miss Margaret Benson, returning from Durham, was robbed of half a guinea. When she arrived in Gateshead, she advised the postman, who was going the other way, to fetch a guard. He refused. After a few miles, he was joined by another man, who he also warned about the highway robber ahead – only to have the stranger pull a pistol and demand the mail bags. The thief, Robert Hazlett, was later captured. He claimed that, while he had indeed robbed Miss Benson, the mail coach robbery had been committed by an accomplice. However, he was able to tell the judge where to find the mail bags, and handed over the money. He was found guilty and hanged. After execution, his body was placed in a gibbet near the site of the crime. This remained in place for many years, a reminder to all who passed by on that road that crime does not pay. (Phillips, M., *A History of Banks, Bankers and Banking*: 1894 / Sykes, J., *Local Records*, i, 1833)

August 15th

1859: On this evening, William 'Captain' Hall came to a sticky end above Felling. A professional aeronaut and acrobat, he'd begun his evening well. A large crowd gathered in the Bath Lane Cricket Ground, Newcastle, to watch Hall's balloon rise up into the air. When it was 1,000ft up, the costumed performer lowered a trapeze, and performed an acrobatic act that apparently terrified onlookers with its risky manoeuvres. The *Newcastle Chronicle* reported, 'it was a relief, having seen him suspended by the foot from his fragile machinery … to perceive that he had retaken his seat'. But ironically, it was while performing what should have been a much safer action that things went wrong. Having crossed the river, the balloon had landed in a field. Hall was stepping out, but at the same time the grappling hook lost purchase and the balloon tipped, releasing some of its ballast and causing it to shoot up again. Hall's feet became entangled in the rope. He was dragged upwards 120ft … and then fell into the clover below. Surprisingly, he was conscious, if not entirely coherent, and there was no sign of injury or broken bones. Many thought that he had had a miraculous escape … but he died a few days later. The balloon itself was never found … and nor was the unfortunate dog which had accompanied Hall. (*Newcastle Chronicle / Monthly Chronicle of North Country Lore and Legend*, 1889)

AUGUST 16TH

1967: On this day, the *Evening Chronicle* announced that Gateshead officials were to be put into stocks as public targets. It was reported that townspeople would be given the chance to buy rotten tomatoes and hurl them at councillors and senior council workers. This was not, however, a popular uprising in favour of returning to medieval law! Instead it was one of the events in Gateshead's two-day town festival, designed to raise money for the elderly. Other events included fencing exhibitions, children's rabbit and dog shows, a flower contest and sheepdog trials. The festival would also include a parade of jazz bands, followed by a battle of the bands, a display of Wearside Beagles and Newcastle Police Horses and an Olympic-style games competition. Unfortunately, the weather put a literal dampener onto both days, as it had in the previous year. On the Friday, rain meant that only 800 people came, and on the Saturday only 8,000 of the expected 20,000 made it through the deluge. Of the events, however, only the fencing had to be cancelled, for fear of electrocution via the electronic scoring system. The poor attendance meant that this year's festival operated at a loss. Ironically, one punishment for debtors in times gone by was to be placed into the town stocks! (*Evening Chronicle*)

AUGUST 17TH

1764: On this day, Dr James Oliphant, his wife and servant girl, were found not guilty of murder. They lived in a rather unusual house, literally perched on the Gateshead end of the Old Tyne Bridge, hanging over the river on the western edge of the bridge. The four-storey building rose above an arch in the bridge – and also dropped down below it, a wooden cellar being positioned below the bridge, with doors opening to the water. Dr Oliphant and his wife had gone away to Scotland for a month. When they came back, they found that their maid Dinah Armstrong was accused of theft. She denied it, but the evidence in her suitcase was suggestive. But the Oliphants kept Dinah on. Then their other servant found the cellar door open, and – it being low tide – saw Dinah's body on the sand below. The corpse was later found to have marks on the neck, perhaps suggestive of violence. Dr Oliphant, with his wife and surviving maid, were all accused of murder, but no substantial evidence was found, and they were soon acquitted. Too poor to sue the coroner for not quashing the case sooner, Oliphant vented his anger in a book. His luck didn't get better – his home was destroyed in the flood of 1771 (although at least he wasn't in it at the time) and he headed back to his native Scotland with his wife. (*Monthly Chronicle of Lore and Legend*, 1887)

AUGUST 18TH

2004: On this day, the red kites of the Derwent valley were left to fend for themselves. A month earlier the Northern Kites initiative had released twenty red kites, the first to grace the area for around 170 years. Beautiful russet-winged birds of prey with a wingspan of around 5½ft, red kites were an unmistakable addition to the sky. These youngsters were taken from the offspring of a similar, and successful, project in the Chilterns. Since kites are scavengers, rather than catching their own prey, it was relatively easy to provide for them. But, as had been hoped, after a few days they began to explore and spread away from the feeding centre, fending for themselves, so the decision was made to stop providing. Nineteen birds were seen after this, so they must have been ready (though one did have to be taken back into care after it crashed into a factory in Birtley!) Sadly, another was found to have been poisoned in October. Seventy-four more were released in 2005–6, and in 2006 the first local chicks were hatched. The red kite is now fairly well established in the area. Although the heavy rain of 2011 and 2012 has made for disappointing breeding seasons and some deaths, the population is still steadily increasing. (www.gatesheadbirders.co.uk)

AUGUST 19TH

1932: On this day, the press reported the tribulations of the inhabitants of Old Fold Road. Apparently they were troubled with what was described as a 'plague of flies'. Fifty residents signed a petition asking the Corporation to look into the problem, which they said was caused by dustcarts tipping rubbish onto waste ground alongside the road. The Corporation responded by covering the ground with a layer of soil, and spraying disinfectant into the air (before the disinfectant ran out). But it didn't seem to help. Indeed, one letter writer called the soil used 'very questionable' and concluded that 'these operations are a mockery of sanitation'. A reporter went to investigate, and was horrified by what he saw. He writes of an invalid woman 'lying in bed ... tortured by flies ... the room was black with flies'. He saw flypaper become black within minutes, and women feeding their children while flapping around them with a towel to keep flies off. In one room 'within a few seconds my face was covered in flies. I was stung on the face and neck'. No wonder the residents were driven to appeal directly to the Ministry of Health, to plead for an immediate fumigation of the houses. (*Evening Chronicle*)

August 20th

1803: On this day, the *Newcastle Courant* reported on the continued success of the military recruiters. They said: '... the business of volunteering goes on most successfully in the parish of Whickham and the adjoining districts. Not fewer than 700 have already entered their names, and several of the men, particularly those employed in the ironworks of Messrs Crowley, Millington, and co. have begun to learn their exercise. In fact, the spirit of the country seems now rowzed to a pitch, that will, no doubt, convince the adversary, in the day of trial, that British valour will always be sufficient to repel the attacks of ambitious and barbarous invasion.' The ironworks on the south bank of the Tyne notoriously produced tough men, and the army must have been glad to have them. Indeed relatives of the soldiers of Hawks ironworks passed down the story from mouth to mouth for generations. Of course, in their version, not only did they personally win the Battle of Waterloo, but it only took twelve 'Harkses' men' to capture Napoleon himself! On the other hand, it was partly a conversation with Stella-man George Silvertop that persuaded Napoleon to flee Elba, and thus led to the Battle of Waterloo in the first place ... (*Newcastle Courant* / Dodds, M., *Low Fell History*, www. asaplive.co.uk / Bourne, W., *History of Ryton*, 1895)

AUGUST 21ST

1860: On this day, John English – better known as Lang Jack, or the Tyneside Samson – lay dying from consumption in his Whickham bed. Born in Chester-le-Street, he'd moved to Whickham when in his thirties. His size and strength had made it easy to make a living as a mason, and he'd worked on the biggest public buildings of the area, like Newcastle Jail and the Scotswood Suspension Bridge. Standing 6ft 4in tall – a massive height for the era – his party piece was to jump up and down on the spot until his head hit the ceiling. On one occasion the floor collapsed, tipping him into the cowshed below! He was certainly easily spotted, especially in the political rallies that he frequented enthusiastically. At one meeting he led a gang of men, armed with oak-saplings or 'peel grains', who surrounded the reformist speakers to prevent another group from breaking up the meeting. It worked, and the agitating pit men fled the scene. Jack built his own cottage in Whickham, dragging the stone from a quarry a mile away. Shortly before his death, his popularity led to a public subscription fund for a monument by his house, and that spring, an 18ft-high monument was unveiled in a cheerful ceremony led by a brass band. The hand-built cottage was destroyed by a fire in 1907. The monument, however, has been restored and survives to this day. (www.sunnisidelocalhistorysociety.co.uk)

AUGUST 22ND

1858: On this day, celebrations were held when rail communication was established over the Tyne, via a temporary bridge. This wooden structure was built in parallel to the High Level Bridge, which replaced it on completion. To test the bridge, the previous day engines exerting around one ton of weight per foot were driven across the bridge, this being about four times the pressure that any train was expected to create. The bridge passed the test and to celebrate flags decorated the line, its stations and the bridge. Many thousands gathered to watch the first train to cross from Gateshead over the bridge. It was made up of eight carriages full of local notables. Among them were only four ladies, who, the *Courant* says, 'are deserving of honourable mention for the courage they displayed in accompanying the train'! The report continued, 'as the train passed steadily over the approaches to the bridge, the anxiety of the immense multitudes was intense, and the scene was truly exciting, yet fearful – not only from the lofty eminence occupied by the train, but from the apparent narrowness and nakedness of the platform on which it rolled along. It seemed, from its noiselessness, rather an aerial flight than the rattling sweep of the iron horse.' It reached the other side amid a cannon salute, and the cheers of the crowd. (*Newcastle Courant*)

AUGUST 23RD

1825: On this day, the church of St John's, Church Road, Sheriff Hill, was consecrated. It was not quite finished – the Gothic Revival-style walls and roof were in place, but the tall elegant spire was not yet complete. But people may have felt they had waited long enough. It was first decreed, and land set aside, in the Enclosure Act of 1809, but the foundation stone was not laid until 1824. It was built on the highest point in the whole of Gateshead – then known as 'Sour Milk Hill' – so as an additional benefit, it could be seen from the sea, and so would aid navigation in the area. Many of the town's great and good gathered to watch – the church was intended to seat 1,000, but on this occasion around 1,200 were packed in. And the large size was praised – after all, this was a much-needed church in a fast-growing area. But it's worth noting that only 500 of those seats were 'free sitting' – the rest were reserved for specific local families. The ceremony was performed by the Lord Bishop of Oxford, in what was described in the press as an 'impressive manner'. He also consecrated the churchyard as a cemetery. The first organ was installed in 1824 – and the first organist, David Shafto Hawks, was blind! (*see* January 25th) (*Newcastle Courant* / Wikipedia)

AUGUST 24TH

1939: On this day, Canon Harry Stephenson made it clear that, for Gateshead, despite the approaching Second World War, business should continue as usual. In the parish magazine, Stephenson opens with, 'My Dear Friends, I refrain from any comment on international affairs.' Instead, he goes on to inform his flock about the day-to-day parish news: the profits raised from a flower show in the Rectory gardens, the upcoming consecration of Lobley Hill All Saints' church, a sale of work by the St Mary's Infant School pupils and changes to the calendar of the local Boys' Club! (*Parish Magazine*)

❖

2012: Also on this day, Gateshead Council excitedly announced the arrival of a life-sized fully inflatable version of Stonehenge. 'Sacrilege' was designed by Turner Prize winner Jeremy Deller. Linda Green, Gateshead's Councillor for Culture, said, 'If anything can prove that modern art can also be fun, then surely this is it … It's a great honour to be included in this prestigious national tour. This promises to be a truly memorable event.' It had originally been scheduled to appear in Saltwell Park on August 15th. Unfortunately, terrible wind and rain led to the initial cancellation of the event. Two weeks later, however, children and adults alike were given the chance to bounce on part of one of the nation's most famous ancient landmarks.

AUGUST 25TH

1951: On this day, John Croft, vicar of St Andrew's, Lamesley, died at home in the vicarage. He was the oldest working vicar in the country - at 100! Croft was born in Arkengarthdale, Yorkshire. His earliest memory was of the family knitting socks to send to British soldiers serving in the Crimea, and he started work as a shepherd on the dales as a child. Coming to Tyneside in 1898, he had ministered to the parishioners of Lamesley for over half a century. He certainly didn't let age slow him down, only asking for support from others in his last few years. At 98 years old, he read the entire New Testament in Greek – and in the same year, he fell from a ladder while out pruning fruit trees! He was survived by his 96-year-old wife, with whom he had enjoyed over 75 years of marriage, and many descendants including his son – a Workington vicar – and four great-grandchildren. Lamesley church itself dates from 1758 (remodelled in Victorian times), but was constructed on the site of an earlier chapel, built in 1286, and the modern church incorporates medieval grave covers and the bowl of a font which may be as early as twelfth century. (*The Times*)

AUGUST 26TH

1755: On this day, Elizabeth Montagu travelled from her home in Denton out to Sunderland. In a letter to a friend, she described the Gateshead section of the journey as 'a wild country full of moors, under which lie the coal mines; the river Tyne gave some ornament to the scene, and the frequent cottages on the moors, which are built for the pitmen, take off something of the solitariness of the desert … The vestiges of agriculture are not to be traced there, and one pities the inhabitants of such an ungrateful soil, till one recollects that the mines reward the labour of the industrious in full as ample, though not so agreeable a manner, as arable lands.' (*The letters of Mrs Elizabeth Montagu*, vol. ii)

1792: On this day, heavy rain caused the Tyne to flood, and rainwater ran down the streets of Gateshead in torrents. At Bottle Bank and Pipewellgate, many houses and shops were flooded, and the able-bodied inhabitants had to carry others out on their backs. The current was so strong that one woman, carrying another, was bowled right off her feet, and the two were carried some distance by the current until they were able to right themselves. This was only a month after an unseasonable hailstorm in which pieces of ice fell from the sky large enough to break windows. (Sykes, J., *Local Records*, i, 1833)

August 27th

1813: On this day, residents of Gateshead would have been forgiven for thinking that the Napoleonic Wars had come to British shores. William Hawks & Co., a local iron and steel manufacturers, were a major supplier for the Royal Navy. They had been trying some new ordnance, but the cannon completely missed the intended target. Instead it went over the wall and landed just outside someone's house, breaking eleven panes of glass in his windows! (Sykes, J., *Local Records*, ii, 1833)

—◆—

1955: Also on this day, Gateshead Youth Stadium was opened by Jim Peters, a marathon runner who had recently broken the 2 hour 20 minute barrier. Back in 1955 the track was little more than a single cinder running track, and a parallel asphalt cycling track. Floodlights and a bit of seating didn't come for a few months, and it didn't hold any major meets until 1961 – although even then, 'major' is a relative term, and Gateshead remained a minor track until the 1970s (*see* August 3rd). (Wikipedia)

AUGUST 28TH

1640: On this day was fought the Battle of Stella Ford (or Newburn Ford, if you were on the northern river bank!) – the only battle of the Second Bishop's War. The Scottish leaders declared they were not against the king, only against those who were misleading him. This was largely to do with religion, and bitterness stemming from an attempt to impose Anglicanism in Scotland. Around 4,000 English troops had been sent to guard the ford at Newburn, and bar passage to the Scots army, all 20–25,000 of them. They dug in on the south side of the Tyne, and hastily built defensive structures, but they were not well positioned. They were also ill-equipped, and often reluctant, conscripts. The Scots, much better prepared and motivated, were able to take higher and less open ground on the northern side, in and around Newburn village. From here, they began a bombardment. The tide ebbed, the ford became passable, and the Scots army crossed the river to finish off the now-demoralised English. Around 250 soldiers were killed, but most surrendered. Two days later, Newcastle was surrendered to the Scots. Charles I tried to get Parliament to raise more taxes to fight the Scots army, but failed. In the end, he more or less had to buy the town back – and the Civil War drew one step closer. (Melia, S., *The Battle of Newburn Ford*, Tyne Riverside Country Park: 2004)

AUGUST 29TH

1865: On this day, Marley Hill farm worker Joseph Leybourne was murdered outside the Granby Arms (now the Marquis of Granby) in Gateshead. It was early morning, and celebrations were continuing following the previous day's flower show. But an argument broke out, with several men seen threatening Leybourne. He was siding with a young farm servant of his acquaintance, against a wandering cobbler, Jack Bee (whose reputation, far from good at the time, seems to have also grown blacker with the retelling). As the group dispersed, a neighbour heard a voice swearing that he would 'knock [Leybourne's] soul out'. Later, as the last revellers made their way home, they spotted a man propped up against the hedge, opposite the Union Inn, Streetgate, about 500m away from the Granby Arms (now the Rose, Shamrock and Thistle). It was Leybourne, dead from a head wound. A rock was found nearby, with blood and hair on it. A verdict of murder was returned, but insufficient evidence was ever found to bring anyone to trial. It didn't help that most of the potential witnesses had been drunk. Tradition has it that the Earl of Ravensworth, who was a magistrate and also benefactor of the flower show, was so horrified that he sacked all of his workmen who had attended the dance – he certainly cancelled all future flower shows. Some even today believe that the ghost of Joseph Leybourne haunts the Marquis of Granby. (http://bpears.co.uk)

AUGUST 30TH

1933: On this day, those attending Gateshead Police Court were surprised by the presence of Mohinder Singh on the magistrates' bench. Singh was a Sikh, and a magistrate from the Punjab town of Ludhiana, holidaying in England. The *Evening Chronicle* reported that Singh, 'wearing a picturesque turban', caused 'surprise and much speculation'. He told the paper that he was impressed with justice dispensed at the court, where 'everybody is given a very fair trial'. (*Evening Chronicle*)

———◆———

1930: On this day, a ground-breaking game of football was played at Redheugh Park Stadium. It was the first game played at the new stadium, and the first match for a team which had over the summer been uprooted wholesale from South Shields. The team's fortunes had plummeted over the previous decade, and it was time for a change – and Gateshead welcomed the team with open arms. As the new stadium took shape in Low Teams that summer, the team officially changed its name to Gateshead FC. And on this day, dressed in claret and blue, they played Doncaster Rovers at home, their first match in the Third Division North. They won 2-1, with centre forward Maycock scoring the first goal – he had also scored the last goal at the South Shields stadium at Horsley Hill. (Esther, G., *Requiem for Redheugh*, Gateshead Borough Council: 1984)

AUGUST 31ST

1805: On this day, the *Newcastle Courant* reported on a recent case of aggressive dogs. At a special session of the magistrates' court, Gateshead, miller Anthony Boggin of Windmill Hills was convicted of allowing his mastiff dog to walk the public road by or on the bridge without wearing a muzzle. He had to pay 30s, amounting to 10s for each of three offences, and court costs. But more seriously, he also had to pay a surgeon's bill – the mastiff had attacked a young woman and severely bitten her arm. It appears that the magistracy was engaging in a bit of a crackdown. The magazine *The Athenaeum* noted that, 'several persons have lately been found by the Magistrates of Gateshead, for riding and drawing carriages on the footpath, and suffering bull and mastiff dogs to go about unmuzzled, and swine to go at large.' The same clause of the Tyne Bridge Act, aiming to remove nuisances from the Gateshead streets leading to the bridge, also bans a mind-boggling array of other activities. You were specifically not allowed to take a sledge on a footpath, kill sheep or cows on the bridge, wash a barrel, saw wood, bait bulls, or light fires. Modern celebrants might be surprised to know that you also weren't allowed to 'let off or throw any squib, serpent, rocket, cracker, fire balloon or other firework whatsoever'. (Brand, J., *History and Antiquities / The Athenaeum / Newcastle Courant*)

September 1st

1939: On this day, the Second World War began when Germany invaded Poland. Closer to home, the first effects of war hit very hard and very fast, with the evacuation of thousands of children to the countryside. This included around 10,600 from Gateshead. This was only 71 per cent of those eligible, probably because some parents did not want to see their children go. They were sent right across the North, many to Cumbria, Teesdale, and North Yorkshire. The whole process was planned with great precision. For example, on this day 715 boys and girls from Low Fell Mixed and Infants school gathered at Gateshead West station and caught the chartered 1.45 train to Ormsby in Yorkshire. Many of them would never have left Gateshead before. Robert Ray, evacuated to Spennymoor from Gateshead, remembers of that day: 'we trekked around town looking for kindly foster-parents, to offer us accommodation. Surprisingly, accommodation for evacuees had not been pre-designated but simply left to prospective foster-parents to pick and choose ... finally, the kind lady at Number 9 must have taken pity on me and took me indoors, much to my relief. I don't remember much about the next day, Saturday, 2 September, apart from examining the contents of my emergency rations cardboard box and finding there was a chocolate "Kit-Kat" bar, something I'd always fancied but was never able to afford ... delicious!' (www.genuki.org.uk / www.bbc.co.uk/history/ww2peopleswar)

SEPTEMBER 2ND

1916: On this day, the famous Blaydon Races was held for the last time – and it ended with a bang, rather than a whimper. In the early twentieth century, following the death of chairman J. Cowen, things had begun to change. The crowds were as big as ever, but rumours began to spread of sharp practice amongst the officials. The First World War got in the way, of course, but in 1916 permission was granted by the Ministry of Munitions for a two-day event provided a substantial donation was given to the British Sportsmen's Ambulance Fund. The first day was attended by over 4,000 people, and all was going well. But on the second day, things changed. In the first race, the ironically named 'Anxious Moments' had been heavily tipped to win, and did indeed come home six lengths ahead. But then an objection was lodged, and the horse was disqualified, without a reason given. The crowd reacted with anger, and this being wartime there were no police on duty to hold them back. They smashed the weighing house, throwing equipment into the river. (Winlaton and District Local History Society, *A History of Blaydon*, Gateshead Council: 1975)

SEPTEMBER 3RD

1970: On this day, MGM was most of the way through filming gangland movie *Get Carter* – often considered one of the best British films of all time – in Tyneside. While locations across the region were used, from Blackhall Colliery to Newcastle's Scotswood Road, it is the Gateshead scenes that have become iconic – and especially those filmed in the car park of Trinity Square, which was forever after known as the 'Get Carter Car Park'. This Brutalist concrete structure had been built in 1967, by which time its severe lines were beginning to go out of fashion. Four years later it was already looking patchy as the concrete began to wear. The rooftop café had never found a tenant, and still looked half-finished – perfect for scenes between London gangster Jack Carter (Michael Caine) and corrupt businessman Cliff Brumby (Bryan Mosley). The car park became defunct in the 1990s, and arguably an eyesore; but at around the same time a campaign began for it to be designated a listed building, both as a cinematic landmark and as a representative of the Brutalist movement. Nonetheless it was demolished in 2010, with the council selling off pieces of concrete in commemorative tins, for £5! Coburg Street was also used for the Las Vegas Boarding House, where Carter stays, and the betting shop scene was filmed in Hebburn. The featured juvenile jazz band were the Pelaw Hussars. (www. movie-locations.com / Wikipedia / *Newcastle Journal*)

SEPTEMBER 4TH

1838: On this day, Gateshead pipemaker Thomas Cowley walked to the middle of the Tyne Bridge and jumped into the fast-flowing waters. While many of those who have jumped into the Tyne over the years had their own demise in mind, Cowley was instead acting on a bet. Perhaps underestimating the cold, or the strong underwater currents, he quickly drowned. That didn't stop others from similar antics. Just over twelve years later, Williamson, a worker at the important foundry of Hawks and Crawshay, also jumped into the Tyne, this time from the new High Level Bridge, before swimming to safety. It was put about that he had done it on a wager, for a quart of ale. Of course, there are many other ways to enjoy hair-raising activities in or around the Tyne. Each year money is raised for charity by those who bungee jump or abseil above the river (though you've not been allowed to abseil down the Tyne Bridge itself since 2008). In 2012, adventurer and television presenter Bear Grylls completed one of the most unusual legs of the journey of the Olympic Torch when he took it over the Tyne by zip wire. (Fordyce, T., *Local Records*, 1867)

SEPTEMBER 5TH

1864: On this day, a rowing match on the Tyne was spoiled by the north-eastern weather. Tyneside and World Sculling Champion Robert Chambers was competing with Robert Cooper, for substantial prize money of £400. The match was set over 3½ miles, from the High Level Bridge to the Scotswood Bridge. Chambers was champion – but it was predicted to be a close race, and a lot of money was bet on low odds. Local factories closed at midday, and workmen gathered on every vantage point (and by every sporting pub!) so thickly that the police could hardly get past. There were even people clinging to the girders of the High Level Bridge. Nineteen packed steamers had turned out onto the water. But the wind was rising, and soon the normally calm Tyne looked more like a rough sea than a river. The two boats smashed into each other, and then Chambers, pulling ahead, clashed with a keelboat that had moved from its moorings. He was taking on water, and the match had to be stopped. Amid much argument, the match was rearranged for the following day, with each man in a new boat. In spite of his previous soaking, Chambers went on to show better form in the continued rough water, and won the match comfortably. The scene, with both boats struggling to stay afloat, was later vividly painted by John Warkup Swift. (*Newcastle Courant*)

SEPTEMBER 6TH

1920: On this day, the Gateshead Magistracy gained its first female members. Four of the new Justices of the Peace sworn in were women, and the mayor remarked on this in his speech. He said he saw it as in harmony with the spirit of the times, now that there was a female MP, and women would soon be qualified as barristers. Women had performed great deeds in the recent war, had an important role in social and charitable works, and served well recently on the Gateshead Education Committee and Board of Guardians. Still, this wasn't exactly equality – the mayor remarked that the women would be of particular value in cases involving women and children! Interestingly, one was a former mayoress; one was involved in Wesleyan Charities; and another with the Suffrage Movement and social work. The first case before the bench was of a 63-year-old decorated war veteran, before the court for the first time, for drunkenness. The mayor told him: 'It is rather an important day for Gateshead. We have ladies on the bench for the first time. You are the lucky individual this morning, and we are going to let you off scot free. I hope you will not give the police reason to fetch you back again'! (*Gateshead Post*)

SEPTEMBER 7TH

1920: On this day, there was considerable confusion at the Gateshead Board of Guardians, where the posts of medical officer and vaccinator for Whickham, and for Ryton, were being re-appointed. The two outgoing men were brothers Dr J. Smith and Dr Andrew Smith senior. So far so good – but the two appointees were the two men's sons – Dr Andrew Smith junior, and his cousin, also called Dr Andrew Smith! To make matters even worse, the cousins were apparently so similar in appearance that, as one of the panel said, 'it was like talking to twins'.

———◆———

1962: On this day, the Bowes Incline was used for the last time. The Bowes Railway was a 7-mile stretch of railway line which ran from Dipton Colliery, via several other collieries, to staithes on the Tyne. The route had been used as a railway of sorts since the seventeenth century, when the Tanfield Railway – the oldest in the world – carried coal in horse-drawn wagons along wooden rails. The Bowes Incline had a 1:11 gradient down from Sunniside. Coal wagons were lowered using a self-acting incline, with the momentum of the full wagons travelling downhill providing enough energy to pull the empty wagons up the hill. Recently, the Bowes Incline has been reopened, demonstrating some of the historic technology once used on the site. It is now the only operational preserved standard-gauge rope-hauled railway in the world. (www.bowesrailway.co.uk)

September 8th

1797: On this day was born songwriter Robert Gilchrist. His father was a Gateshead sail maker, and it seemed that he would follow his father's footsteps, being apprenticed to another sail maker. Indeed he did eventually take over his father's business. But his true love was writing, even if only as 'the offspring of a few leisure hours'. When he was 21, his friends gave him a silver medal as a mark of appreciation of his writing. His biggest publication, aged 27, was the two-part *Collection of Original Songs, Local and Sentimental*. He also wrote hymns, and was published in the Tyne Mercury and collected in song anthologies. Most of Gilchrist's songs were written in local dialect, and features north-eastern subjects. His themes were romantic – love, loss, and landscape, perhaps in emulation of Robert Burns. He also performed his own pieces, and it was said that he used the 'odd cast in one of his eyes' to great effect during his more comedic numbers. But not everyone was happy at someone from such humble origins publishing high-minded poetry, even if they kept their day job. Sunderland poet T. Ferguson argued that the immature and derivative works of labouring-class writers like Gilchrist could only have a negative impact on literary standards! This in spite of Gilchrist being of a respectable status, and a Freeman of Newcastle. (Gilchrist, P., 'Bard of Tyneside', www.paulgilchrist.net)

SEPTEMBER 9TH

1864: On this day, entertainer George 'Geordie' Ridley died. With little schooling, he started as a trapper in Oakwellgate Colliery, Gateshead, at 8 years old, to help the family coffers. He moved to Friar's Goose Colliery a couple of years later, but was already amusing himself and his friends by performing a comedy act – from inside a rabbit shed with an improvised 'curtain'! In 1858, one 'Dr Airey', self-proclaimed 'wonder of the medical world' advertised in the *Newcastle Courant* that he had successfully cured George Ridley of a long-standing severe cough. But worse was to come – around 1860, he suffered a major injury, crushed between two of the wagons he worked with. Forced to seek a new source of income, he fell back on the one thing for which he had won prizes – comedy singing. He first entertained in the Grainger Music Hall, and later the Wheatsheaf (later Balmbra's) in Newcastle and elsewhere. He not only sang traditional and original songs (*see* June 9th), but also performed comedic interludes and mimicry. His compositions included commentary on local events and also local culture, like Cushie Butterfield (a tribute to the sturdy Tyneside lass) and Johnny Luik-up the Bellman. Copies of his song lyrics sold well in cheap editions, and children sang his songs on the streets. But he never fully recovered from his injury, and died at his home in Grahamsley Street, at only 30 years old. (Harker, D., *Gannin' to Blaydon Races!*, Tynebridge Publishing: 2012)

September 10th

1842: On this day, world champion rower James Renforth was buried, in East Gateshead Cemetery. Renforth was actually born in New Pandon Street, Newcastle, but moved across the river at around a year old. In his early twenties we find Renforth at work rowing materials and men out to the Tyne Bridge, which was being demolished. He took up sculling at 24 and was soon beating all comers. Only two years after first rowing competitively, he beat Londoner Henry Kelley on the Thames, and became Champion Sculler of the World. He retained this title until he died. Renforth began to race in pairs and fours, and the Tyne team was soon known as the best in the country and perhaps the world. In 1842 his crew of four – including his old rival Kelley – travelled to Canada for a challenge race. But the Tyne boat gradually fell behind, and then Renforth's oar dropped from his hand. He died that evening, aged only 29. Although his death was probably caused by heart failure following an epileptic fit, rumours persisted for years that he might have been poisoned. Renforth's funeral procession was led by the Newcastle and Gateshead Operatic Band. Estimates of the number of mourners who turned out range from 50–100,000! His memorial, paid for by public subscription, shows Renforth in Kelley's arms, in an Egyptian reed boat. (Whitehead, I., *James Renforth of Gateshead: Champion Sculler of the World*, Tynebridge Publishing: 2004)

SEPTEMBER 11TH

2010: On this day – the ninth anniversary of the bombing of the World Trade Centre – six young men burned two copies of the Muslim Holy Book, the Quran, outside The Bugle pub, Felling. The men, with head scarves covering their faces, poured petrol on the books and set them alight, cheering wildly. One shouted, 'this is for the boys in Afghanistan; September 11, international burn-a-Quran day'. We know about this because they also filmed their actions, and published them on YouTube. A few days later all six were detained on suspicion of inciting racial hatred, under the 1986 Public Order Act. The crime here was not the actual burning of the Quran, but the posting of the video, which was classified as 'distributing ... a recording of visual images ... which are threatening, abusive or insulting ... intending thereby to stir up racial hatred, or ... racial hatred is likely to be stirred up.' The pub had previously been subject to police investigation because of suspicions that some regulars had connections to the far-right English Defence League (although the EDL claimed not to condone book-burning). On a wider scale, security experts warned that it would endanger British lives, at home and in conflict zones. However, the Crown Prosecution Service decided that there was not enough evidence to provide a realistic chance of conviction, because no threatening behaviour was shown, and there was no way to identify the person who recorded and uploaded the offending material. (*Guardian* / www.bbc.co.uk)

September 12th

1884: On this day, the *Tyneside Chronicle* produced a report highlighting a remarkable new innovation taking place in the schools of Gateshead. This was the 'Penny Dinner' scheme, the brainchild of Revd Moore-Ede. It was one of the first in the country, although the idea was taking root across the country and would soon spread. Before year's end, Moore-Ede was providing school dinners for over 6,000 Gateshead children. In theory each would pay a penny, but in practice they soon found that some of the children could not afford it, and had to be given their meals for free. To make ends meet, the meals had to be quite basic. Moore-Ede's recipe on a 'meat day', to feed 117, involved one and a half ox heads, ham bones, pea flour, onions, rice, and potatoes, with bread to mop it all up. That cost just over 9*s*, and was so bulked out with water that after everyone was fed, there was still 44 quarts of the mixture left – this was sold to parents for 1/2*d* a quart. The best days were probably those with pudding – made with jam or rhubarb, or rice pudding with treacle. Moore-Ede also published *Cheap Food and Cheap Cookery*, with recipes to help others with penny dinner schemes, and designed a new form of gas-powered slow cooker to help things along. (Smith, F., *The People's Health*, Weidenfeld & Nicolson: 1990)

SEPTEMBER 13TH

1894: On this day was born, in Japan, a remarkable man. Konni Zilliacus was an unlikely figurehead for post-war Labour politics. Son of a Finnish revolutionary and an American, Zilliacus grew up in Sweden, Finland and the US, spending only three of his first 21 years in England. During the First World War he worked in a military hospital, and in Russia gathering intelligence (it helped that he could speak six languages). Later he worked for the League of Nations. Zilliacus first stood as Labour MP for Gateshead in 1939, but was not voted in until 1945. As a communist, supporter of the United Nations, and opponent of the anti-Soviet policies of Cold-War-era government, he found himself increasingly isolated. In 1949, he was expelled from the Labour Party for not towing the party line on the formation of NATO. In the same year he was also refused entry visas by both the USA and the USSR! He stood as an independent candidate for Gateshead, but was not voted in, and in 1952, newly returned to the Labour fold, he became MP for Manchester. In the 1960s he helped to found the Campaign for Nuclear Disarmament. Zilliacus was only in Gateshead for seven years, but in that time he was a busy man and a household name. There is barely a week in this time when he was not in the local papers, making statements on politics local, national and international. (Potts, A., *Zilliacus*, Merlin Press: 2002)

September 14th

1914: On this day, 30-year-old Gateshead man Thomas Sewell was charged with illegal gambling 'in a public place' as well as 'dishonestly acquiring food to the value of 10/0'. Each morning, he would make his way to Newcastle Barracks, where he would run a game of Crown and Anchor, an eighteenth-century dice game enjoying a revival in the army at the time. The barracks were full of soldiers mobilising for the Western Front, and Sewell would persuade the richer ones to bet. They would have been well advised to avoid playing Crown and Anchor, which always favours the house! (Hewitson, T., *A Soldier's Life*, Tynebridge Publishing: 1999)

———◆———

2012: Also on this day a Ugandan choir recorded an album in Gateshead. The Pearl of Africa choir (named after Winston Churchill's description of their country) arrived the previous day in Newcastle in order to begin a tour of the UK. The choir itself was mainly made up of schoolchildren, many of whom had been orphaned by civil war and poverty. Their first venue was the Broadwater Studios on Kell's Lane, where they recorded their African gospel-style album. After Gateshead, they moved around the country, performing in churches, schools and cultural venues. The aim was to raise money for children's education – the previous tour raised over £100,000, which was distributed among seven schools in Uganda.

September 15th

1683: On this day the diary of Jacob Bee of Durham has the following cryptic entry: 'There was a man, a glasier by traid, came from Gateshead and stood in the pillery in Durham about one hour and one half (his name was Simpson), for taking a bribe from a quaker.' Gateshead was a centre of Quakerism. But in 1681 the faith was declared illegal, and six Gateshead men were fined. Several local Quakers were imprisoned or fined over the next few years, and in 1684 one man was whipped naked through the streets for trying to stop constables from seizing the property of his Quaker master. (Hodgson, J., Six North Country Diaries, *Surtees Society*, 118: 1910/ Sansbury, R., *Beyond the Blew Stone*, Newcastle Preparative Meeting: 1998)

❖

1949: Also on this day, a major theft took place at Marley Hill Colliery Offices. The money – £12,900 in cash, worth around £320,000 today – had been put into 1,540 wage packets the previous night. But when the strongroom was opened the following morning, the whole lot had gone. That was no mean feat – the money included coins weighing over a hundredweight. In the short term, fourteen staff members worked to get new wages sorted out. Meanwhile, detectives offered a £500 reward for information leading to arrest and the recovery of the stolen money. But no promising leads were ever found, and the mystery remains unsolved. (www.webwanderers.org)

SEPTEMBER 16TH

1967: On this day, a Gateshead youth group gave a Viking-style 'funeral' to a houseboat moored at Ryton Willows. The boat had been bought the previous year by club leader James Hart, as a project for members of the Wrekkers Youth Club. The teenagers had spent months cleaning, painting and repairing, and professional joiners were brought in for the trickiest jobs. The plan was that the lads could spend weekends in it, once it was finished. But there were problems. The council wanted to clean up Ryton Willows, and ordered all houseboats to move. Hart complained, and heard nothing more. But when Hart return from holiday, he found that vandals had moved in – and found only one houseboat remaining, as an easy target. Anything valuable had been taken, and all the rest, inside and out, had been smashed up. Rather than leaving a wreck stuck on the Tyne, the club decided that the best solution was to finish the job by giving the boat a good send off – and setting it alight, as if it were a Viking ship taking a noble to his last resting place. (*Evening Chronicle*)

September 17th

1937: On this day, Gateshead footballer Hughie Gallagher scored an impressive five goals in his fifth match for the team. Scotsman Gallagher had lived in the area before, signing for Newcastle United as a cocky 20-year-old from the coal mining districts of Scotland. Here he broke records for goal scoring, before being sold on. Meanwhile he maintained an international career for Scotland. He always had problems with aggressive play, and was full of little tricks like imitating the voices of other players as a confusion tactic. In the mid-1930s, he was passed from team to team until in 1937 he returned to Tyneside, to Gateshead, where he continued to score prolifically. He would stay in the area for the rest of his life, but the story has a sad end. Gallagher never really recovered from the death of his wife in 1950, and in 1957, during an argument, threw an ashtray at one of his beloved sons. He drew blood and was accused of assault. Once his allies, the press attacked, accusing him of a much wider pattern of abuse and neglect for which there was no clear evidence. Shamed by his own attack, kept from his son and expecting the worst from the courts, in June 1957 Gallagher committed suicide by jumping in front of a train. His last word was an embarrassed 'sorry' to a couple of nearby train-spotters. (*Independent* / www.world-football-legends.co.uk)

September 18th

1986: On this day, Felling man Don Reid beat thirty other men to win the Northern Counties Ratings and Valuation Association's annual golf tournament. That might not seem terribly impressive, until you learn that Reid only had one arm! He lost the other as a boy, but took up golf in his thirties and found that he had a natural gift. He told reporters that having only one arm didn't worry him when driving, or indeed doing other things, although 'some chaps get a bit upset when they can't beat someone who's not all there ...' There are actually enough one-armed golfers in the country to have their own society, which has been around since 1932 (it currently has almost 200 members). Reid served as their chairman between 1982 and 1994, and wrote a detailed history of the society. When not golfing, he played badminton and also found time to chair the Gateshead and District Association! (www.onearmgolf.org / *Newcastle Chronicle*)

———— • ◆ • ————

2012: On this day, a new sports scheme, supported by Dame Kelly Holmes and aiming to inspire a new generation of athletes in the wake of the London Olympics, began in Gateshead College. For its first event, more than 450 students were given master classes in boxing by Olympic gold medallist Nicola Adams, and in football by world freestyle football champion Andrew Newman. (*Newcastle Journal*)

September 19th

1877: On this day, the first underground telephone system in the world was demonstrated, in Addison Pit. Amazingly, the engineer on the spot was Alexander Graham Bell himself, who had been demonstrating the phone in Newcastle Town Hall the day before. Around 500 yards of wire were laid, running from a cabin at the pit mouth, down nearly 100 yards and then along the tunnel. At the other end, the cable was taken to Hedgefield House – probably the first house in Britain to have a phone installed. It is thought that Bell was related by marriage to the house's owners. A primitive telephone was then attached to each end of the wire, and experiments began. Professor Bell stood with the miners, while Mr Heansilly of the Post Office led the group on the outside. Each found that their words and identity were easily distinguishable. Bell sang 'God Save the Queen' and 'Auld Lang Syne' down the line, and in turn was able to hear Hedgefield House's piano. All parties considered the whole thing a success, and parted contemplating the many useful applications for the telephone within the mines. (Letter from Mr J.B. Simpson to Dr Siemens)

SEPTEMBER 20TH

1965: On this day, Gateshead geophysicist Arthur Holmes died, aged 75. In his early years, the 'age of earth' controversy was at its peak. As Holmes grew up, he was fascinated by the problem, and specialised in physics and geology. At only 21, he came up with the first uranium-lead analysis specifically designed for the purpose, combining recent discoveries in radioactivity with his own fields of interest. But his family were not rich, and he struggled to make ends meet as a research scientist. He took a job in Mozambique, but became so ill that after only 6 months a telegram was sent home reporting his death! He survived, however, and on his return, in 1913, the publication of *The Age of Earth* confirmed Holmes' place as the world's leading expert on the subject, against entrenched opposition who did not accept the new theory of chemical isotopes. And yet it didn't bring in money – and a failed mining expedition led to bankruptcy and a stint selling far-eastern knick-knacks! Fortunately he was offered the headship of Durham's new geology department – a department of one. His later work was on continental drift, and he was the first to postulate the continents moved due to slow-moving currents within the earth's mantle. However, while his work on geological time was soon accepted, Holmes was for many years considered a maverick for his continental drift theories, which were only being rediscovered and validated around the time of his death. (Lewis, C., 'Arthur Holmes', *GSA Today*: 2002)

September 21st

1896: On this day, the Metropole Theatre opened on Gateshead High Street. Entrepreneur Weldon Watts already owned the Queen's Theatre, but he believed that the rapidly expanding population could support more theatres. Certainly the opening night of the Metropole helped his argument, as the crowd that gathered for admission that first night amounted to more than twice the available seating in the theatre. The *Era* reported that 'the press circle presented an animated experience, being occupied to its utmost extent by a gathering representative of the town' (or at least its aldermen and officials). The National Anthem was sung before the opening play – *The Sign of the Cross* – was performed. Watts then gave a speech, saying that he had started small, with the Queen's Theatre, and could now move to a larger endeavour – in spite of those critics who had told him 'we are afraid you have made a mistake; a theatre would never pay in Gateshead'. The theatre manager also spoke, saying that in all England there was no comparable theatre in any town of a similar size. The Metropole was certainly an impressive building, a new red brick structure with marble staircases, elaborate plasterwork, hot water, and early electric lighting provided by a gas engine (if the engine stopped, the lights simply went out). With seating for 2,500 people, it was Gateshead's biggest ever theatre. (*The Era*)

SEPTEMBER 22ND

1711: On this day, Thomas Wright was born in Byers Green, Durham. Wright is claimed by Gateshead Grammar School as their first famous old boy, having attended Revd Pickering's school in the 1720s. Son of a carpenter, Wright founded his own school at an early age, but over time became absorbed in many fields including astronomy, instrument making, architecture and garden design, designing several grand country house gardens. It was in the first of these areas that he was to have a lasting impact, with his 1750 work *An Original Theory or New Hypothesis of the Universe*. This was the first publication to correctly explain the appearance of the Milky Way, as 'an optical effect due to our immersion in what locally approximates to a flat layer of stars'. He also suggested that faint nebulae, barely visible, 'may be external creation, bordering upon the known one, too remote even for our telescopes to reach ...' – in other words, other galaxies. Both of these ideas were new – and both were taken up by Immanuel Kant, to whom they are usually attributed. He also speculated, from a theological viewpoint, about the possibility of life on other planets. For him, the sun was no longer the centre of everything, and the earth and its inhabitants were insignificant on the scale of creation. (stardate.org)

SEPTEMBER 23RD

1823: On this day, the glassmakers undertook one of their spectacular processions through the streets of Newcastle and Gateshead. There were several glass-houses along the banks of the Tyne and the Wear, who got together in a display of their work. While several guilds did this sort of thing, the glassmakers' one must have been particularly fine. As well as the usual music and flags, every man's clothing was decorated with glass ornaments and the best, most beautiful examples of their art. The effect was enhanced by the rays of sunshine on a gorgeous late summer day; Mackenzie described the 'glittering column' as possessing a 'richness and grandeur of appearance that defy description'. An extra dimension came from the music of a glass bugle, played to sound the halts, and its 'rich and sweet tone' – and the finale was a salute from a 'fort mounted with glass cannon'. Large crowds turned out to watch and admire the spectacle. Interestingly, Mackenzie contrasts the procession with that of 1789. Rivalry between guilds was evidently high, and he calls the earlier display a 'ludicrous and boyish shew … (intended to ridicule the silly exhibition of the cordwainers)', complimenting the glassmakers on their improved taste! (Mackenzie, E., *Historical Account of Newcastle-upon-Tyne*, 1827)

September 24th

1946: On this day, an essay competition for children was opened as part of Gateshead's road safety campaign. The inspiring title was 'Youth's part in road safety'. Winners would get a half crown saving stamp, and tickets to the Scala cinema – as well as being published in *The Times*! Children's road safety seems to have been a major concern to the council, a concern which probably began in January 1945, when three Gateshead children were killed by a lorry during the blackout. The first salvo of the Gateshead Prevention of Accidents committee was the film *As easy as A-B-C*, a short animation that all Gateshead children were expected to learn by heart ('A is for accident, hated by all …' and so on). But it didn't end there. There was 'pedestrian crossing week', an additional 'child safety week', and a 'cyclists' week' (with fancy dress cycling parade). The press bemoaned the low turnout for Gateshead Youth Organisations Safety Week. The council even spent £445 on a 'Universal Trainer' (described as a road safety training machine, though quite what that was is not recorded). Children were taught the 'Children's Highway Code' and 'Teddy Tells You'. And indeed the number of road casualties does seem to have reduced, although whether the campaign was directly responsible is less clear. (www.movinghistory.ac.uk / *Gateshead Times*)

SEPTEMBER 25TH

1851: On this day, work began on the laying of the first cable to run under the English Channel – using Gateshead-made wire. The man behind it was engineer Robert Stirling Newall, a Scotsman who set up R.S. Newall & Co., and moved it to a factory in Gateshead. Here, in 1840, he patented new methods of making wire rope, and made great improvements to underwater telegraph cables, adding a hemp element to the copper wire and gutta percha (natural latex). This was definitely needed – the first attempt at a trans-channel cable had lasted roughly an hour! Another impressive piece of engineering made possible by Newall's of Gateshead was the Edinburgh 1 o'clock gun. For eight years, the city's Nelson Monument had featured a time ball, which dropped at one each day and so told sailors in port the time. When a different method, the 1 o'clock gun, was introduced, the two were mechanically synchronised with a Gateshead-made cable over 4,000ft in length. Newall's works also made around half of the cable that first crossed the Atlantic, and began actually laying underwater cable, for instance around Sebastopol during the Crimean War. (*See* October 19th for Newall's interest in astronomy.) (www.1oclockgun.org.uk / atlantic-cable.com)

September 26th

1760: On this day, Sir George Bowes, owner of Gibside and Streatlam Castle, died. With money coming in from both land ownership and coal rights, Bowes started life with every advantage. As a young adult 'handsome George' was a cavalry officer, a ladies' man with a penchant for gambling. But when he inherited the Bowes' fortune he settled down surprisingly quickly. At 23 he married 14-year-old Eleanor Verney – and when she died within three months, he stayed unmarried for over twenty years. He was involved in the building of the Causey Arch in 1725, and became MP for Berwick, though he rarely visited the House of Commons. He collected paintings and furniture, and his main hobby seems to have been gardening – keen on fashionable trends in country house garden layout, he helped design the garden in Gibside. He made Gibside his main home, and as he began his final illness, gave instructions for the building of a chapel there, for his first wife Eleanor and himself. But it was only just begun when he died, and his body was buried in Whickham church for over fifty years, before being moved to Gibside chapel in 1812. When Bowes died, his only child was 11-year-old Mary Eleanor Bowes (*see* March 7th). He left her a fortune of £600,000 – at least £70 million in today's money. (Parker, D., *The Trampled Wife*, Sutton Publishing: 2006)

SEPTEMBER 27TH

1825: On this day, glassmaker Joseph Price died. He had been a big influence in the development of glassmaking in the town, starting with a patent for 'new methods of making glass' in 1814 and the opening of the Durham Glass Works factory in Pipewellgate. This new factory manufactured flint glass, a durable glass containing lead, notable for purity and brilliance. In 1819, Price donated a beautiful stained-glass window to St Mary's church, incorporating the coats of arms of local notables. By 1827, he'd got involved with the British Flint Glass Company and was also manufacturing a patented plate glass in another works next door. But he didn't limit himself to glass. In 1815 he got involved in what he called the 'Steam Boat speculation on the Tyne', and three years on claimed to have been responsible for a great success. A steam boat had towed a sailing ship for the first time! He'd more-or-less invented the steam tug. Others were not impressed – the tug itself had been damaged, and Price was even told that he had ruined the port! Many years later, after his glass-making venture had also failed, he noted that he had spent £2,000 on experimenting with steam tugs. He wondered whether, now that steam tugs were more popular, some of the money might be repaid him. He hadn't given up on the venture – in the same year, he took out a patent for adapting steam boilers to wooden ships.

SEPTEMBER 28TH

1849: On this day, the royal family visited Gateshead ... sort of. They were on the way back from a holiday in Scotland, and what they actually did – in the pouring rain – was travel by very slow train through Newcastle and Gateshead. In the centre of the High Level Bridge, a platform had been erected to seat dignitaries from both towns, various ladies and gentlemen and a regimental guard. A triumphal arch also marked the spot, bearing the motto 'Welcome on both sides of the Tyne'. The royal train stopped for fifteen minutes to take in the view, and listen to addresses from the two mayors, the Queen apparently delighting all with her 'animated manner ... and beaming countenance'. This is thought to be the first visit of a Queen of England to Gateshead since 1461, when Queen Margaret of Anjou headed for Scotland, fleeing the Yorkist victory at the Battle of Towton. But does it really count, since Victoria never set foot off the train? Either way, it is often thought of as the official opening of the High Level Bridge, which certainly didn't have another one. (www.gateshead-history.com)

September 29th

1847: On this day, a group of churchwardens from Lamesley Parish went to the magistrates of Durham with a problem. Apparently the parish authorities of Gateshead were 'fitting up a house in Eighton Banks for the reception of persons infected with fever'. Eighton Banks was in Lamesley parish, and the parishioners were not impressed with their neighbours quietly passing over all their own contagious parishioners. They met on the 28th to discuss it, noting that the proposed fever hospital was close to the turnpike, in an area well populated by 'poor industrious men', and less than 100 yards from a school. But also on the 28th, the first patients had been moved in, thus 'an infectious disease was introduced unnecessarily into the parish'. The Gateshead relieving officer said in their defence that they had previously been able to take infectious people to the Newcastle Fever Hospital, but this was full; they had looked for alternatives for those who needed to be instantly taken from their homes, but found nothing suitable in Gateshead. The Bench decided that, while they disapproved of the actions of the Gateshead committee, they 'were sorry they could not interfere with it'. The Lamesley deputation said that they had achieved, at least, the aim of making the situation better known, but that if the hospital was not removed, they would further proceed against it in law. (*Newcastle Courant*)

SEPTEMBER 30TH

1836: On this day, a grisly murder took place in a glass house in Pipewellgate, Gateshead. The victim, Mr Lee, was from Newcastle, and a member of the Northumberland and Newcastle Volunteer Cavalry. Lee was on service with his fellow volunteers, and he'd spent the evening drinking. He'd found his way into the glass house and fallen asleep on a large box. Three young men – who vaguely knew him – found him there, and acted in the cruellest of ways. They covered him with straw and hot cinders from the furnace, adding more and more, until the whole thing caught light. Perhaps they had not meant things to go so far, but when the straw went up in a blaze, Lee had no chance. They had left the room as the flames rose, but were swiftly met by Lee himself, awake, ablaze, and running around screaming 'fire'. Others, drawn to the scene, put Lee out, but he died a few days later from his injuries. He was buried with full military honours, while one of his attackers was sent to Australia for ten years, and the other two were imprisoned for two years each. Many thought this to be inadequate considering the crime. (Latimer, J., *Local Records*, 1833)

OCTOBER 1ST

1528: On this day, William Tomlinson and his son Thomas were jointly appointed clerks of the Bishop of Durham's coal and lead mines. The bishop had several Gateshead coal mines in the early sixteenth century, and probably did better out of the coal trade than anyone else living on the south side of the Tyne. Three new pits were opened at 'the Cornfield' in 1511, and another pit dug on Gateshead Moor in 1528. For William, today's promotion was perhaps the crowning achievement of a lifetime of advancement in the service of the Bishop of Durham, including working along with another son, Anthony, as keeper of the Tower of Gateshead and Bailiff of the Town. By the 1520s, the family had leases on several Gateshead coal mines, and were basically controlling the vast majority of the coal trade in the Gateshead and Whickham area. Curiously, at this time all coal was called sea-coal, even though most of it came from drift mines or shallow pits dug straight down. Perhaps the name – originally for the coal eroded by the waves and washed up on the shore – stuck because almost all of Tyneside's coal travelled by sea, down to London. (Newton, D. and Pollard, A., eds, *Newcastle and Gateshead before 1700*, Phillimore: 2009)

OCTOBER 2ND

1817: On this day, St Mary's vestry minutes contain details which provide a fascinating insight into the life – or at least the diet – of the inmates of Gateshead Workhouse. The whole building was actually illegal, as the terms of its original bequest had been for an almshouse, a quite different institution. It took almost 100 years before this was questioned, in 1841, and it reverted to being an almshouse. In the meantime, up to fifty inmates lived in tough conditions, within the early eighteenth-century house on the High Street. Here they were served what can perhaps best be described as monotonous and non-nutritious stodge. Five days a week, breakfast was hasty pudding – a wheat flour and milk porridge. On the other two days, it was boiled barley with milk and bread – so basically, more porridge. There were four main meals on offer over the course of the week – potato stew, bread and dumplings, bread with boiled milk, and as the highlight of the week, beef and pease pudding in broth. Then you'd get the broth dregs with more bread, or bread with milk or barley, for supper. Records show that inmates were given a clean blanket every six months, and had to wash every day. (St Mary's vestry minutes / www. workhouses.org.uk)

OCTOBER 3RD

1705: On this day, thirty-nine lives were lost in an explosion and fire in Stony Flatt pit, Bensham. Although there had been isolated deaths in mines before, this was the first massive set of deaths in a pit accident anywhere in the country. Thirty-one of them were buried in St Mary's churchyard, and some victims must have lingered before death, as the recorder writes 'these were slain in a coal-pitt in the Stony Flatt which did fire' after burials from the 4th to the 18th. This was a close-knit community, living cheek by jowl in miserable huts provided by their masters. In many cases, family members were buried together, including a Jackson who was buried with his daughter, the only female casualty. Women were allowed to work underground until 1842, but we don't know if Abigail Jackson was working, or just visiting her dad. In this part of Gateshead, coals were 30–60ft down. We don't know whether this pit was a large bell pit, or an early attempt at something deeper and more complex. Either way the explosion was probably caused by a build-up of flammable gas catching light – perhaps, ironically, when it reached a fire which had been set to encourage a through-current of air. (www.dmm.org.uk / Clepham, J., 'Coal Mining in Old Gateshead', *Archeologia Aeliana*: 1886)

OCTOBER 4TH

1827: On this day, at half-past one in the morning, a distinguished group – which included Sir Walter Scott and the Duke of Wellington – arrived in Ravensworth Castle. Sir Walter Scott wrote all about it in his diary, describing the castle as 'half-built ... chiefly modern, excepting always two towers of great antiquity'. He was right – the oldest sections of the castle date from the fourteenth century, but the main house was less than twenty years old. The group had been to a political rally in the afternoon, then on to dinner and dancing in Durham. On the morning of the 4th, understandably, Scott didn't rise until 10, and found that most of the others were not yet up (only the day before, he had been speculating that 'my morals begin to be corrupted by travelling and fine company'). After a chat with Wellington about his experiences in France, the two were joined by the rest of the group for a day trip to Sunderland, ending in yet another dinner party and ball. This time, they didn't get back to Ravensworth until half past two! The 5th was a rather gentler day, 'giggling and making giggle among the kind and frank-hearted young people' ... although one group of young women 'sang "The Campbells are coming" in a tone that might have waked the dead'! ('The Journal of Sir Walter Scott', www.online-literature.com)

OCTOBER 5TH

1947: On this day, guitarist Brian Johnson was born. His miner father and Italian mother lived in Dunston, and in his autobiography he reflects on time spent as a child exploring the corners of the industrial land: 'there were places we were told not to go, that's where we went, basically, anywhere dangerous. The power station was definitely off limits because of the slag heaps, which held water and also created a form of quicksand. But between the dangerous bits there were old army trucks and old railway carriages. The carriages, they were red and cream with wood linings inside and beautiful lamps over the tables … I was completely in love with both the trains and the trucks.' Johnson was always musical. But it wasn't until 1972 that he hit the big time, as a founder member of the Tyneside glam-rock group USA – who soon changed their name to the more appropriate Geordie. Over the next couple of years they had several hits, the biggest of which – 'All Because of You' – reached number 6 in the charts. But success became elusive, and in 1976 the band called it a day. They were on the verge of reforming in 1980 when he was invited to audition as a new vocalist and guitarist for metal group AC/DC. The band's next album, *Back in Black*, is one of the best-selling albums of all time. (Johnson, B., *Rockers and Rollers*, Penguin: 2009)

OCTOBER 6TH

1854: On this day, the warehouses, shops and houses packed along the quaysides of Gateshead and Newcastle alike were devastated by fire. Beginning in Wilson's worsted factory in Hillgate, the fire soon spread into other warehouses filled with a lethal mix of noxious, flammable and explosive chemicals, and sharp objects. It would be hard to create a more dangerous combination, and although fire precautions had been taken, they were nowhere near up to the task. As the blaze spread, spectators gathered on the High Level Bridge, and the Newcastle quay, to watch the explosions, the purple and green flames, and the streams of molten lead and liquid sulphur pouring into the Tyne. But then came a huge explosion, big enough to be heard 20 miles away. Almost every fireman in Tyneside was trying to fight the flames, and most died in that moment, while the rest were seriously injured. The blast also sent large quantities of stone and flaming material into the timber structures on the northern shore. In Gateshead, most of Hillgate was destroyed – still, earlier that year it had been described as 'one of the dirtiest and most unwholesome places in the kingdom'. St Mary's church was damaged badly enough that starting from scratch on a new site was considered. The fire blazed on, visible 50 miles away, and did not die down until well into the morning of the 7th. (Rewcastle, J., *A Record of the Great Fire of Newcastle and Gateshead*, 1855 / *Illustrated London News*)

OCTOBER 7TH

1911: On this day, a terrible murder took place at Lintz Green station. This isolated spot comprised only a railway station and the stationmaster's house. Here the elderly and respected stationmaster, Joseph Wilson, his clerk Fred White and porter John Routledge waited for the last train. Four men got off; one stayed with White as he locked up, while the other three started up the road. Wilson headed for home, but a short time later a shot was heard from the direction of his house. Wilson was found mortally wounded and unable to name his killer. A gag and cosh were found nearby. The motive was assumed to be theft – usually he would have had the day's takings on him in the evening, though for some reason today he had dropped them off early. Over 200 men were drawn into the massive police investigation. Eventually relief porter Samuel Atkinson was arrested, as several people said they had seen him hanging around nearby. Atkinson appeared before Durham Assizes – where, to much surprise, the chief constable in charge requested that Atkinson be discharged, as no evidence would be brought. The police had forgotten to caution him, and that made many of his statements inadmissible in court. The case was then dismissed, Atkinson's guilt or innocence left uninvestigated. (Middleton, T., 'The Lintz Green Murder', www.bpears.org.uk)

OCTOBER 8TH

1897: On this day, Whickham steelworker William Collingwood died. He was well known for miles around as a source of gardening advice, especially on vegetable growing – and with good reason. In 1865 he had grown a red cabbage which has gone down in legend as 'the Swalwell Cabbage' – it was a staggering 125cm high, over 6½m in circumference, and weighed 8st. 10lbs. This was a world record which lasted longer than Collingwood did, not being broken until 1989 (in case you're wondering, the current record holder is just a fraction under 9st., so improvement has been slow!) The story goes that it required a handsaw to cut it out and a handcart to carry it to the Buck Inn – conveniently next door to Collingwood's house – where it was shown. Apparently they also had to take down the gateposts of the garden in which it had been growing. Collingwood also grew giant leeks, producing one over 10ft long for entry into the leek show at the Buck Inn, Swalwell, in 1876. His fame was such that others issued challenges that he could produce better and bigger leeks than anyone else in the world, for a prize of any sum – and no one took them up! (www.swalwell-online.co.uk)

OCTOBER 9TH

1928: On this day, on the eve of the opening of the Tyne Bridge, a very unusual radio play was broadcast by the BBC. Written by local antiquarian Mr G. Spain of Jesmond – father of 1950s author Nancy Spain – *The Bridge of Tyne* featured specially commissioned chamber music. This was a serious play, very different from the music-hall style creativity that earlier bridges over the Tyne had tended to inspire. Made by their fledgling Northern Service, *The Bridge of Tyne* was a fantasy, mixing music with speech from characters such as the river god of the Tyne, and the spirits of the old Roman bridge and the new Tyne Bridge. Another character was the Emperor Hadrian, who spoke a prayer that Spain imagined he might have spoken at a dedication ceremony of the Roman bridge over the Tina (Tyne): 'I pray that the future may bring prosperity and trade to this new port I name this bridge, and the quay, and the fort Pons Aelii!' The Tyne Bridge may well be the only bridge in the world to have had a radio play written about it! (Goulding, C., *Hidden Newcastle*, Tynebridge Publishing: 1995)

OCTOBER 10TH

1928: On this day, the Tyne Bridge was officially opened. Newcastle and Gateshead town councils had for decades been considering building a high level road bridge, especially as it became clear that the High Level Bridge was making good money from tolls well after the costs had been recouped. But though various committees met over the years, no one was willing to put their money behind the proposals. In the 1920s, as traffic increased and the government put money into schemes for the unemployed, the idea became more appealing than ever. Dorman, Long & Co. of Middlesbrough eventually won the contract. They had recently finished a design for Sydney Harbour Bridge, and utilised much of the same design over here (so while the Tyne Bridge was finished first, because it was much smaller, it wasn't started first). The whole thing (including buying land) cost around £1,200,000, of which the government paid 60 per cent. The granite towers were intended as five-storey warehouses, but in the end the internal floors were not built, leaving massive empty spaces (apart from lifts). The bridge was opened by George V with much celebration and the novelty of a camera crew for British Movietone News. (Manders, F. and Potts, R., *Crossing the Tyne*, Tynebridge Publishing: 2001)

OCTOBER 11TH

1966: On this day, Matt Heslop, proprietor of a West Street joke shop, was in hot water with Gateshead Council. He had run the shop for ten years, and it had recently gained a new street lamp close to the building, after the previous one was knocked down by a lorry. He was painting his shop front bright yellow – and decided to paint the lamp post yellow too! No one interrupted him as he painted an undercoat, and the following day a top coat, over the lower 8ft of the post, so that it would 'blend in' with the shop. But the council were not impressed, and order him to remove it, or pay the expenses of having council workmen do it. He settled for the latter – after all, he said, 'who knows, I might damage the lamp ...' The mayor commented that Heslop's actions were 'not far short of vandalism ... We can't allow him to get away with it, otherwise people throughout the town would be painting lamps all colours.' Only a month later, Heslop was in trouble again, this time for displaying posters on bill boards outside his shop. The argument was that they might be distracting to motorists – but he'd been displaying posters in this way for ten years. Heslop responded by instead displaying the letter from the council, surrounded by comments like 'Gateshead Council crucifies joke shop'. As he put it, 'I harm no-one unless they take a poke at me. But when I'm right, I fight'. (*Evening Chronicle*)

OCTOBER 12TH

1887: On this day, two Gateshead brothers were arrested in New York as part of an international theft investigation. Apparently the two – 'tall, intelligent-looking young men' of 27 and 30 – were sons of the chief tax collector of Gateshead, and sometimes helped him in his work. This time, however, William and Robert Chapman helped themselves instead. In May, rumours started to build up that there were irregularities in the books, which were shown, when investigated, to amount to a deficit of $25,000 (around £5,000). That day, William and Robert disappeared. Initially the manhunt was centred on England, but police moved their attentions to the United States when they found out that a third brother lived there. They were eventually found in an apartment in Pineapple Street, Brooklyn. Police in England were cabled, and then an officer had to actually travel to America by sea, on board the *Germanic*, to bring the relevant arrest warrant. The two men were arrested and sent to await trial. We do not know what happened next, or how Chapman senior took his sons' betrayal. (*The New York Times*)

OCTOBER 13TH

1943: On this day, the Little Theatre in Saltwell Park opened its doors for the first time. It was the only English theatre to be opened during the Second World War. The theatre can trace its roots to 1920, and the formation of the Gateshead Independent Labour Party Drama Society (*see* March 17th). But the accommodation, in Westfield Hall, was far from ideal – the temporary stage had to be dismantled every week to make way for dances. Over the 1930s, tensions grew with the hall owners, and a building fund was begun. In 1938 the Dodds sisters, Hope, Sylvie and Ruth, donated enough money to start work in earnest. By the time the war broke out, the Players had a building and a neighbouring vacant plot, and many of the fittings they would need. While the dilapidated house was commandeered as a balloon barrage for a while, building work began on the vacant plot – and the Players continued to perform. For instance, in 1941 they entertained the troops in Gateshead Town Hall. By 1943, the Little Theatre was nearly finished, though a nearby bomb explosion was a setback, blowing in the doors and windows and sending a tree crashing through the roof! By October, they were ready to go, with an opening production of Shakespeare's *A Midsummer Night's Dream*, a great piece of light relief amid the struggles of war-torn Gateshead. The Little Theatre is still open, and is Gateshead's only theatre. (www.littletheatregateshead.com)

OCTOBER 14TH

1621: On this day, Richard Backas (perhaps Backhouse?) was buried in St Mary's churchyard. His death is thought to be the first recorded fatal accident caused by firedamp – the build-up of flammable gas within a mine. The burial register records 'Richard Backas, burn'd in a pit.' This danger had been known of for some years, though – as collieries grew deeper in the mid-sixteenth century, Dr Keys of Cambridge commented that in some northern pits, 'the unwholesome vapour whereof is so pernicious to the hired labourers that it would immediately destroy them if they did not get out of the way as soon as the flame of their lamps becomes blue and is consumed.' Backas was not, though, the first known English pit fatality. That dubious distinction goes to James and Thomas Thompson, who were killed earlier in the same year – also in Gateshead. (Galloway, R., *History of Coal Mining in Great Britain*, 1888)

◆

1914: On this day, the War Office officially sanctioned the creation of the Tyneside Irish and Tyneside Scottish brigades. Initially the War Office rejected the idea of these units but on this day, Lord Haldane decided to allow it, and recruiting meetings began. By November 4th the Tyneside Irish had over 5,000 recruits, enough for a brigade. In 1916, they were in the thick of the Battle of the Somme, and suffered extremely heavy casualties. (www.tyneside-scottish.co.uk)

OCTOBER 15TH

1346: On this day, King David II of Scotland brought an army to Gateshead. His goal was to provide a diversion on behalf of his ally, King Philip VI of France, who had recently lost badly at Crecy. Believing most of England's forces were still in France, David was happy to oblige. He entered England on the west side of the country, then moved east, taking Lanercost Priory and sacking Hexham Priory. The army obviously wanted to avoid the bulwark of Newcastle itself, and so turned southward shortly before reaching it, fording the Tyne at Ryton before setting up camp in Bearpark on the 16th. Legend has it that as David passed through Ryton (possibly while he was sacking its church) St Cuthbert appeared to him in a dream, and told him that his expedition would come to a bad end if he destroyed any part of Durham, St Cuthbert's own land. Perhaps he should have listened – on the 17th, the English nobles gathered their forces and crushed the Scots army at Neville's Cross. David was captured – but at least his life was spared as he was ransomed, unlike many of his troops! (Bourne, W., *History of the Parish of Ryton*, 1896)

October 16th

1916: On this day, Winifred Laver started up the Vine Street Mission. Two previous attempts to get it going had failed – but then, Laver was no ordinary woman. As a young adult, she had hoped to become a missionary in China, but she was turned down because she had tuberculosis. So she set her sights on Gateshead. Rather safer, you'd think, but her doctor warned her 'if you go there, you will only live for one year!' At least she didn't have to worry about catching tuberculosis since she already had it in her system, even though it was rife on Rabbit Banks. On this day, she arrived, and went straight to the mission building. She recalled, 'there was nothing but a dilapidated old building. I just knelt down in the bare hall and prayed, "Heavenly father, you and I can do this work. Show me where to begin!"' She provided spiritual guidance, basic medical help and – after a lad began to eat the bread poultice she'd put on his foot – meals whenever she could. Seemingly inexhaustible, she ran Christmas parties and summer day trips for 1,200 children at a time, and the biggest Girl Guide troop in the country. For her services to the people of Gateshead, she was given the Freedom of Gateshead, and an MBE. She kept on working with Gateshead's poor until shortly before her death when tuberculosis finally claimed her at the age of 92. (www. localhistorygateshead.com)

OCTOBER 17TH

1764: On this day, Revd Leake of Stanhope came to an unfortunate end. He was travelling from Newcastle to Whickham, where he intended to stop the night, but he got lost. Trying to ford the river Team, his horse became stuck fast in the mud. When the pair were found the next morning, the horse was barely alive, and Leake himself was dead. (Sykes, J., *Local Records*, i., 1833)

1867: On this day, the foundation stone was laid for the Abbot Memorial Ragged and Industrial School. The Abbot being commemorated here was local industrialist John Abbot. It was his wife who funded the Ragged and Industrial School, and who laid the first stone. The stone laying was complemented by the ringing of local church bells, and a massive parade through the streets with regimental bands. Schools like this were intended to get children off the streets and instil in them Christian morality. The hope was to keep them from a life of crime, by teaching them a trade. So, the Catherine Terrace site was soon laid out not only with classrooms, but with a garden, workrooms and kitchens. Boys learned trades like tailoring and shoemaking; girls learned knitting, sewing and laundry work. There was room for 150 boys and 150 girls. The school closed in 1930 and was demolished in 1968. (*Newcastle Courant*)

OCTOBER 18TH

1297: On this day, the people of Ryton suffered for their arrogance. The Scottish army of William Wallace was rampaging along the north bank of the Tyne. According to one chronicler, Ryton's inhabitants thought that the river kept them safe, and shouted insults across the water at the soldiers. The Scottish troops were so incensed they forded the river and burned the village to the ground! (Bourne, W., *History of the Parish of Ryton*, 1896)

———◆———

1745: On this day, twins William and Barbara Scott were born in Heworth. These were interesting times to be born, as news had reached Newcastle of the rapid advance of the forces of Pretender Bonnie Prince Charlie, still pressing his claim to the throne. In the event, he never made it to Newcastle, but the town was a mass of activity. The Scotts' father, also called William, was worried for his heavily pregnant wife, but the gates were already boarded up – so she was put in a basket and lowered down from the top of the town wall! From there she took a short boat trip to her father's country house at Heworth, but the excitement had triggered labour, and the two were born later that night. The family's fortunes were already rising – William Scott the elder was a coal fitter who became a respected merchant – but his children went on to greater things. William the younger ended up as Baron Stowell of Stowell Park, Gloucestershire, and the twins' brother became the Earl of Eldon! (Latimer, J., *Local Records*, 1857)

OCTOBER 19TH

1869: On this day, York instrument maker Thomas Cook died. A pioneer of British telescope-making, Cook was at the time working on a telescope for Robert Stirling Newall, a rich Scottish engineer and keen amateur astronomer. Pending movement to a higher, more clear-aired location, it was sited in a private observatory in Newall's garden, Ferndene, Gateshead. Tyneside's industrial smog made it a far-from-ideal location, and Newall only used the telescope's full aperture once in fifteen years! Sadly, Cook died before seeing his telescope completed, but the 'Newall', when finished, was for some years the largest refracting telescope in the world. It weighed nine tons, yet was so well balanced that it could be easily repositioned, and fine-tuned, by a single man. It was 32ft long with a lens of almost 25ins across. *Nature* magazine said at the time that its construction 'marks an epoch in astronomy', and praised the English manufacturers for once more leaping ahead of foreign rivals. After Newall's death, his son Hugh wanted to use the telescope more. He made an offer to the University of Cambridge – he would move the telescope, and work for five years without payment as its main observer, in exchange for a plot of land close by, where he could build a house. The telescope was moved to Cambridge in 1891, and was used there until the 1940s. In 1957, it was donated to the National Observatory of Athens. (Ré, P., 'The 25-inch Newall refractor', www.astrosurf.com / www.hasi.gr)

OCTOBER 20TH

1988: On this day, the *Gateshead Observer* reported on the strange adventure of a Pembrokeshire pigeon. Keen pigeon racer Joe McGarr was surprised to see a lost-looking racing pigeon in Gateshead town centre in early September. Because of a postal strike it took him weeks to track down the bird's owner. Apparently the pigeon – which McGarr named Lucky – was well off course, having been racing from Kent to Cardiff. McGarr then sent the pigeon back – by airmail! Lucky was indeed lucky to be found by a pigeon racer, but Gateshead does at least have plenty of them – pigeon racing is a traditional pastime in the mining villages of the North East. (*Gateshead Post and Times*)

———•◆•———

1982: On this day, Rabbi Leib Gurwicz died. Gurwicz was born in Poland and spent his early adulthood studying in yeshivas (Jewish traditional schools) across Eastern Europe and Russia. He moved to London in 1932 and in 1948 accepted a post at the growing Gateshead yeshiva, where he stayed for over thirty years (*see* June 14th). In his time, the yeshiva became the leading centre in Europe for study of the Torah. When Gurwicz died, his coffin was carried through the streets of Gateshead, and a procession of a thousand people followed his body to Newcastle Airport. (Wikipedia)

OCTOBER 21ST

1990: On this day the Gateshead Garden Festival closed its doors for the last time. Since opening in May, the festival had attracted over 3 million visitors. It was the fourth of the United Kingdom's five National Garden Festivals and the biggest cultural and horticultural attraction in Europe that year. Showcasing 100 gardens from around the world, and twenty-five national horticultural shows, it involved the planting of 2 million trees and shrubs, and around 1 million bulbs. Additional attractions included funfair rides as well as around 25,000 hours of events in dance, music, theatre and sport. Over seventy art installations, fifty newly commissioned, graced the site. A narrow-gauge railway (with replica early nineteenth-century trains) crossed the site, and a monorail was built between Norwood and Eslington. Additionally a ferry service was put in place between Dunston Staithes and Newcastle Quayside. All this was a massive change from what had gone before – the 200-acre festival site had, two years previously, housed a disused gasworks, coal depot and coking plant. The staithes provided a rare point of continuity, although even these were restored. All this renovation and improvement cost around £37 million. This, however, was part of the point of Garden Festivals – not simply to provide a transitory entertainment, but to regenerate large areas of industrial land, making possible new beginnings. Much of the area is now under housing developments. (McLanders, F., *The Life of the Dunston Staithes*, Wimpey Homes: 2007)

OCTOBER 22ND

1644: On this day, Scottish army captain John Cunningham was buried at St Mary's, Whickham. He was the second soldier buried in Whickham that year – the first is recorded in the parish register as 'a man that was shot by the Scottish sentries in the meadows, as he was coming up the water in a boat'. This was probably on The King's Meadows, a large island in the Tyne. Scots forces had held the area and kept Newcastle under siege since August (*see* August 12th), so the unnamed man was taking his life into his hands going so close to their army – perhaps he was spying? The Scottish army entered Newcastle on October 19th, as the Royalist survivors pulled back, holing up in towers to snipe at the invading army and staging a desperate stand in the Bigg Market. It was presumably in this conflict that Cunningham met his end, though the casualties were much higher on the other side – we don't know why he was buried over the river. Whickham wasn't left alone for the rest of the Civil War. An army camped there in September 1648 as Cromwell headed north to make a treaty in Edinburgh. One soldier died there, and was also buried in St Mary's. Cromwell himself is rumoured to have stayed in Dockendale Hall. (Serdiville, R., and Sadler, J., *The Great Siege of Newcastle 1644*, The History Press: 2011)

OCTOBER 23RD

1919: On this day, Gateshead Council debated an interesting offer. The War Office, presumably with a lot of spare artillery on their hands, was offering it to town and parish councils, with mixed results. Gateshead had been offered two heavy German guns – but with the First World War less than a year over, it's hardly surprising that some councillors wanted nothing to do with them, rejecting the offer 'on the grounds that they would remind those who returned what they had been through'. In Fulwell in March, a similar debate took place in a parish council, where 'there was considerable difference on the matter'. One gun was 'dumped' outside the cemetery gates in Ryton. Further afield, two guns were accepted by Durham Council, but Stockton turned down the offer of a tank. And in Stanhope, locals removed the German gun and ran it into the River Wear! Perhaps that's why the one in Sunderland briefly had an armed guard … Finally, returning to Gateshead, three German machine guns were stolen from the Brighton Road Territorial Army Drill Hall in December 1921. These, too, were souvenirs from the First World War. Whether they were stolen for scrap, destruction or private collection, we will never know, as the military and police investigations drew a blank. (www.newmp.org.uk)

October 24th

1900: On this day, fire engulfed the Dunston Lodge Lunatic Asylum, almost completely gutting the brick building, collapsing the roof and some sections of walls. Fortunately, the asylum had closed just a few months before, and so no lives were lost in the blaze. A crowd of onlookers watched room after room catch light, but the Gateshead fire brigade soon arrived and were gradually able to bring the flames under control. The cause of the blaze remains unknown. Ironically, a fire station was later built on the same site, and used until the 1960s. (*Northern Echo*)

1947: On this day, the small New Zealand town of Te Aroha arranged to send food parcels to Gateshead. A public scheme had been set up to send food to Britain, and Gateshead had been selected as the first recipient! The parcels would contain tinned tongue, honey, cooking fats and cocoa, and would be sent to the mayor, who would then distribute them as he saw fit. This would be 'a small token of appreciation ... for the many years of hardship and danger experienced by the people of Britain'. Gateshead's mayor gratefully accepted the gifts, saying that the people were 'determined to win through the crisis'. (*Gateshead Weekly Pictorial Post*)

OCTOBER 25TH

1824: On this day, two young men – bricklayer James Wallace, and butcher Thomas Dunn – met on Barlow Fell, near Ryton, to compete in a prize fight, for winnings of 20 sovereigns. At half-past one the ring was formed, and an enthusiastic crowd of, as the *Courant* put it, around 2,000 'persons of every description', gathered to watch. The contest would have been fought under Broughton rules. These were devised by a boxer who, in 1741, accidentally killed his opponent, and wanted to make sure this never happened again. That meant that the men boxed with open fists, and when one hit the deck, they were not hit again; their second had thirty seconds to get them back to 'scratch', a marked spot at the edge of the ring, or the match was lost. The contest would go on until this happened, however long that took, but in this case it took only eight rounds, and the crowd were apparently disappointed at Wallace's easy victory. Unfortunately, the magistrates had been alerted. Wallace fled the country, but Dunn was prosecuted. He pleaded guilty and was let free on condition of good behaviour. (Pears, T. and B., 'High Spen and District', www.bpears.org.uk)

OCTOBER 26TH

1893: On this day, the popular satirical magazine *Vanity Fair* published, within its series on politicians, a caricature of William Allan, 'the Gateshead Giant'. Allan had been elected Liberal MP for Gateshead in February; his portrait matches the description in his *Telegraph* obituary, 'with his sturdy powerful figure, his well-known soft hat, and bearded like a Viking'! This might have been enough to grant a measure of fame, but Allan also boasted a decidedly murky past. He was born in Dundee, and worked as an engineer in the Royal Navy and merchant navy. During the American Civil War, he was chief engineer of a steamship gun-runner, engaged in getting weapons past a military blockade! After hair-raising adventures, the ship was captured and Allan imprisoned. Released on parole, he settled in the North East, founding the Scotia engine works in Sunderland, where he notably introduced an eight-hour working day. This hints at his radical and humanitarian politics, which drew him towards Parliament. The Liberal Party had been struggling in Gateshead when Allan took the seat, but he engineered a revival in its fortunes and remained in post until his death in 1903. He could talk with equal conviction about Home Rule (he was for), or the perils of using water-tube boilers (he was against), but thought of himself as a poet first and foremost. He wrote several volumes of verse, all harking back to his Scottish ancestry and a love of nature. (*Vanity Fair / Daily Telegraph*)

OCTOBER 27TH

1899: On this day, William Sadler junior dived into the Tyne to save a man in distress. At the time, a single rowing boat, run as a ferry by the Sadler family, plied the crowded waters between Paradise, Benwell, and the Delta steelworks, Raines. It was extremely busy and essential to daily life for many workers in the industry along the riverbank. Near Benwell, the tide was running strongly and the water was around 12ft deep, when J.T. Errington accidentally fell in. When Sadler saw what was happening, he dived into the swirling waters, fully clothed, and pulled Errington to safety. He was later awarded a bronze medal by the Royal Humane Society, an honour given to those who place their own lives at great risk to save, or attempt to save, another. The Sadler family were well known in the area not only for the ferry but also as landlords of the Boathouse Pub, Scotswood, and owners of a boat builder's yard in Dunston. Sadler Square – a square of two-up, two-down houses, with toilets and water supply in the middle – was named after the yard, and was demolished in the 1950s. (www.webwanderers. org / Life Saving Awards Research Society)

OCTOBER 28TH

1853: On this day, the last normal interment took place at St Mary's, Gateshead, when labourer and cholera victim Nicholas Urwin of Low Bensham was buried. The graveyard was packed full even before the cholera outbreak of autumn 1853, and the rector tried to encourage their relatives to go elsewhere. But 140 families could not be persuaded, due to what he called their 'anxiety to have their dead interred by the side of relatives'. After this final burial, the General Board of Health ordered the closure of the graveyard, pre-empting by four months the general order of Queen Victoria for burials to cease within towns. In fact, however, St Mary's welcomed one more body, on March 5th 1854, when Mrs Akenhead gained special dispensation from Sir George Grey, the Secretary of State, to be buried alongside her husband in his vault. The graveyard received a facelift a few months later, thanks to the great fire (*see* October 6th). A lot of money was forthcoming to start the process of restoring the church, and a small amount was left over – this was used to sow more grass, and plant larch trees in the graveyard. (Lang, A., *The St Mary's Story*, Gateshead Council: 2009)

OCTOBER 29TH

1769: On this day, Dr Askew had a fright on the road to his Whickham country house. Some lads had climbed on the back of his carriage, so the doctor ordered his driver to scare them off. Unfortunately it was the horses that panicked – the lads jumped back, but the horses ran over a steep cliff at full gallop. The coach was overturned, but the horses continued to drag it behind them until the front wheels separated from the body. Dr Askew was much bruised, and one good thing may have come out of the incident – four months on a Newcastle ironmonger patented a design which allowed easy uncoupling of horse and carriage, in cases of panicking horses. (Sykes, J., *Local Records*, i., 1833)

———◆———

1869: Exactly 100 years on, a tragic shooting took place in Leopold Street, Gateshead. Photographer Thomas Skelton apparently kept a loaded pistol under his mattress – which does rather sound like an accident waiting to happen. And happen it did, when his wife, airing the bed, left the gun on the windowsill. It was spotted by their eleven-year-old son William, who took the pistol into the kitchen, and 'in a playful manner', pulled the trigger – and hit his thirteen-year-old sister right above the heart. (*Western Mail Cardiff*)

October 30th

1946: On this day, in a grand ceremony, Revd Henry Stephenson, the rector of Gateshead, was made an honorary Freeman of the Borough. At 74 years old, Stephenson was well known as a 'grand old man' of the local church, with thirty-seven years of service under his belt. (*Gateshead Weekly Pictorial Post*)

1970: On this day, the papers reported on Gateshead council's plans to deal with the problem of vandalism. This wasn't just the odd bit of graffiti, but thieves breaking into derelict and empty council houses, and stealing wiring, lead pipes and other valuable goods. Some houses were apparently being left in such a state that there was little choice but to pull them down. The council's plan was simple – to send in their own 'thieves' first, to do a more careful job of stripping anything of value. And to protect the houses that would soon be inhabited, they had a different strategy – they would be 'booby-trapped in such a way that if any vandal does break in he will get one or two unpleasant surprises'! (*Evening Chronicle*)

OCTOBER 31ST

1831: On this day, a group of glass workers held a public meeting in Gateshead Town Hall. Their purpose was to protest in favour of the glass works, and against the series of recent prosecutions which had been made against them because of the large amount of smoke they produced. The chairman argued that when men came and invested in the area, the people were naturally pleased, and that a return could not be made on this investment without the production of a certain amount of smoke. But now, some council members were seeking to prosecute the owners of the Neville Glass Works 'because the furnaces that he had adopted were not the ideal furnaces of a certain gentleman'. They were asking him to pull down the chimney, and replace it with another that would trap smoke better. The chairman queried whether it was right to make these demands – especially since some works would not be able to afford it, leading to works closures and job losses (and the increase in parish rates that would come from a rise in unemployment). He claimed that this had already happened to a firm in Pipewellgate – which had been replaced by the even more unpleasant spectacle of a guano works! In short, it was argued that smoke was in effect putting bread on the tables of tens of thousands of working men, and that was a small price to pay. (*Newcastle Courant*)

NOVEMBER 1ST

1907: On this day, John Patterson was killed during a robbery at the Windy Nook Co-op, Howard Street. Over the previous few weeks, joints of meat had been going missing. Since the local Co-op committee feared an inside job, they didn't want to involve the police. Instead, the committee took it in turns to lie in wait. The culprit arrived at around 4 a.m. – but when a group tackled him, he pulled out a gun and fired twice. John Patterson was killed instantly by a bullet in his head, and Christopher Carr was left permanently disabled. George Ather chased the killer down the street, joined by his wife, who had been roused from her house next door by the noise. Despite the tragic circumstances, this made for a farcical scene, as the intruder was wearing a slouch hat and false beard, while Mrs Ather was dressed in a petticoat and wielding an axe! Suspicion soon fell on colliery blacksmith and gunmaker Joseph Noble. He fitted the bill, with recent wounds, professional burglary tools, keys to the Co-op, and a house filled with far too many Co-op goods. The defence argued that this was all circumstantial, and the surviving committee members were initially unsure, as they thought they would have recognised Noble. But they were persuaded by the weight of evidence – and so was the jury. Noble was hanged the following year, protesting his innocence to the last. (Oxberry, J., *Windy Nook Village*, Co-operative Society: 1924)

NOVEMBER 2ND

1968: On this day, the *Northern Echo* reported on filming in Gateshead for the adaptation of D.H. Lawrence's novel *Women in Love*. The novel is set in 1910s Beldover – an amalgam of Midland towns Belper and Andover. But when director Ken Russell went there, he found the towns had changed too much in the intervening years, and were now too 'romantically pretty', so opted for Gateshead instead. The *Northern Echo* thought that Russell was attracted by 'the drabness of Gateshead ... its dereliction, dirt and slums'! For one key scene, Glenda Jackson, in an Oscar-winning role as Gudrun Brangwen, is seen walking along Half Moon Lane in central Gateshead, from the Half-Moon Bar to the Central Bar. She is propositioned crudely, before being rescued by Oliver Reed's character. The 'flat-iron' block that houses the Central Bar was built as business premises for wine merchant Alderman Potts in 1854, but became a hotel around 1890. Very little had changed by 1968! Since 2009, sympathetic renovation has brought back many of the Victorian features as well as adding a rooftop terrace. As well as using Gateshead itself, Russell recreated Beldover Market in North Shields, and went to Bedlington Colliery for the mine scenes. Some early machinery had to be restored for the film, but that was still easier than trying to use the actual locations of the book, which had modernised greatly. (http://www.movie-locations.com / *Northern Echo*)

NOVEMBER 3RD

1948: On this day, years after the end of the Second World War, the Gateshead coroner recorded a verdict of 'Death by enemy action' on the bodies of two unknown men. The bodies – now buried in Swallwell cemetery – have a strange history, and to this day no one can be certain who they were, or where they had come from. They were found inside the fuel tank of the HMS *Malines*, which was awaiting destruction in a Dunston breakers yard. Built by Armstrong, Whitworth & Co. in 1921, as a ferry for the Great Eastern Railway Company, she was requisitioned in 1940 and took part in several evacuations, including Dunkirk. On July 22nd 1942, HMS *Malines* was in the Mediterranean escorting convoys when she was hit by a torpedo and badly damaged. She limped into Port Said and was out of action for about six months. So the likelihood is that the unfortunate men had been victims of the attack, lying dead for six long years. But questions remained. Who exactly were they? How had they remained undiscovered while the ship was extensively repaired, and used for warfare and for training? And what were they doing inside a fuel tank? (Local press)

NOVEMBER 4TH

1769: On this day, Richard Byron was made rector of Ryton parish. He was the brother of William, 5th Lord Byron (who was also known as 'the Wicked Lord' and 'the Devil Byron' after he killed his cousin in a duel, and also deliberately ruined the family estate), and the great-uncle of the famous poet, George, the 6th Lord Byron. Richard Byron stayed in post for twenty-five years. Other notable rectors of Ryton have included Thomas Secker, who started as a non-conformist, and prior to his ordination had studied medicine and worked as a London apothecary. After ordination in the Church of England he became rector in Houghton-le-Spring, but found the damp air poor for his wife's health, and was transferred to Ryton in 1727, staying for five years. He worked his way up through the Church of England, winning favour with his sermons, and in 1758 was made Archbishop of Canterbury. Another rector of Ryton was Charles Thorp, a Gateshead man who held the post from 1811. In 1832 he became the first warden of the University of Durham, and in some senses can be seen as its true founder. Ryton Church is itself worthy of note, dating back to around 1220 and housing a thirteenth-century sculpture. (*Oxford Dictionary of National Biography* / Wikipedia)

NOVEMBER 5TH

1571: On this day, John Heworth of Gateshead, about to share his wife's death by plague, dictated a will bequeathing his goods to his daughter and the poor. On the same document, his friend James Cole wrote some interesting expenses. 'To the apothecary for treacle and certain other things, 3s. 10d. ; for straw and candles, 4d. ; for soap and coals, 1s. 4d. ; for the bearing of John and his wife, for the church and for making their grave, 5s. 4d. ; to the priest and the clerk for the burial, knolling and ringing the bells, 3s. ; for frankincense, juniper, and broom, for smoking the house, 1s. ; for cleansing the house, for meat and drink to him and her in time of sickness, and to two servants, a child, and two dressers of the house, 40s. 1d.' (Welford, R., *History of Newcastle and Gateshead*, 1884)

———◆———

1832: On this day, William Ridley, furnace-man at Felling Colliery, was working at the bottom of the pit. Having lit two furnaces, he filled a corf (large basket) with ashes to take up to the surface. Ridley shook the chain attached the corf, which was the signal to the men at the top to draw it up – but unfortunately his leg was caught in the coils of the chain, and as the men drew the corf up, Ridley went with it. He was carried, unharmed, up the shaft for about 220m! (Sykes, J., *Local Records*, 1833)

November 6th

1770: On this day, a massive block of ore, 'extracted from sundry matters', was tested in Mr Cox's refinery, Bill Quay. It was found to contain 667lb of precious gold and silver, the largest quantity ever tested for in one go in the country. It was exhibited in Newcastle before being sent on to London; over £8 was raised in 1s entry fees. (Sykes, J., *Local Records*, i, 1833)

———— ◆ ————

1922: On this day, the Shakespeare Fellowship was founded. One of the three founder members was the unfortunately-named J. Thomas Looney, a Gateshead schoolmaster. In the 1910s, Looney was a leader in Tyneside of the Religion of Humanity, a secular system of belief and ritual based around the veneration of humanity, and emphasising altruism, order and progress. When this failed locally, he turned his attention to the question of the authorship of the works of Shakespeare. In 1918 he theorised that Shakespeare's works were actually written by the Earl of Oxford, placing a paper on the subject in a sealed envelope in the British Library. He expanded on this in his 1920 *Shakespeare Identified*. In 1959 the Fellowship became the Shakespearean Authorship Trust, which survives to this day; additionally the Shakespeare Fellowship was re-founded in 2001, and cites as one of its mission objectives promoting research and education on 'the Shakespearean authorship question' with emphasis on Looney's theory.

NOVEMBER 7TH

1859: On this day, the Town Hall was the venue for the first general meeting of the Gateshead Rifle Club. This was not a shooting club for the promotion of sport shooting, but rather, as its chairman Alderman Hawke put it, 'an association of gentlemen, who organised themselves to defend their households, their wives, their property and their children'. He did not expect that many of the young gentlemen present had wives and children; but he believed they were all aspirants in that direction. It was associated with the Rifle Corps movement, which he stressed was defensive, rather than associated with any political faction. He said that he did not think the French would cease being England's allies, but since they were 'keeping up their military discipline, he thought it was incumbent on them to keep up the same system, and be prepared for anything that might happen'. The movement would 'keep up the spirit of the nation' as well as providing a large body of troops if it came to pass that they were needed. The forty drilling members and twenty honorary members all agreed to a dark green uniform similar to those of the non-commissioned officers in the Rifles. (*Newcastle Courant*)

NOVEMBER 8TH

1897: On this day, Gateshead boxer Will Cawley – better known as Will Curley – fought American Patsy Haley. The place was the Standard Theatre, Gateshead (on the corner of Sunderland Road and High Street), and at stake was the world 118lb title. He was only 19, this was his third professional bout, and he still hadn't fought beyond Tyneside. Still, he won quite comfortably, especially when Haley grew angry that his claim of a foul in the ninth round was rejected. *Sporting Life* called it one of the best bouts ever seen in the North. Curley went on to defend his title the following year, and in 1899 went to Brooklyn to challenge American George Dixon (only 5ft 3in, performing name, 'Little Chocolate') for the World Featherweight title. He narrowly lost that one, but continued to win titles at various specific weights, retiring in the early 1900s (not before one final bout with George Dixon, where, both past their prime, he could only manage a draw). By this point – like many other boxers of his generation – he was also running a bar, in this case Phoenix Bar on Gateshead High Street. He ran the bar for over forty years, and was still its publican when he died in 1937. Many years later the pub was renamed Curley's Bar in his honour. (boxrec.com)

NOVEMBER 9TH

1841: On this day, a grand dinner was held to celebrate the opening of a new suite of public buildings on Durham Road, Low Fell. Designed by Thomas Oliver, a single roof housed a reading room, and a lecture theatre. It was paid for by a mixture of public subscription, and the sale of 5s shares. Initially, you could also get in and out of the reading rooms via a staircase leading straight to the Crown Inn! Above-stairs was a schoolroom for the children of Low Fell, the only provision for them and one which lasted until 1891. The whole thing had been organised by local author and dialect poet Thomas Wilson, and Mr Hetherington, the landlord of the Gateshead Arms. Wilson also headed up the council of trustees, and was keen to make achievement more attainable for a new generation of children than it had been for himself. He started work down the pit at 8 years old, but worked his way up within engineering firm Losh, Wilson & Bell, eventually being made a partner, as well as a Gateshead town councillor – a truly self-made man. (*See* also April 22nd and July 17th. (www.gateshead-history.com)

NOVEMBER 10TH

1838: On this day Eleanor Brownlee died, better known as 'Pot Nelly' or 'Deaf Nelly', a door-to-door seller of nuts, oranges, and pottery around Gateshead Fell. This day, she was returning from Ravensworth when she was caught in heavy rain. She asked for shelter at a farm near Cow Close, but was refused entrance. It is assumed that she died soon after. Her body was found some weeks later in Ravensworth Woods, so much damaged that the lads who found her ran straight home. She was 102 years old, and locally famous for remembering the Rebellion of 1745. She was also a survivor of the floods of 1771, when she escaped from the medieval Tyne Bridge down a ladder held in place by some keelmen. (Gateshead Library Local Collections)

1891: On this day, the premises of Clarke Chapman engineering works were gutted by fire. The Gateshead firemen – an offshoot from the police – had turned out quickly, but their best efforts had little or no effect, and it took the combined efforts of Gateshead and Newcastle firemen to bring the fire under control, at considerable risk to their lives. Crucially, Newcastle had powerful fire engines – horse-drawn carts with 2 tons of complex steam-driven pumping equipment – and Gateshead did not. This fire was a major spur in the following year's formation of a proper fire service, with its own engine. (March, G., *Flames across the Tyne*, Peterson: 1974)

NOVEMBER 11TH

1843: On this day, composer John Selkirk died in unfortunate circumstances. A barber's son born in 1782, legend has it that he was born in a house on the bridge, just to the south of the blue stone which marked the official dividing line between Newcastle and Gateshead. As a young man Selkirk worked as a clerk for Straker & Boyle on the Newcastle Quayside. It was in this period that he began writing, his first songs being published around 1806. His main creation was Bob Cranky, a habitual braggart who commented on the sights of Tyneside, for instance in Bob Cranky's ''Size Sunday', in which Cranky watches the annual procession of the Assizes judges. Another song was 'The Swalwell Hoppings'. Selkirk moved to London in his thirties and worked as a merchant, but something must have gone wrong, and in 1830 he returned to the North East destitute. In spite of the popularity of his songs, he lived in poverty for the rest of his days. Refusing parish relief, he was eventually reduced to living on others' charity, and sleeping on the shavings on a joiner's shop floor. On this day, he was reaching into the Tyne with a tin bottle, to get a drink, when he slipped, fell, and drowned.

NOVEMBER 12TH

1948: On this day, Thomas Mead, a butcher with premises on Gateshead's Old Durham Road, was fined £100 for two offences concerning the sale of horse flesh to the public. Despite three years of peacetime, rationing of meat was still in force, and actual meat was still in short supply. Substituting horse meat for beef was a common trick of the black market. Horse meat could be sold, and was not rationed, but you had to have a special license, be clear about what it was, and label it 'fit for human consumption'. Mead had done none of these things. As magistrate Edward Scott said, 'it is a distressing thought that people who are getting little enough already should go into a butcher's shop and be sold horse, that we know most people abhor'. The fines were £50 for bringing horse meat into a butcher's with intent to sell it, and £50 for preparing sausages containing horse flesh. And we're not talking small quantities. The meat discovered by two sanitary inspectors amounted to 98lb of horse flesh and 200lb of sausages containing horse! Mead initially claimed that it did not belong to him, and tried to bar the investigators from taking samples. Later he admitted the crime, but said he was bowing to pressure. People expected him to have sausages, and when he did not, they were turning elsewhere … to butchers who, he believed, were selling horse. So he followed suit! (*Gateshead Post*)

November 13th

1898: On this day, Eunice Crook (later Bowman) was baptised in Lancashire. Not much to do with Gateshead you might think – but in 1905 the decline of the textile industry led her father to seek work as a coal miner in Felling. He, his wife and twelve children, all made the move northward. Eunice then lived in Gateshead for a remarkable 105 years. When she died, in 2010, she was almost 112, and the oldest person in the country. She put her longevity down to not smoking or drinking alcohol – her main vice was a 'tipple of honey'. As a young woman, she would walk across the Tyne seven days a week to work twelve-hour shifts making fuses in the Armstrong Munitions factory. After raising her children, she worked in a Gateshead fish shop until she was 84. She may not be the oldest woman to have lived in Gateshead though – at least not if we believe John Sykes, whose *Local Records* (1833) lists many somewhat unlikely centenarians. For him, the honour would go to Mary Tate, who allegedly died in Gateshead in 1783 – aged 116! But then, Sykes reckoned that others across the region made it well into their 120s … (www.bbc.co.uk / Sykes, J., *Local Records*: 1833)

NOVEMBER 14TH

1841: On this day, the church of Whickham St Mary's was almost completely gutted by fire. It started when a stove flue got so hot that it set fire to one of the wooden box-pews. From here the flames spread via the galleries to the roof. The fire brigade were called, but the engine – simply a cart with a hose, a water barrel and a two-man pumping mechanism – failed to work, perhaps through long disuse. A second engine arrived – but was also found to be broken. In the end, it was a combination of time and the labours of the parishioners that brought the blaze under control. But the structure was unsafe, and the north wall had to be rebuilt. Coincidentally on the same day, another large fire took place at Friar's Goose Colliery, right on the other side of the borough. Fortunately no one was hurt, but a lot of damage was done to wagons and sheds. (Fordyce, T., *Local Records*, 1876 /www.stmaryswhickham.org.uk)

———◆———

1870: On this evening, the Alexandra Music Hall opened for the first time, on the corner of Oakwellchare and High Street. It was the first music hall in the borough. Performers on the first bill included a female impersonator and clog dancers. (www.twsitelines.info)

November 15th

1896: On this day, Alexander Petrie – thought to be the oldest workman on Tyneside – was celebrating his 92nd birthday. He had been apprenticed in Scotland, but then began work for the metalworkers, Abbots of Gateshead. The company was at the start of a boom period, which by mid-century saw the foundry employing up to 2,000 men and boys at the massive Park Works riverside site (now the site of the Sage building). They made a wide range of metal goods, from small things like tin tacks to cranes, anchors, and the copper tubes inside the engines of Stephenson Locomotives. They also provided materials for the construction of the High Level Bridge and Newcastle Central station. One of their specialisms, especially in the early days, was the making of pewter vessels, from serving dishes to tankards. This was where Petrie came in. He must have been one of their best, as he was sometimes asked to make pieces as formal gifts to local dignitaries. When he was 90, he stopped working in the main room, but remained with the company in a separate room making small pewter measures. In 1898, he had been working at Abbots for seventy-one years; we do not know how much longer he stayed there! (*Daily Chronicle* / www.ellisonplace.co.uk / www.pewterbank.com)

NOVEMBER 16TH

1771: On this morning, it started to rain heavily across the region – and it kept on raining. Residents going to bed on this Saturday night would have had no idea what awaited them the next morning – though those living near to the river cannot have slept easy. In the event, by midnight the river was at 12ft higher than would be caused by the highest of tides. As the water rose, boats were pulled from their moorings, and many were smashed or swept out to sea, while timber and other goods were lost to the water. Soon, buildings at the river's edge were completely underwater; in Dunston, boats were launched to rescue people from the roofs of their houses. And shortly after midnight, the Tyne Bridge – standing since around 1250 – gave up the struggle. The middle arch, and two other arches on the Gateshead side, along with seven shops (with houses above), were simply swept away, along with six people. Another family were left stranded between two fallen arches for six hours, until they were rescued in a bold scheme involving narrow timbers laid from pier to pier to reach the side of the house, where an opening could be forced. Pieces of one house were later found 8 miles downstream, empty but for a cat and dog, alive but bedraggled! (Garrett, W., *An Account of the Great Floods of 1771 and 1815*, 1818)

NOVEMBER 17TH

2010: On this day, Gateshead vicar Jim Craig had to bow to pressure from his congregation and tone down a proposed art exhibit. For six months previously, he had been helping local artists to use a section of St Edmund's Chapel as a display space. But the sensitivities of the congregation always needed to be taken into account, and when the ideas of artist Jonathan Scott Blood were presented as the forthcoming attraction, many parishioners were up in arms. The chapel itself has some fine thirteenth-century sections, and was once attached to a medieval hospital – but it had never seen anything like this before. The main point of contention was the plan for a large crucified Jesus – made of lard! Blood, and Craig, argued that 'Christianity is messy … there is fascinating potential dialogue there with the nature of Christ'. But aside from the practical difficulties of getting hold of that much lard, and keeping it stable (and non-smelly!), the congregation were simply unconvinced by the whole idea, and unhappy that it had been agreed upon without consultation. Craig decided that it was best to give ground on this point, and the rest of the exhibition, titled Raw Dog, went ahead as planned, including large colourful canvases and sculptured grotesques daubed with blue paint. The Sanctuary Artspace is still going strong. (www.bbc.co.uk)

NOVEMBER 18TH

1837: On this day, the *Gateshead Observer* was published for the first time. This was the first time Gateshead had had its own paper, rather than having to look to papers in Newcastle or Durham. It wasn't the first paper published in Gateshead, though – that distinction goes to the *Newcastle Gazette*, the first newspaper in the whole of the North of England, which Joseph Button of Pipewellgate printed from 1710 to 1712. But the *Observer* – available weekly for *4s ½d* – was the first one focussing on news in and around Gateshead. The *Observer* was the brainchild of William Brockett, a politician who was later mayor and was also influential in getting Gateshead parliamentary representation (*see* April 28th and December 31st). The editor, from 1837 to 1860, was James Clephan of Sunderland; after that, Brockett edited the paper himself. Until his death in 1867, the *Observer* had a reputation as one of the best newspapers in the north of England. But in the 1870s it declined, becoming little more than a catalogue of lurid crime and disaster. It ceased publication in 1886, and no other Gateshead paper succeeded in establishing itself until 1939. (Manders, F., *History of Gateshead*, Gateshead Corporation: 1973)

NOVEMBER 19TH

1923: On this day, postman James Hopewell went absent without leave somewhere near High Spen. When he failed to come into High Spen Post Office that morning, investigations were made, and it was found that he hadn't made any deliveries in the village at all – and worse, he was carrying a package containing £50 – well over £2,000 in today's money. Despite being a married man with two children, Hopewell had disappeared. Two days later his overcoat and bag were found in a hedge ... and then things went quiet for a few weeks. In late December, Hopewell handed himself in, confessing to having succumbed to a temptation to run off with the cash. In March 1924, he was sent to prison for four months. (Pears, B., *High Spen and District*, www.bpears.org.uk, 2010)

———•◆•———

2003: On this evening, flames were spotted licking against the Dunston Staithes. Sixty-seven fire fighters worked into the early hours of the 20th to put out the intense blaze, but by the time they were finished a significant amount of damage had been done to the staithes, the largest wooden structure in Europe, as burning timbers collapsed into the Tyne. It is estimated that 20 per cent of the fabric of the staithes was destroyed and a further 20 per cent was seriously damaged. Further damage was sustained in 2010, but in 2012 a project was begun to look for the best way to secure the staithes' future. (BBC News / *Evening Chronicle*)

NOVEMBER 20TH

2000: On this day, the Millennium Bridge was brought up the Tyne. The second low-level bridge across the Tyne in Tyneside, and the only one for pedestrians and cyclists only, the Millennium Bridge was the brainchild of Gateshead City Council, aimed to bolster the newly developing Gateshead Quays and tap into Millennium Commission funding. Six designers followed a complex brief intended to link communities while providing no further impediment to river traffic. There was one clear winner: its pivoting structure is a world-first in bridge design. Fabricated in sections in Bolton, the bridge was put together and painted in Wallsend. When the time came, it took all the power of the *Asian Hercules II* – one of the largest cranes in the world, with a deck the size of a football pitch – to bring the span of the bridge upriver and into position. Its final placing had to be accurate to less than 2mm; yet at 126m long, it had to be brought up the river sideways, as it is wider than the Tyne in places. Approximately 100 million people worldwide watched the journey on television, and thousands watched in person from the river banks. It was another seven months before the Millennium Bridge was ready to tilt for the first time; the public could step on it in September 2001, and it was not officially opened until April 2002. The Millennium Bridge has won several prestigious awards and been praised for its elegance and efficiency. (www.gateshead.gov.uk)

NOVEMBER 21ST

1910: On this day, Gateshead and District Camera Club held its first meeting. Very little is known about the first decade of the club, but it was certainly successful, and has continued to support Gateshead's photographers ever since, even meeting during the First and Second World Wars. By 1922, the club was regularly organising outings to rural locations like Winlaton Mill and Seaton Sluice, funding them with whist drives and especially the annual Whist Drive and Dance. The quality of the club's work was perhaps first recognised in 1923, when they held an exhibition at the Shipley Art Gallery, grandly if not entirely accurately described as the National Photographic Exhibition. You had to be rich to take part, as advanced exhibitors paid a shilling for each print they entered, while beginners paid half that. Women were welcomed, but rare, despite a reduced membership fee. Things remained very formal even after the Second World War. Photographs taken on a visit to Saltwell Park in 1952 show nine men in shirts, ties, and in several cases trilby hats – apart from a 'Mr Judd', who is wearing a flying jacket and goggles. Presumably he arrived by motorbike! (www.gatesheadcc.com)

NOVEMBER 22ND

2006: On this day, a permanent sculpture was unveiled in honour of famous Tyneside fiddler James Hill (*c.* 1811-1853). Often considered one of the most talented fiddle players of his age, Hill was from Scotland, but lived most of his life in Gateshead. Sometimes called the 'Paganini of the hornpipes', Hill composed at least fifty tunes. Some of these, like 'Beeswing', a hornpipe, are now very much viewed as key pieces of the genre. Several were named after local pubs or racehorses, like the classic 'Hawk', named after the Hawk pub down the road from his home. The High Level Hornpipe, written for the opening of the High Level Bridge in 1849, is used across the world as a test piece in fiddle competitions. Peter Coates' sculpture features a 9ft tall fiddle made of Blaxter Stone, the same material as the wall of the Tyne Bridge against which it leans, as it overlooks the High Level Bridge. Incorporated in the sculpture is also a bench inscribed with the titles of Hill's tunes. As part of the same celebrations, the Sage music venue ran a programme of education about the life of James Hill, including a concert by children from Blaydon West Primary School. (www.folknortheast.com)

NOVEMBER 23RD

1839: On this day, John Davies took up his post as rector of Gateshead. He brought with him his family, including his nine-year-old daughter, Emily. As she grew up, Emily chafed at the restricted roles available to a woman of her class. She is best known for what happened after she moved away in 1862, when she founded women-only Girton College, Cambridge, and was active in the suffrage movement. She was also involved in the Society for Promoting the Employment of Women from 1860. (*Oxford Dictionary of National Biography*)

1937: On this day, seven years after Gateshead AFC moved in, greyhound racing was first held in Gateshead's Redheugh Park Stadium. By coincidence, one of the stadium's stands was a second-hand model which had already served time on a greyhound track, in Carlisle. The addition of a 440-yard track around the Gateshead pitch's perimeter brought financial security, but reduced the crowd capacity. It wasn't unusual to combine greyhound racing with another sport, though – for instance, the White City Stadium in Blaydon hosted rugby and greyhound racing, and in 1938 even staged an England versus Scotland women's football match! (www.heedarmy.co.uk / Pearson, L., *Played in Tyne and Wear*, English Heritage: 2010)

NOVEMBER 24TH

1935: On this day, Alderman John MacCoy died, aged 92. A marine engineer, he had been owner of the Prince line of steamers, and went into business with Sir George Lunn of Newcastle to form the shipping company Lunn & MacCoy. But he was to be remembered for his work for Gateshead Council. He was Mayor of Gateshead on eight occasions between 1912 and 1923, a record to which no one else has come close (and especially remarkable since he was aged 75 before he started!). In 1922 MacCoy had the distinction of being the first and only Mayor of Gateshead to be knighted, and in 1930 he was awarded an Honorary Freeman of Gateshead. But MacCoy's personal life was full of tragedy. His wife Rebecca was killed in a motoring accident in 1914. Two years later, he presented the council with a drinking fountain, in her memory. This four-sided monument, with a bowl on each side, was originally located in Brunswick Terrace, but when that street was demolished in 1986 it was moved to its present site on Ellison Street. On top of that, his son, Lance Corporal Percy MacCoy, was killed in the First World War. (isee.gateshead.gov. uk / www.dmm.org.uk)

NOVEMBER 25TH

1848: On this day, the clock on the tower of St Mary's church, Gateshead, was illuminated for the first time. Improvements had certainly been needed, but it's possible that such a cosmetic improvement wasn't tackling the real problem. Certainly that is the impression given by this poem, published in the *Gateshead Observer* in response to the previous year's plan to illuminate the clock, and add a minute hand and chiming bells:

> Mistress Mary,
> Quite contrary,
> Why do your Wardens so?
> Your clock don't tell,
> With hand and bell,
> The time – for it won't go!

Still, in late 1848 the bells were rehung and the clock face illuminated by gaslight. Presumably the more fundamental problem of the clock 'not going' was solved at the same time. Negotiations on paying for the gas continued into the following year – eventually the Gas Company agreed to provide the gas for £20 a year. (Lang, A., *The St Mary's Story*, Gateshead Council: 2009)

NOVEMBER 26TH

1858: On this day, notice was given for the proposed Gateshead Quay Second Act. This was intended to extend and revive the powers granted in the first Gateshead Quay Act, 1855, which largely concerned the ability to buy lands and houses by compulsory purchase, in Newcastle and Gateshead. This was needed so that a new quay, and works behind, which had been authorised in the 1855 Act, could be carried out. This was badly needed in the wake of the 1854 fire (*see* October 6th), which had left large swathes of the quayside devastated. The new act was also about making enough money to pay for it all – it allowed the Tyne Commissioners to raise money upon the security of the borough of Gateshead, considered provisions for the repaying of money borrowed, and granted the levying of rates upon the people of Gateshead. The Commissioners were to be given permission to work out contracts with the North East Railway Company, over what they could do on the newly built roads – 'the management, working, interchange, and direction of the traffic, and the loading and unloading of goods … and the payment of the tolls, rates, and charges arising therefrom'. (www.london-gazette.co.uk)

NOVEMBER 27TH

1957: On this day, police were investigating the suspicious death of Ernest Wilson. Wilson had been married only a fortnight when he died – which might not have been suspicious, except that for 67-year-old Mary Elizabeth Wilson, he was husband number four. Number three, Oliver Leonard, had also lasted a mere fortnight, earlier that year – and husband two had only managed a few months. At the time, she'd asked the undertaker, apparently in jest, about getting a bulk discount. This time, when she married Ernest Wilson, she even joked that any spare sandwiches should be saved for the funeral! No wonder she was gaining the nickname 'the merry widow of Windy Nook'. So, alarm bells ringing, the police arranged to exhume Leonard and Wilson. Traces of phosphorus were found in both men's systems, suggesting beetle poison. Later it was discovered that the other two husbands had also showed signs of poisoning. Mary was convicted of two murders, and sentenced to death. She only avoided being the last woman executed in Britain due to a last-minute reprieve by the Home Secretary, who cited her age and gender as making her execution undesirable. (Seal, L., 'Public Reactions to the case of Mary Wilson', British Criminology Conference Papers: 2008)

NOVEMBER 28TH

1757: On this day – allegedly – Matthew Beck wrote a letter of recommendation for a visiting quack doctor, which was then published in the press. He says: 'I Matthew Beck, at the Queen's-Head, in the Bottle-Bank, Gateshead, in the County of Durham, was afflicted with the Rheumatism, and tried the most eminent of the Faculty, without any Relief; by applying to Dr. Long, and taking six Doses of his Medicines, I am cured.' This recommendation, along with other similar praises from Tyneside, was an ideal advertisement for Dr Long as he attempted to sell his cure via booksellers in Manchester and Liverpool. It was matched, of course, by Long's own self-promotion – his cure 'is the only Specifick as yet known for the Cure of the Rheumatism, Sciatica, Gout &c' and apparently so 'innocent a Nature, that a Child may take it without Danger' (an important point in a time when some quack remedies really could prove lethal). But the mention of 'operation by perspiration' and 'discharging the humours' tell us that – like many 'remedies' of the time – all it probably contained was a strong emetic or purgative … no use at all for the rheumatism sufferer! (Local press)

NOVEMBER 29TH

1917: On this day, the Shipley Art Gallery was formally opened. Solicitor Joseph Shipley had collected paintings throughout his life, with special interests in early Dutch and Flemish work, landscapes, and moral content. By the time he died, in 1909, his entire house – Saltwell Park Towers – was dominated by paintings, packed in boxes and displayed on every wall surface. There was even a room set aside for a full-time conservator! But his will was to cause something of a stir. It stipulated that his collection would go to Newcastle Council, provided they built a new gallery to house the paintings. This caused a split among Newcastle's councillors, between those who wanted to retain the collection, and those who argued that the money that came with it was too small, the collection not good enough in quality – and in any case the Laing Art Gallery had only been open a few years, so a second gallery would be an excessive near-duplicate. The latter faction won, and by the terms of the will, the collection was then offered to Gateshead. The council was again divided, but eventually decided to go ahead with building a new gallery. They selected around 500 paintings, selling the others to help with costs. In spite of wartime shortages in manpower and material, by this day in 1917 the Shipley was ready. It opened to the public the following day. ('The Shipley Bequest', www.gateshead.gov.uk)

November 30th

1886: On this day, a government inspector visited Gateshead Workhouse. Here he found material to furnish a damning report into the conditions endured by the inmates. The building discussed here was on Union Lane. When it had been built, the site had been in the fresh air of Bensham suburb, but in the forty-five years since, the town had encroached. It was also overcrowded, housing more than the 276 inmates for which it was designed. Still, it was found to be 'clean and well ventilated', its children 'in a clean and healthy state'. Some might have expected to stay for some time. In 1861, thirteen of the inmates had been there for more than five years (and in one case, since the place opened). Their problems ranged from insanity and mental deficiency to blindness, deafness, and paralysis. The problem was with the workhouse hospital, a wooden building built on the grounds to house unwell children. Here, the inspector said, twenty-eight sick boys and girls 'suffering from different diseases ... of both sexes (not separated)' shared a damp-floored room. Twenty-two were sharing beds, and all were of 'dirty and uncared-for appearances'. Fortunately in 1886 plans were under way for building an alternative workhouse, with school and hospital, at High Teams Farm – although this might have discouraged the authorities from worrying too much about improving the existing situation. (*Daily Chronicle* / Carlton, I., *A Short History of Gateshead*, Gateshead Metropolitan Borough Council: 1998)

DECEMBER 1ST

1920: On this day, Gateshead Council debated whether or not children should be allowed to play on the swings in Saltwell Park on Sundays. The debate was close. On the one hand were those, supported by the Parks Committee, who saw it as a desecration of the Sabbath, and the thin end of the wedge – if this was allowed, then the next thing would be condoning Sunday football, 'of which there was already a lot in the town'. On the other side were those who thought it no worse than an adult listening to a band in the park, or 'being driven along a country road in a motor car by a chauffeur'. Additionally, they should be retained because 'they were being used by children from the slums'. The council was split right down the middle on the issue, and it was left to the mayor, Alderman Clough, to give the casting vote. He voted in favour of a ban, and the swings were henceforth banned on Sundays. While the council became more relaxed over time, Sunday activities in the park continued to be in dispute well into the 1950s. In September 1953, the Lord's Day Observance Society protested about the Sunday opening of the Horticultural Show, calling it morally and spiritually irresponsible. The council argued that the display of flowers and vegetables would do no harm to the public. (Local press)

DECEMBER 2ND

1860: On this day, Gateshead man John Wilson, better known as 'Cuckoo Jack', died. He got this name from his father, a repairer of clocks (cuckoo and otherwise). Jack himself was a bargeman with a knack for finding precious things in the river. He would take them to the authorities, who often rewarded him in cash. He was also known for his skill at recovering dead bodies from the Tyne, which he took to the Dead House on Newcastle's City Road. The corpses were paid for too, and it's been suggested that this might have made him better money than his day job! It was not uncommon for men to slip into the Tyne and drown, and Jack is thought to have brought in between 150 and 200 bodies over the years. Cuckoo Jack might have been lost to history were it not for 'The Deeth o' Cuckoo Jack' lyrics in the Geordie dialect, written by Edward Corvan to fit to a series of existing local tunes. This praises him as 'a genius o' the grappling line' who 'cared little for sowls, so he but got the bodies'. In the song, Jack hopes that auld Nick will not, in turn, be grappling for him. His name appears in at least seven other songs of the era, including 'Steam Soup', an imagined complaint by Jack about the low quality of soup being distributed by the soup kitchens of Tyneside. (Corvan, E., *et al*, *A Choice Collection of Tyneside Songs*, 1863)

DECEMBER 3RD

1886: On this day, a huge explosion in a tar boiler at Redheugh Tar Works killed four men. Two were badly burned, the other two so damaged as to be almost unrecognisable. A court case ensued in which the wife of one of these men, Robert Porthouse, sued the Redheugh Tar Products Company for £268 for the loss of her husband. This was three years' wages, the maximum allowable sum under the Employers' Liability Act. It was argued that he had done everything in his power to prevent the explosion once a blockage was discovered. The boiler in question was a closed vat of tar, 7ft deep, with an agitator inside and a furnace underneath. Vapour came off, which in this instance was condensed as creosote in a long pipe or 'worm'. The worm had to be kept at the right temperature – if too cold, the creosote could crystallize and block up the mechanism. But the temperature was down to guesswork, which in this case proved fatally incorrect. The defence argued that safety valves and thermometers were not necessary for boilers of this type, and countered that the cause was instead negligence on the part of Porthouse himself; therefore, although they had paid compensation in the cases of the other men, they had no need to do so now. The jury did not agree with this, and the compensation was paid. (*Newcastle Weekly Courant*)

DECEMBER 4TH

1894: On this day the Gateshead Board of Guardians met to discuss a burning issue – whether or not the men of the local workhouse should be allowed to have beer with their Christmas dinner. A few days before, the Workhouse Committee had met and decided that they should simply have their usual tea and coffee. The press blamed the presence of 'the ladies, who would perhaps be better employed within their own province at home', and were glad when a second meeting of the whole Board reversed the decision and allowed the beer to flow once more. Some women of the Temperance movement saw the beer – a gift from the brewers – as just one more dose of the same drug that had caused 'nearly all the crime and insanity of the country'. Others argued that the anti-alcohol campaign should focus on the young, rather than 'good old people' – so an attempt was made to limit the Christmas beer to only the older inmates, but this failed. Even those who had ended up in the workhouse through drink, it was thought, should be allowed to indulge in controlled conditions at Christmas. The *Courant* enjoyed describing all of this, seeing beer as better for the digestion than tea or coffee, and arguing that the teetotallers did damage to their own cause when it was an 'absolute despotism, on people who will have nothing to do with it'. (*Newcastle Weekly Courant*)

DECEMBER 5TH

2011: On this day, the Turner Prize was awarded at the Baltic Art Gallery. Over the course of three months the gallery had displayed work by the four artists on the short list – painter George Shaw, installation artist Karla Black, sculptor Martin Boyce and film-maker Hilary Lloyd. This was only the second time the Turner Prize exhibition was held outside London, and the first non-Tate venue (Tate Liverpool did the honours in 2007). In the first weeks, queues often stretched back to the Millennium Bridge, and overall an impressive 150,000 visited – the highest ever Turner Prize exhibition turnout (the fact that it was free might have helped). The prize – £25,000 – was awarded to Martin Boyce, narrowly the bookies' favourite. Boyce's Modernist transformation of his gallery space involved angular metal trees made from the columns of the building, with park benches and free-standing sculpture, aluminium leaves dappling the light and paper leaves texturing the floor. As has become traditional, the Turner Prize showcased a wide range of different aspects of contemporary art – Boyce's competitors fielded paintings of a Coventry housing estate carefully evoked with Humbrol model paint, huge installations of crumpled forms of paper and plastic smeared in colour, and multiple projections of snatched footage combining into patterns. (*Guardian*)

December 6th

1837: On this day, at about nine in the morning, an accumulation of gas caught fire inside Springwell Colliery, causing a large explosion. Twenty-nine men and boys were working in that section of the Hutton seam, the youngest aged only 12. Twenty-seven of them died, along with three horses. The two surviving lads were severely injured. Several families had lost more than one member, and one man died alongside his two sons. The tragedy was all the harder because it followed hot on the heels of another disaster, which had claimed forty-seven lives in the same pit on May 9th 1833. This was also due to poor ventilation, and so attempts had been made to add extra tunnels to increase the circulation of air. After that, it was considered to be relatively safe, even though candles were still regularly used at the coalface. Notably, safety lamps were always used in removing pillars of coal, the time thought to be most likely to produce dangerous gases. But the inquest, studying the remains of the pit, concluded that something happened which could not have been predicted. Miner Edward Price seems to have dropped his safety lamp, which then fell across the rolley way – where it was run over, and broken. This, it was thought, was the start of the fire. A verdict was returned of accidental death. (*Newcastle Journal*)

DECEMBER 7TH

1889: On this day, Davidson's glassworks patented the techniques behind 'pearline glass', a material which became synonymous with glassmaking in the region. Glass production had been important across Tyneside for a long time, especially after Sowerby invented a new pressed glass method. George Davidson was a butcher, but was so inspired by the pressed glass technique he switched careers completely, opening the Teams Flint Glass Works in 1867. He started off making glass chimneys for paraffin lamps (at the time usually imported from Belgium), but soon branched out into making highly praised – and surprisingly cheap – pressed glass bowls and jugs. He improved Sowerby's technique for 'malachite' glass, made by marbling clear and coloured glass, before perfecting a workable technique for the famous pearline style. Much copied and much prized, pearline glass comes in turquoise blue, acid yellow, and 'moonshine', a pearly white. Another revenue stream, from 1894, was the production of lampshades made of prismatic glass like that now found in car headlights. This was for the designers Holophane, who had patented the idea of using tiny prisms to direct and magnify a light source, but were not themselves manufacturers. A later technique which also found many devotees was 'cloud glass', a marbled glass invented in the 1920s by George Davidson's son. George Davidson himself died in 1891, while walking to church. His obituaries praised him for his kindness and charity. (1st-glass.1st-things.com / www.cloudglass.com)

DECEMBER 8TH

1988: On this day, Metro Radio was floated on the London Stock Exchange. A commercial radio station catering for the Tyne and Wear area, Metro Radio opened in 1974, playing not only the entertainment and pop music that dominated other fledgling radio stations of the era, but also specialist music programmes, drama, documentaries and news. It broadcast from a studio in Swalwell (nearby to the site which would later be the Metro Centre), remaining there until 2005, when it crossed the river to Newcastle. During its time in Gateshead, Metro Radio launched the careers of controversial DJ James Whale, Britain's first 'shock-jock' (who presented the ground-breaking and popular *Night Owls Show* until 1980), and Radio 2 broadcaster Jeremy Vine, who co-presented once a week from 2 a.m. during the mid-1980s. Others who used Metro Radio as a springboard to greater fame include Mark Goodier and Gabby Logan. As regulations changed over the decade, so too did Metro Radio's output, and by the time of the floatation it was largely a chart hits broadcaster. In October 1988, the frequency was shifted slightly and the Burnhope transmitter boosted, to give a better signal in marginal areas. And on this day, shares were sold and the company went public. (metroradio261.blogspot.co.uk / *Gateshead Post*)

DECEMBER 9TH

1881: On this day, elderly Ellen Hart was sent to jail for nine months – three months for 'frequenting the streets for unlawful purpose' and six months for fortune telling. Her method seems to have been to prey on the insecurities of the young servant girls of central Gateshead and Bensham. Apparently the police knew of many such cases, but only three women were willing to come forward. All three had wanted to know about their matrimonial prospects. Sarah Armitage was lucky; she had her palm read and learned that she had two suitors, without charge. For sixpence, Charlotte Dyson heard that two dark young men were fond of her – but she would have to pay more to be able to see them in the 'glass' that Hart kept in her pocket. And poor Elizabeth Wilkinson was the most gullible of the lot. Hart asked for Wilkinson's black dress and petticoat, in exchange for her fortune. The girl fetched them, and Hart said that she would be back in a couple of minutes with a piece of paper, which Wilkinson must place under her pillow to dream of her sweetheart. Unsurprisingly, Hart walked away with the dress and never came back. (*Northern Echo*)

DECEMBER 10TH

1888: On this day, William Waddell was hanged for the murder of his former sweetheart, Jane Beadmore. Beadmore lived in a single-roomed cottage in Birtley with her mother, stepfather and half-brother, below a loft used for pigeons. She had gone out on September 22nd, to buy sweets to take away the nasty taste of the medicine for her heart condition. She never came home. The following day, her body was found by a railway line at Birtley Fell. She had been stabbed in the breast three times, and virtually disemboweled. What made this case shine particularly brightly in public consciousness was that this was at the height of the Jack the Ripper murders. Had the Ripper moved north to Gateshead? A London CID inspector and police surgeon were dispatched to Birtley, but characterised the crime as a 'clumsy piece of butchery', not comparable to the Ripper's work. Police suspicion instead settled on Waddell. Beadmore had told friends a few days before that she had 'found someone nicer'. What really looked odd was his behaviour late that night – he ran from Birtley, reaching Corbridge by the next morning and Berwick a few days later! While some Ripperologists have continued to try to include Beadmoor's death within Jack's tally, there seems little doubt that Waddell was indeed the 'Birtley Ripper'. He confessed shortly before the execution, blaming drunken frenzy. Interestingly, he had been reading accounts of Jack the Ripper shortly beforehand. (www.casebook.org)

DECEMBER 11TH

1686: On this day, architect Robert Trollope was buried under a lavish monument in St Mary's parish churchyard. Starting out as a Yorkshire brickmaker, at some point Trollope moved to the North East, working on several Northumbrian country houses, and building a new guildhall for Newcastle after the medieval building was damaged during the Civil War. Much of the interior survives, though hidden and altered by later architects. Other buildings have been attributed to him because of ornate stylistic details, but this is rarely certain. He certainly did design his own vault, though – complete with a figure, reputedly himself, pointing across the river to the Guildhall. He also wrote his own epitaph, based on a rhyme he had often used while alive:

> Here lies Robert Trollop,
> Who made yon stones roll up.
> When death took his soul up,
> His body filled this hole up.

He is also commemorated by the Bob Trollop pub, a seventeenth-century timber-framed building on Newcastle Quayside, which may well also have been designed by its namesake. Oddly, his name is usually spelled with the 'e', but his gravestone has it without and the pub, perhaps, took its cue from that.

December 12th

1832: On this day, Gateshead elected its first Member of Parliament. It had been granted its own MP as part of the Great Reform Bill of 1832 – although it's arguable how much democracy was really being served in the borough, since Cuthbert Rippon of Stanhope Castle stood unopposed! There had been some opposition to Gateshead getting a seat in Parliament. When it was debated, the Marquis of Londonderry argued that Gateshead 'was a mere suburb to the town of Newcastle – a most filthy spot, containing the vilest class of society, and that description of population least worthy to enjoy the right of voting for a Member to serve in Parliament. He could not give their Lordships a better proof of the description of the inhabitants of the town of Gateshead, than by alluding to the effects produced in that town by the visitation of cholera [...] He could not but advocate the claims of the town of Stockton-upon-Tees, in preference to those of Gateshead. The former contained a most intelligent, respectable, and wealthy population.' Lord Durham countered this with, among other arguments, praise for the industry and diligence of the working men of Gateshead, and the rising influence of those who owned its factories. Londonderry may have picked up some filth prancing through on his Arabian but this was not the general state of the town! (*Hansard*)

DECEMBER 13TH

1912: On this day, the railwaymen of Gateshead were in the midst of a strike, a local incident in the period just before the First World War that has become known as the great unrest. Unusually, the grievance here was not pay or conditions, but something more specific – the demotion of a North East Railways train driver, on a charge of drunkenness while on duty. The railwaymen called for a retrial, but they were ignored; their next move, from December 6th, was to strike. It is perhaps telling that it took just eight days for the Home Secretary to send magistrate Chester Jones to investigate the case. Jones overturned the previous verdict, and the driver was reinstated. On the 14th, the strike was called off. Rudyard Kipling was distinctly unimpressed with this legal verdict. On the 25th – Christmas Day! – he wrote to his friend, American author Edward Lucas Wright, describing these events as 'a parting of the ways at which this land took the downward lawless plunge … One of those rare cases where one can distinctly *see* a nation turning a corner. And nobody seems to care very much either. They will in a generation.' (Kipling, R., *The Letters of Rudyard Kipling*, University of Iowa Press: 1990)

DECEMBER 14TH

1955: On this day, hundreds of thousands of homes were left without power when Stella South Power Station, on the Stella Haugh near Blaydon, failed. Work on the power station, and its smaller sister across the river, Stella North, had begun in 1951. Both were what were known as 'brick cathedral' power stations, with 73m-tall free-standing cooling towers on the river bank. They both became operational in late 1954, but a year later building was still on-going to expand the sites. Indeed, Stella South was not operating at full capacity until 1957, by which point twenty-two railway sidings were bringing in 2,000 tons of coal a day. Innovative silica technology was used in the turbines, and the whole thing was lit by what was then the most powerful lighting installation in the North East. But at about 8.30 on this morning, something went wrong – switches exploded, and the generators closed down. Dunston Power Station could not handle the additional load alone, and shut down under the strain, leading to a total blackout across Tyneside. It has been estimated that around 400,000 people were affected, including 20,000 miners who were trapped underground until power could be restored. This process was begun by midday, and complete by 6.30, but meanwhile more than £1 million had been lost in missed time. (Wikipedia / sine.ncl.ac.uk)

December 15th

2009: On this day, the Mayor of Gateshead visited the home of composer William Shield, in Hood Street, Swallwell, to unveil a commemorative plaque. Born in 1748, violinist Shield studied as a young man under Newcastle's Charles Avison, a leading light of late eighteenth-century music. During a later stint as lead violist at Covent Garden, his compositions – over thirty operas as well as other works – found favour with royalty, and in 1817 he was appointed Master of the King's Music. His best-known composition is *Rosina*, an opera whose use of spoken word sections, English lyrics, and a mix of light tune styles, can be seen as a precursor to light opera and even the musical. Shield can also be credited – arguably – with the tune of 'Auld Lang Syne'. The tune can be found within *Rosina*, written six years before Robert Burns wrote down the song. However, the words are known to be based on earlier poems, so perhaps the tune was older too? Shield, like other composers of the time, was not above plundering the folk music of his native region – but this in turn raises the possibility that the tune started life as Northumbrian! Shield died in 1829, giving all his worldly goods to 'my beloved partner Ann, Mrs. Shield'. This was a quiet deception, however – when the will was proved, the claimant was revealed as 'Ann Stokes, alias Shield, Spinster', Shield's long-term mistress. (*The Journal* / Wikipedia)

DECEMBER 16TH

1831: On this day, Mary Hymers (or Hindmarsh) was buried in St Mary's churchyard, along with a Springwell blacksmith whose body had been brought to town. These two corpses were the town's first ever cholera victims; the first of many. The deadly disease had arrived in England only two months before, and quickly travelled from its point of entry at Sunderland into the slums of Gateshead, with their poor sanitation and inadequate sewage system. Hymers was a poor woman from Bottle Bank. She grew ill on the 14th, but still went to work 'selling small articles, rags and shoes'. On the 15th, her condition worsening, her husband sent for Dr Brady, who 'gave her medicines'. When she died the doctor claimed that 'broth and small beer was the cause of her death, and were sour upon her stomach'! Things remained quiet for a while, but on Christmas Day Gateshead's water supply must have become heavily infected. By the 26th, B. Bell was writing to her parents that, 'six persons had died in the Beggars Entry, two in Hillgate, one in Jackson's Chair and there is several ill of it in the last place mentioned. The doctors have been running about all the day.' And by the 27th, over forty people were dead. (archivesalive.ncl.ac.uk / Morris, R., *Cholera 1832*, Taylor & Francis: 1976)

DECEMBER 17TH

2004: On this day, the Sage Gateshead opened the doors to its three performance spaces for the first time. Transforming a derelict stretch of the bank of the Tyne into an impressive piece of modern architecture, the Sage had already won awards for its curved glass-and-steel design, which changes in appearance as it reflects the colours of the sky. Paid for with what was at the time the single largest Arts Lottery award granted outside London, it was an ambitious project to build a new music venue which would work on the principle of a value in all genres, showcasing among other things folk, blues, classical, and world music. As a nod to this respect for diversity, the opening weekend was not marked with a massive concert, but with a wider showcase of varied styles, which the public could freely dip into. Hall One holds 1,700, and has ceiling panels which can be adjusted to make the sound profile of the room, in theory, perfect for any type of music. The smaller Hall Two may be the only ten-sided performance space in the world. The official opening was in October 2004, ten months later, when the Queen and the Duke of Edinburgh toured the building.

DECEMBER 18TH

1907: On this day, over 600 unemployed men marched through the streets of Gateshead. Earlier that day, a special meeting of Gateshead Town council had been called to discuss 'the unemployment question'. They were debating how many genuinely unemployed men there were in the borough, and whether a special bureau should be set up to find out. At the time unemployed men were supposed to register with the Distress Committee, but some were put off by the stigma of doing so, and the figures were in doubt. One man declared that the unemployed were exaggerating their numbers by inviting employed friends to meetings! Things degenerated from there, as each side accused the other of lying. Representatives of a group of unemployed men asked the Council to find them work – they did not want charity, only jobs. They then returned to a meeting of the unemployed, where the debate continued – should they register with the Distress Committee, or wait for work? Should they become more militant and refuse to pay rent on council property? The group had little faith in the Council, who repainted schools by 'sweated labour' while painters were out of work. The large group of men then marched from the Queen's Theatre to the Town Hall, and stampeded into the building itself. They seem to have gone into the building, along the corridor, and out the back door, doing no harm – and all were gone by the time the police arrived! (*Northern Mail*)

DECEMBER 19TH

1864: On this day, an inquest was opened into a murder in High Spen. Matthew Atkinson had been to a pigeon-shooting match with his nephews. When he got home, as far as neighbours could tell by the sounds coming through the walls, he began to argue with his wife, and then began to beat her. Some neighbours tried to get in, but were dissuaded by threats from within the house. The violence continued until Eleanor Atkinson was dead. Matthew was arrested, and the inquest began. *The Times*, conveniently forgetting the violence of London, was damning of the neighbours: 'We verily believe that … no other population … would have allowed a fellow creature to be murdered almost before their eyes.' The defence tried to get a reduction to manslaughter, arguing for Atkinson's previously good character, and his wife's dissolute habits – but this didn't wash with the jury. The drama wasn't over, though – when he was hanged, the rope broke and he fell 15ft. The crowd speculated on the legal implications of this for twenty minutes until a second rope was put in place. Even then, Atkinson did not break his neck but was slowly strangled, causing letters of outrage about execution to the press. The curious thing is, the faulty noose was the first 'hanging rope' to be made inside the prison, by prisoners. Could they have botched it deliberately? (Pears, T., *High Spen and District*, www.bpears.org.uk)

DECEMBER 20TH

1892: On this day, at 3 o'clock, the Mayor of Gateshead, Walter Wilson, officially presented to the Borough of Gateshead the clock tower which stands just outside the Town Hall, as what the *Courant* describes as a 'substantial and acceptable Christmas gift'. Wound by hand, it had been set in motion earlier that day by Wilson's wife. A Gothic-style tower 25ft tall, painted in striking black and gold, it is an exact facsimile of the clock tower of Victoria station, London, which stands at one end of Victoria Street. This was erected earlier in the same year by the same company, Gillett & Johnston of Croydon. It was intended to mimic, on a smaller scale, the tower of the Houses of Parliament which houses Big Ben, at the other end of Victoria Street. Thus both the Victoria station clock, and the Gateshead clock have been affectionately titled Little Ben. At the time it was not just a decorative feature to the town, but very practical as most people did not have watches – the *Courant* described it as 'a boon to the inhabitants of the town'. Walter Wilson's other legacy for the region was the foundation of the chain of Walter Wilson's (sometimes called Willson's) grocery stores. The chain spread right across Tyneside and County Durham, styling itself the 'smiling service store'. (*Daily Chronicle / Weekly Courant*)

DECEMBER 21ST

1916: On this day, Belgian policemen faced a near-riot … in the streets of Birtley! The story goes back to the previous year, when the government had realised it needed to rapidly increase armament production, and also to house hundreds of Belgian men, and their families. Their solution was to build pre-fab houses for 6,000 people, and a massive arms factory – and put a huge fence around the whole thing. Outside was Birtley; inside was Elisabethville, or Little Belgium, where over the years 3,500 men, 85 per cent of them disabled by war, made 2¾ million shells, far more than their target. The community had its own hospital, cemetery, school, church, nunnery and Co-op, and used Belgian law, language, and currency. The new housing, which boasted electricity and indoor toilets, was clearly better than that enjoyed by most of the locals! But workers chafed against their regulated lives, and their twelve-hour shifts in difficult and dangerous conditions which killed at least thirteen. Today 2,000 of them marched on the gendarmes. Things grew sufficiently heated for a shot to be fired, but this protest seems to have cleared the air. Over time, the Belgians generally settled (some even began to grow leeks, and keep whippets!), and around thirty stayed behind to marry when the rest returned home after the war. (Bygate, J., *Of Arms and the Heroes*, History of Education Project: 2006)

DECEMBER 22ND

1900: On this day, interested locals were given a sneak preview of the transport of the future – the electric tram! The new 'Liverpool Car' was painted yellow and red, and divided into smoking and non-smoking sections. It was a double-decker, with an open top and advertising hoardings at the front. The first trams were steam-powered, and were brought in by the Gateshead and District Tramways Company in 1883. In 1897 a controlling interest was bought by the British Electric Traction Company, who, after years of legal preparations, began to construct electric tramways, and convert the existing tracks in June 1900. The trams seen on this day were not in action until May 9th 1901, with trams running to Heworth, Sheriff Hill, Dunston and Low Fell. It was very popular – in 1908, 12 million tickets were sold, almost ten times the number who had used the steam trains in 1900 (though this was admittedly disrupted by the conversion process). At around the same time an innovative 'Fair-Fare' scheme was introduced, in which the passenger simply paid a farthing per stop travelled. And in 1912, the company launched the first pay-as-you-enter system in Europe – though increased delays at platforms in busy periods were a severe drawback. (*Daily Leader* / Hearse, G., *The Tramways of Gateshead*, G. Hearse: 1965)

DECEMBER 23RD

1822: On this day, writer and philanthropist Francis Elizabeth King (*née* Bernard), known as Fanny, died in her daughter's Gateshead home. Born in Lincoln in 1757, Fanny's father left to take up the position of governor of New Jersey, America, when she was one year old. Left with distant relatives and instructed in feminine behaviour, Fanny seems to have developed an unusual degree of self-reliance. At 20 she wrote *The Rector's Memorandum Book*, a novel whose heroine's triumph over her cruel husband is purely in her continued Christian virtue. King herself was to marry a vicar, and fully embrace the ideal of a godly parson's wife. Books on a stay in France, and the role of Christian temper in domestic bliss, followed, and she helped her brother to establish the Society for Bettering the Condition and Improving the Comforts of the Poor. She moved to Gateshead in 1810, where her memoirist says she was 'a mother to the poor ... She not only established a large Sunday school, a Sick Fund and Clothing Society, but was constant in her superintendence of these institutions, and in visiting the poor at their own houses.' Whilst conformist in many respects, seeing a woman's place as in the home, subordinate to her husband in all things, she thought that men more often failed in their domestic duties than women, and that the education of women should go beyond mere 'accomplishments'. (*Oxford National Dictionary of Biography*)

DECEMBER 24TH

1813: On this day, at one thirty in the morning, an explosion shook Brandling Main colliery, Felling. Of the forty-three men and boys underground at the time, half (all of those in the southern half of the pit) died. To the north, another twelve suffered serious burns. Only one pony, out of thirteen, survived. It happened just as a new shift was coming down into the pit, and had it occurred just a few minutes later, the death toll would have been even higher. The cause of the explosion is not known, but that part of the mine was known to have fissures in the ground which sometimes discharged hydrogen so quickly that the nuggets of coal on the floor actually danced around. Usually the risk was kept to a minimum by maintaining a through-draught so strong that it was difficult to even keep a candle alight. Nonetheless a gas build-up remains a strong possibility. Something certainly caused a wave of flame to race through the tunnels, so fast that while men died, the wood within the mine appeared untouched by fire. Eight widows and fifteen children were left behind, doubly tragic in a community which had lost another ninety-two miners only nineteen months previously (*see* May 25th). (www.dmm.org.uk)

DECEMBER 25TH

1913: On this day, Emily Matilda Easton died. Born in 1818, Easton was from a privileged background – family members owned several coal mines including Oakwellgate, and also passed land in Layton, Yorkshire to her after their deaths. She spent much of her childhood, and also her later years, at the Nest House, a manor house in Felling. She never married, and rarely spent money on herself. She was sufficiently frugal that in 1891, she only had two live-in servants, where others of her status often had a dozen. Instead, she gave to charity. She founded St Chad's church, Bensham, offering the money initially as an anonymous donation, and a few years later had built the twelve aged miners' homes still known as Easton Cottages. Still, at the time of her death it was estimated by the *New York Times* (hence the use of dollars) that Easton was worth over $5 million– well over a billion in today's money. She gave her lady's companion $8,000, and her gardener $3,000. She also gave to twenty-two local charities, to the Newcastle Medical College and Armstrong College of Science, to the chapel of the Royal Victoria Hospital (on condition that it only hosted Church of England services) and founded a charity (still extant) to help elderly Church of England women. She is buried in Ryton. (*Whickham Magazine / The New York Times*)

DECEMBER 26TH

1891: On this day, tragedy struck a festive pantomime performance at Gateshead's Theatre Royal. Around 1,200 people – mostly teenagers – had packed in to the theatre to watch *Aladdin*. But then a shout of 'Fire!' echoed through the building. This was in response to smoke from a lad's illicit pipe smoking, which had indeed started a very minor smoulder in a floorboard – a problem, but not a catastrophe. But even as the actors and theatre owners urged calm, panic spread amongst the audience as they fought to get out. Several jumped from upper windows. A small baby was thrown to safety over the crowd. But as hundreds of frightened people ran down the stairs, stumbling and pushing each other, a human blockade began to build up, and no one could stop it. When things finally calmed down, the mass of humanity was gradually untangled – and it was found that ten people had died in the crush. Nine were teenage boys – the tenth worked at the theatre, and had been opening a door to help people leave when he found himself at the bottom of the pile. Fate was particularly unkind to one policeman involved in the rescue, who found the body of his own son. Ironically, in December 1922 the building did indeed fall prey to a major fire. (*Birmingham Daily Post*)

DECEMBER 27TH

1860: On this day, slater Thomas Lankie Smith was executed for the murder of miner John Baty. The two had been drinking together in a Blaydon pub one evening after a pigeon shoot in Blaydon Burn, well into the small hours. And a few hours later, Baty was found dead in a field, his head smashed. Oddly, he seemed to be wearing someone else's clothes. Smith was arrested when he was recognised near Whitby a week later, and found to be actually wearing some of Baty's clothes. He claimed that the two of them had drunkenly agreed to have a fist fight, and so stripped to the waist. Smith said he had won the fight, but Baty had still been alive when he left. The judge suggested the real motive was theft, and the jury convicted Smith, though they did recommend leniency. The Home Office disagreed, and he was hanged outside Durham Prison. Five years earlier Smith had been a suspect in another murder (*see* August 5th), but disappeared for a time – so he may have killed before. And even stranger, his fellow lodger Matthew Atkinson was five years later himself hanged as a murderer! (*see* December 19th)

DECEMBER 28TH

1836: On this day, at a public meeting held in the Town Hall and convened by the mayor, a petition was created, which would be left in seven shops across the borough for people to sign. The petition, to Parliament, was for 'the immediate and total abolition of Church rates' (a local property tax for the upkeep of Anglican parish churches). The supporters' argument was that it was coercive and unjust, since it forced those who differed in their doctrines and practices from the established Church to nonetheless pay taxes for the maintenance of that Church. They thought this was against Christian values and indeed was harmful to the reputation of the Church of England itself. Any attempt to reduce, rather than end, the tax would – the petition said – be seen as aggravation, as this was a matter of conscience. In Gateshead, this worked, and the Church rate was abandoned. Nonetheless, in April 1841, the *Courant* reports a second near-identical meeting, also in the Town Hall and convened by the mayor, to consider the propriety of petitioning Parliament on a wider abolition of the rate. Several impassioned speeches were made on the subject, which discussed the effect upon the finances of the Church in Gateshead. Church rates were not, however, universally abolished until 1868. (*Newcastle Courant*)

DECEMBER 29TH

1793: On this day, the populace of Swalwell took part in a nationalist demonstration against Thomas Paine, hated for his revolutionary views and criticisms of Christian doctrine. An effigy was made which was tried for his crimes, hanged 'for the usual time' then burnt to ashes, 'with the emblem of his trade in one hand, and his most detestable pamphlet in the other, surrounded by the judge in his robes, and all the principal officers that attended the procession and trial'. The whole thing was apparently done very calmly (apart from timed volleys of gunfire), by a mass of people wearing black cockades, and labels in their hats displaying phrases like 'God Save the King', and 'King and Constitution'. The whole thing was rounded off with a chorus of the National Anthem. Hundreds of similar Paine-burnings happened across the country that winter, many with complex and varied rituals associated – the following week, for instance, Swalwell got involved. The *Newcastle Chronicle* reported that 'Paine's effigy has been burnt, shot, hanged, and undergone the greatest marks of popular resentment in most of the towns and villages in this part of the country'. (O'Gorman, F., 'The Paine Burnings', *Past and Present*: 2006 / Bourne, W., *The Swalwell Story*, 1893)

December 30th

1815: On this day, the Tyne rose to dangerous heights. While the flood was perhaps not as obviously severe as that of 1771, the damage was arguably almost as great. Two days of rain gradually built up into a massive storm on the night of the 29th, when winds got high enough to blow the roof from a house in Windmill Hills. Thawing snow from further upstream combined with the rain to raise water levels dramatically. An account written three years later states that the sight at around 5 a.m. was 'particularly awful', with boats coming loose from their moorings, and cellars filling with water. Thomas Thompson, a 43-year-old merchant who lived on Windmill Hills, 'was seen repeatedly plunging into the river, anxious to save his floating timber, ere it was swept away by the overwhelming torrent'. He was pulled from the waters but died a few days later, apparently from a severe cold and lung infection caused by over-exertion. Acres of low-lying corn were ruined, and many sheep drowned, as they had been placed on turnip fields alongside the river for December. A man and boy were drowned trying to rescue the crew of a stranded keelboat. And at the Gateshead side of the bridge, the arches became choked with ice, timber, and boats – it was considered lucky that it did not share the fate of the bridge at Haydon Bridge on the same day, and collapse. (Garrett, W., *An Account of the Great Floods in 1771 and 1815*, 1818)

DECEMBER 31ST

1835: On this day, Gateshead Town Council met for the first time, following that year's Municipal Corporations Act. The first mayor was George Hawks, who employed over 900 men in his ironworks (*see* March 1st). The reform of the town governance was not without opposition, largely from those who favoured the existing borough structure and didn't want to hand over any documentation to the new municipal body. But the day was won by W.H. Brockett and his Whig faction, who then dominated the council for the next twenty years. The only Tory to become mayor in this time was John Barras, described by one contemporary Whig as, 'a good-hearted affable benevolent thorough-going Tory ... the wonder is that such a man should be a Tory!' The position of mayor was hardly a popular one – in 1843 four men turned it down! One initial problem for Brockett and company was the lack of a permanent office. This first meeting was held in a solicitor's office, the second at the Anchorage School. After that the next nine years were spent in a rented house in Oakwellgate, before a town hall was built in 1844. (Manders, F., *A History of Gateshead*, Gateshead Corporation: 1973)